DAM RIGHT!

Fred Lynch, Oscar Kendall
&
The Lynch Brothers Diamond Drilling Company

Joseph Edward Fulton

Dam Right!
Fred Lynch, Oscar Kendall & the
Lynch Brothers Diamond Drilling Company

ISBN-13: 978-0979607226
ISBN-10: 0979607221

Copyright © 2014 Joseph E. Fulton

Cover design by Emma Callender

Cover layout by Megan Janssen
Cover photograph of Owyhee Dam courtesy of *Bureau of Reclamation.*
Back cover photo of Ross Dam by Debra Hascall.

Published by Originario Productions
Kings Valley, Oregon USA

This book is dedicated to the memory of
Betty Biner Fulton, (1918-2009),
first grandchild of Dan Lynch, who loved her grandfather
and his brothers and preserved their memories
so that they might be remembered.
I am honored to make her wish come true.

Dan Lynch, the original diamond driller of the Lynch Brothers, with his granddaughter Betty Biner and grandson Billy Biner.

Table of Contents

Introduction

The Lynch Brothers Diamond Drilling Company, unsung heroes in the economic development of the Pacific Northwest, was founded in 1914 (100 years ago this year), and shut down in 1964 (50 years ago this year). Led by the sons of Irish immigrants this small company paved the way for mineral exploration and dam construction in Washington, Oregon, Idaho, Alaska and beyond. Their story, full of triumph and tragedy, is told here for the first time.

This book also presents the first biographical histories of two men who were, in their own times, famous characters in the Pacific Northwest: Seattle's Fred Lynch, the beloved "Singing Policeman" of KOMO during the Roaring Twenties (the heyday of live radio); and his uncle, Portland's Oscar J. Kendall, the ill-fated "steam-dye man," who saw his life change dramatically after an accident with an electric street car in "Stump Town's" wild 1890s.

The story of the Lynch clan might be familiar to other Irish American mining families who followed the big lodes of copper, iron, silver and gold. From Ireland to Michigan's Upper Peninsula to Butte, Montana, these families helped bring prosperity and expansion to their adopted country, while introducing Irish customs and beliefs that are now as American as apple pie. But something about this particular Irish family demanded more than what the daily descent into the mines had to offer.

Dan, Dick, Bill and Pat Lynch moved to the Pacific Northwest, started their own company, and led rugged, but generally good-natured work crews, who operated expensive and temperamental diamond drills in some of the most inhospitable locations, from the Wrangell Mountains of Alaska, to the treacherous gorges of the North Cascades, to the mighty Columbia River, when it still ran wild. Their work would lead to the successful mining of fabulous strikes of gold, silver, copper, coal, oil, marble and more. But most importantly, their work led to the placement of the majority of the dams in the Pacific

Northwest - supplying drinking water to Portland, Oregon (Dams 1 & 2 at Bull Run Reservoir); electricity to Seattle, Washington (the Skagit River Project); and irrigation to the arid Inland Empire (the Grand Coulee Dam). And when they were successful, the projects their drilling inaugurated would lead to thousands of jobs for desperate men during the troubled times of the Great Depression and World War II.

Many of the dams built in the Pacific Northwest have created serious ecological dilemmas. But it is unlikely that the early drillers and other skilled laborers understood the full environmental impact of what they were doing. The corporate bosses and scientists probably had an idea, but specialized workers like the Lynch Brothers thought they were doing something great for our country. It would be revisionist history to condemn them now. Suffice to say that some of the dams the brothers helped build have since been removed. The Lynches were FDR Democrats, progressive in their world-view. It seems likely that if they were alive today they would have understood the need to remove some of those great dams.

Most of our energy comes from coal, natural gas and nuclear power plants. Hydroelectric power accounts for a mere 7% of total energy produced in the United States. But in the Pacific Northwest (Washington, Oregon & Idaho), 70% of power generation comes from the dams that the Lynch Brothers helped create. And despite the legitimate ecological concerns of these dams, hydroelectric power *is* a renewable source of energy.

I like to share my passion for history through storytelling. But I discovered long ago that the people and events that fascinated me most had already been covered exhaustively by far more qualified or scholarly historians. Then something enlightening happened. I inherited a collection of letters written by two ancestors while they were Union soldiers during the American Civil War: letters that had not seen the light of day for a century. It finally occurred to me that the stories I could share- stories that had never been shared before-were stories from my own family.

From Beardstown to Andersonville, the Civil War Letters of Newton and Tommy Paschal was published in 1998, and again, with additional information on troop movements, in 2011, the 150th anniversary of the start of the Civil War. In 2013, I published a second book, *Brewmaster's Bombardier and Belly Gunner, the World War II Letters of Bill & Bob Biner*. These war heroes were the brothers of my mother. They flew over 100 missions during World War II and lived to tell about it.

Dam Right! Fred Lynch, Oscar Kendall & The Lynch Brothers Diamond Drilling Company, is also based upon true stories from my own family history. Dan Lynch, the oldest of the Lynch Brothers, was my great-grandfather. His son, Fred Lynch, another diamond driller, but also a famous Irish tenor, was my godfather; and Oscar Kendall, was my great-uncle.

Neither Fred Lynch nor Oscar Kendall had children of their own, so their colorful stories were not carried on in the hearts or minds of offspring. Yet, the stories of their distinctly different lives add sweet and sour chapters to the early history of the Pacific Northwest's two great cities. The Lynch Brothers, who were much more significant in the history of the Pacific Northwest, are even more forgotten. But in their time they were deeply trusted and depended upon, from corporate bosses seeking great profits, to skilled laborers seeking a job during the Great Depression, to arguably the most powerful American of the 20th century, President Franklin Delano Roosevelt.

The irony is that none of the brothers became rich and none of their descendants ever lived off the profits of the most important drilling company in the history of the Pacific Northwest, despite the fact that the Lynch Brothers went into the wildest rivers and found the ideal and safest locations to build dams that would change America forever. Above all, their drilling determined the site of a dam that would hold back a lake, named after FDR himself, 300 feet deep and 150 miles long; for they were the very first workers on the Grand Coulee, the largest concrete structure on earth. And these salty Irish brothers knew perfectly well that the placement of such a monster needed to be *Dam Right!*

One: Knockmahon to Keweenaw

During the second half of the 19th century an exodus of the young left Eire for the old. Carrying little more than cherished memories and hope, hundreds of thousands of young Irish men and women left their mother country for the United States in search of jobs. 80% of these Irish emigrants were between 18 and 30 years of age. Some were skilled laborers and most had a specific destination in mind; usually where other emigrants from their own Irish county or region had settled.

It was not the first mass exodus of the 19th century from those gray shores of the emerald isle, familiar, and somewhat softened, by pastel-colored shops and thatched roofs. Ireland experienced unfathomable loss from a series of potato famines during the first half of the century. Millions died or fled to America. But famine was just part of a greater misery. Thousands left the island due to religious and political persecution by the ruling English aristocracy. Indeed, little had changed since the previous century when Jonathon Swift lampooned British bigotry with a satirical essay advocating the consumption of Irish babies to prevent them from becoming burdens on the British state as worthless adults. More than one thick-skulled British "statesman" took the proposal seriously.

Although the potato famines had passed, life was no less promising for the Irish people during the second half of the 19th century. The industrial revolution in America and England offered both despair and hope for the Irish. Massive amounts of copper and iron were needed to fuel industrial growth. Waterford County was a mining area. The Knockmahon Copper Mine and later the Tankardstown Mine employed many of Waterford's working poor. However, Knockmahon and Tankardstown were British owned and soon investors turned their attention and money to the extraordinary purified copper deposits discovered in the Keweenaw Range of Michigan's Upper Peninsula. This meant the death of the Waterford mines and the jobs produced and supported by them. The ruins of these once vibrant mines are ghostly and picturesque curiosities today.

Ruins at the Tankardstown Mine in County Waterford, Ireland.
Photograph by Shaun McGuire.

It was widely reported that much of the copper mined from the Keweenaw was instantly ready for use: no smelting or purification necessary. Many Cornish miners had already made the move to Michigan. If a man waited too long he might miss out on the action. Naturally, the desperate Waterford residents began to speak excitedly of Michigan. This included a husky, dark-haired young servant and blacksmith named Cornelius Lynch.

Cornelius, himself the son of a blacksmith, was born in 1836, in Ballyduff, Waterford County, Ireland. On February 16, 1864, then

28 year-old Cornelius married Bridget Harris, the 21 year-old daughter of the local schoolteacher. Bridget got pregnant while the two were making plans to join other Waterford natives in the "Copper Country" of Upper Michigan. But they would delay their trip long enough for their parents to see a grandchild born in Ireland. Named Michael after Bridget's father, the baby arrived on December 18th.

Five months later Cornelius booked passage for his young family on the *S.S. Etna*, a steamer from Liverpool. Unlike emigrants from the potato famine days, they did not have to travel to Liverpool to board the ship. The British government had approved the port town of Cobh in Cork Harbor as a stopping point for British passenger ships bound for America. Without regard to local sentiment they took the liberty to rename the port Queenstown in honor of the ruling British monarch, Queen Victoria. Hundreds of British passenger ships would make their final port at Queenstown before the long journey across the Atlantic, including the ill-fated *Titanic* in 1912.

Ballyduff, Ireland was on the Cork/Waterford border and it was an easy trip physically for Cornelius Lynch to reach the port. But it must have been a difficult trip emotionally. He realized like most young Irishmen heading for greener pastures in America that he would probably never see his parents or the country he loved again. Such sad goodbyes experienced by so many emigrants came to be known as an Irish Wake.

Bridget was a bit more fortunate than her husband. Her brother John was already in Michigan. Another brother, Michael, would follow a year later. And in 1871, after her father passed away in Ballyduff, her mother, Bridget Longe Harris, and her three sisters, Anne, Katherine and Mary, moved to the Upper Peninsula as well, settling near the growing Lynch clan in the Copper Country. The Harris family proved industrious and successful and many descendants of these siblings still reside in Michigan and across the country.

Ballyduff, Waterford County, Ireland in the 19th Century.

*S.S.Etna, the ship that Cornelius Lynch took to America with his wife
Bridget Harris and son Michael in 1865.*

Bridget's younger brother Michael was perhaps the most famous and most successful of the Harris siblings. After working the mines near Hancock, Michigan, he moved to Menominee County where he became a lumberman, opened a general store and supervised the building of numerous charcoal kilns, needed for fueling the blast furnaces of steel mills. Harris was elected to the Michigan state legislature and was so popular that he was re-elected with a plurality from both political parties. Among his legislative successes was the funding of an agricultural school in Menominee, Michigan, which became the Jordan Catholic Seminary. He also established the township of Harris, in Menominee County, and served as justice of the peace and postmaster for twenty years.

But Michael Harris was most highly regarded for his support of Indian rights and for the kindness he showed toward the Potawatomi Indians during a smallpox epidemic in the early 1900s. The following story was written by Margaret Thurston Carlson in 1971, after she interviewed two of Michael Harris's surviving daughters, Lillian and Genevieve.

"It was during the years of the panic toward dread diseases and plagues that Indians living in the country surrounding the Harris Farm near Bark River, Michigan, were inflicted with an epidemic of smallpox. All in the community were fearful of the smallpox spreading, and the Indians were left to their isolation, in the dead of winter with snow piled high along country roads, to die of lack of food or medicine as all persons in the area knew of the smallpox epidemic and would not allow an Indian to approach."

"The Indians were special friends to Michael Harris. They had worked for him cutting lumber on his farm; he paid them fair wages and legislated for their welfare. Upon realizing their plight, he built a structure near the road which led to his farm to wash and change his clothes, and proceeded with his horse-drawn sleigh to deliver food and medicine to the Indians in their distress. His daughter Genevieve reports that the Indians would leave baskets on tree stumps near the road, with notes what supplies they needed. Mike would fill the baskets and return them to the tree stumps, then go home to his impoverished building to wash and change clothes before returning to his family. He was very aware of the danger of contracting smallpox, and even worse, in his mind, passing it on to his family. Yet he could not let the Indian community die. They did survive, and the warrants for the arrest of Michael Harris were never served upon him although it was the sheriff's intention to do so for going to the Indians in this way."

"The Indians (Potawatomi) adopted Mike as a member of the tribe, and named him Makenus, meaning Big Chief or White Chief. His daughter Lillian was called Pale Morning. When Mike died in 1936, the Indians came to the Harris farm in tribal dress to mourn his passing."

The Potawatomi also honored Michael Harris with a beautiful ceremonial blanket, coveted to this day by the descendants of this younger brother of Bridget Lynch, who had preceded him to Michigan by one year, with her husband Cornelius and son Michael, aboard the S.S. Etna.

As a steamship, the S.S. Etna was quicker than the 18th century cargo vessels that brought earlier immigrants. But it was still miserable. While many English passengers crossed the ocean in relative luxury, virtually all Irish emigrants were placed "tween decks" in steerage, a level below deck usually about five feet in height with narrow bunk beds where passengers would store their worldly possessions and try to sleep.

Scant privacy, inadequate toilets and no windows made steerage a brewing pot for disease. It was filthy and dank as the only air came through a narrow hatchway. Death "tween decks" was not unusual during Atlantic crossings. But Cornelius, Bridget and their five-month old baby made it to New York on May 16, 1865, and were processed at Castle Gardens Receiving Station. The more famous Ellis Island would not open until 1892.

It was a momentous time to arrive in America. The Civil War had just come to an end. Northerners still grieved over their slain president, Abraham Lincoln, and called for revenge against the vanquished South. The wounds of war would be slow to heal. And with thousands of Union soldiers returning home there would be competition for jobs.

Michael Harris, (1852-1936), the good-natured Michigan state legislator and advocate of Indian rights, was the younger brother of Bridget Harris Lynch and uncle to the Lynch Brothers.

The only known photograph of Bridget Longe Harris, (1814-1890), the mother of Bridget Harris Lynch and Michael Harris; and the grandmother of the Lynch brothers. She is buried in Republic, Michigan.

Irish immigrants bore the brunt of bigoted nativist hostility during the 19th century and, along with newly freed blacks, became the scapegoats in a contested job market. Like today's Mexican immigrants, the Irish were hard-working to a fault; proud of their heritage and deeply devoted to their families and their Catholic faith. They had built New York's Eire Canal and would be instrumental in the construction of the Transcontinental Railroad, but that didn't stop many Protestant Americans from slandering them as filthy, stupid, lazy drunks.

Arrival in the great port of New York was not the end of water travel for those headed toward the Upper Peninsula. After making their way to Buffalo, either by train or via the Hudson River and Eire Canal, hopeful immigrants might board a steamer to pass through Lake Eire to Detroit and then through Lake Huron to Sault Ste. Marie, Michigan. There the new Soo Locks led travelers into Lake Superior where they braved unpredictable and often treacherous conditions to find their preferred port of entry to the Keweenaw. There is little doubt that many an Irish miner found stormy Lake Superior reminiscent of their own Irish Sea. And many went down with their ships before having a chance to mine the fabled copper. It has been said that Lake Superior is filled with the ghosts of the copper boom.

Cornelius made his way to Michigan's Upper Peninsula through the Portage Entry, on the southeast side of the copper "finger," a sub-peninsula that is home to the Keweenaw Range. The entry had been dredged just five years earlier, making it possible for ships to sail into Portage Lake and the Portage River to the north where the twin copper boomtowns of Hancock and Houghton faced each other from opposite sides of the river. The Lynch family settled in the Franklin Township area of Hancock which was situated on the north side of the river.

The copper towns of Houghton and Hancock, Michigan in the 1860s.
(Photo courtesy of Kevin Musser)

Not only would Cornelius find competition from returning Union soldiers, but as the Irish already knew, Michigan's copper country included a large population of Cornish miners from southwest England, traditional rivals of Irish miners. There were also neighborhoods and whole communities of Swedes, Finns, Norwegians, Poles, Croats and other nationalities. But the

Cornish and Irish accounted for the largest contingents of foreign born people in the Upper Peninsula.

The Irish referred to the Cornish men as "Cousin Jacks" and Cornish women as "Cousin Jennies". The Cornish called the Irish "Micks." They often settled their differences in the hundreds of saloons that served the miners in dozens of mining towns. Boxing and wrestling were almost as common in the saloons as the rot-gut whiskey called "forty-rod." According to Angus Murdoch, author of *Boom Copper*, the term forty-rod originated because, "this type of whiskey would down a tenderfoot standing forty rods (220 yards) from an open bunghole. Even old-timers, it is said, would set fire to their own mothers after downing a shot or two."

Despite their differences, the second and third generations of Cornish and Irish Americans got along fairly well, often intermarried, and the Irish Americans even adopted a Cornish favorite for their own dinner table: the meat and vegetable pocket pie known as the pasty.

It is likely that Cornelius worked for the Quincy Mine of Hancock, Michigan as a blacksmith. He also worked with Bridget to produce the traditional large Irish family. On January 28, 1867, Bridget gave birth to a second son, and the first member of the family to be born in America. He was named Daniel Samuel Lynch, in honor of his paternal grandfather back in Ballyduff.

Over the next three years two daughters would be born; Mary in 1868 (named for Dan's mother, Mary Garan Lynch) and Bridget in 1870 (named in honor of Bridget's mother, Bridget Longe Harris). Baby Bridget became ill as an infant and lost her hearing. She would spend her life as a deaf-mute and would never marry, but she was educated and became the beloved Aunt Bridgy to her nieces and nephews. Remembered fondly for her gentleness and good cheer, Bridgy communicated with sign language and everyone in the Lynch family learned enough of it to converse easily with her.

Mineral exploration in the Upper Peninsula not only revealed massive deposits of copper, but profitable amounts of silver and iron ore, too. When an iron mining boom struck Marquette County, Cornelius moved his family to Ishpeming where several mines, including the Barnum, Cleveland and Cliff Shafts, were in full operation. Unfortunately, tragedy struck shortly after the young family settled in.

On a balmy Friday afternoon, July 23, 1871, the first child, six and a half year-old Michael was playing with some friends on a bluff above the Cleveland Mine. Family oral tradition says that the boys were picking wild blueberries when a terrible accident occurred. According to the July 29, 1871, issue of the *Marquette Mining Journal,* "On Friday of last week, a little son of Cornelius Lynch, while playing with some other boys on the bluff just south of the store at the Cleveland mine, fell over the cliff and was so severely injured that he died the next day."

The family was devastated, none more so than Cornelius. Michael was the last of his Lynch family to be born in Ireland. But Bridget had little time to grieve. She was five months pregnant with her fifth child. John "Jack" Michael Lynch would be born to Bridget in Ishpeming on November 18, 1871, but it is likely that his arrival could not fully erase the loss of her first born. Perhaps an emotional tug-of-war within Bridget caused her to nurture her new baby less than she should have. It cannot be known for sure. What is known is that Jack was destined for a tragic end himself.

Cornelius decided to leave the town where he had buried his first son and move back to the copper country, this time settling in the hamlet of Greenland in Ontonagon County. Greenland, as the name suggests, was founded by Scandinavian immigrants. The town was home to two significant copper mines; Adventure Mine and Caledonia Mine. On August 1, 1873, Bridget gave birth to their sixth child, Cornelius Francis Lynch, Jr. in Greenland.

The family was on the move again two years later and finally settled in a town where Cornelius and Bridget felt at home. They would spend the rest of their lives in Republic, Michigan, where

Cornelius found employment as a blacksmith for the Kloman mine and some of his sons eventually worked for the Republic Iron Company. It was here that his sons would get their first knowledge of mining, leading some of them toward long and successful careers. And it was here that his last four children, all sons, would be born. They were Timothy (1875); Richard (1878); William (1880) and Patrick (1885). Two other children, probably born between William and Patrick, died in childbirth, their names, if they had them, lost forever.

Keeping seven sons on the straight and narrow would be challenging in any setting, let alone a mining boomtown that attracts a transient population of young men serviced by numerous saloons and prostitutes. Cornelius Lynch came up with a simple strategy to keep his boys close to home and hopefully too tired to wander.

Winters are long and hard in the Upper Peninsula. The ground is frozen or covered in snow for seven months each year. Temperatures regularly plunge below zero with an average high hovering at about 20° Fahrenheit during the heart of winter. Homes in the mining towns, particularly those of common laborers, were not particularly well-insulated.

The Lynch home in Republic was heated by wood. Cornelius kept at least a dozen cords stacked neatly in the backyard of the home. But his sons did the stacking. And they were regularly directed to move the cords from one part of the yard to another. The lads couldn't see the sense in this, but dared not defy the sturdy blacksmith; even those sons who towered over him. Whether the mindless work kept them from snooping around the taverns or whorehouses when their father was otherwise occupied is open to conjecture. But boys will be boys.

Cornelius Sr. also attempted to stake some claim in mining exploration during his later years in Republic. He purchased 200 shares in the Gladstone Exploring Association. Virtually every miner would buy shares in some new exploration, sold to them by speculators and con-men who guaranteed a strike like the Calumet & Hecla, the most successful mine in the history of the copper region. Very few struck it rich: most failed to see a return on their investment, including Cornelius. Nevertheless, his sons kept faith in the ever-fluctuating fortunes of the mining world. The price of copper and other raw minerals would regularly plummet, only to rise again with each new invention or war.

Cornelius gave up his blacksmithing business after he reached 65 but he did not stop working. He became the mail carrier in Republic.

The Republic mining shaft and the Roman Catholic Church in Republic, Michigan, circa 1900. The Lynch home is at the far right in the bottom photo. (From the Fred & Mollie Lynch Collection.)

Bridget Harris Lynch and Cornelius Lynch with sons Timothy, Jack, Cornelius and Daniel (L to R in back) and Patrick between them.

On March 3, 1887, twenty year-old Daniel Lynch sat for his portrait by an artist named Osborn (see below). Neatly dressed in suit and tie, the dark-haired son of a blacksmith looks confident, serious and proud; a man with a future. Perhaps it was this confidence that gave him the courage to court a woman quite foreign from his familiar Irish Catholic community.

Five of the Lynch brothers in Republic, Michigan, circa 1895, back row, Tim, Pat and Dick Lynch. Front row, Dan ad Con Lynch.

*Dan Lynch, far left, joking around with some friends in Michigan. Below is
Bridgy Lynch, the deaf-mute sister of the Lynch brothers.*

Two: Deepening the American Roots

Mariette "Mate" (pronounced Mate-ee) Kendall could not have been a more unlikely match for Dan Lynch. She was a Protestant with deep roots in America, none of them Irish. Her father, Jackson Kendall, was a Union veteran, having fought with the 30th Wisconsin during the Civil War. Her grandfather, Asa Kendall, fought in the War of 1812, and was the cousin of Amos Kendall, postmaster general of the United States and closest advisor to President Andrew Jackson. Asa named his own son in honor of his cousin's colorful and controversial boss, who was serving his 2nd term as president at the time.

Mate's great-grandfather, Joshua Kendall, was a soldier during the American Revolution. Joshua was a direct descendant of Francis Miles Kendall, who emigrated from England in the 1630s and was a founder of Woburn, Massachusetts.

As if Mate Kendall's paternal lineage wasn't intimidating enough for the son of an Irish immigrant, her mother's pedigree was even more daunting. Harriet Chipman Kendall was the grand-niece of U.S. Senator Nathaniel Chipman and U.S. Representative Daniel Chipman, both from Vermont. She was a direct descendant of John Chipman, who married Hope Howland, the daughter of Mayflower pilgrim John Howland. Howland signed the Mayflower Compact after surviving a terrifying experience when he was tossed overboard by a violent storm during the Mayflower's epic crossing of the Atlantic. Mayflower pilgrim and historian William Bradford referred to Howland as, "A lusty young man," and though he was referring to his strength in holding on to a topsail halyard to prevent his drowning, Howland did father ten children with fellow pilgrim Elizabeth Tilley and his descendants in America number in the tens of thousands at this writing.

Mate also had a distant cousin in Hyde Park, New York that her husband and his brothers would later admire and in a sense, work for. His name was Franklin Delano Roosevelt.

Jackson and Harriet Kendall lived in Hanover, Wisconsin where they raised three daughters; Philena, Mate and Eva, and one son, Albert. They had cousins in Michigan's Upper Peninsula, children of their father's older sister, Adelina Kendall Durkee. Perhaps it was during a visit with these cousins that Mate encountered Dan Lynch. Whatever the circumstances Dan was confident enough to propose to the outgoing Mate and despite the objections of her family, the two were married on October 2, 1889, in Mate's hometown of Hanover. Two weeks later, on October 17, 1889, the couple renewed their vows, as required by Dan's Irish Catholic faith, at St. Augustine Catholic Church in Republic, Michigan.

Mate's sister Eva took the impressive Kendall-Chipman family heritage most seriously. She was a member of the Daughters of the American Revolution and became the Supreme Oracle of the Royal Neighbors of America, a women's philanthropic organization. Eva founded the Janesville, Wisconsin chapter of the Royal Neighbors of America in 1899, and it is still active more than a century later.

Eva rose quickly in the ranks. After a decade of steady activism on behalf of women, she was named chairman and "Supreme Manager" of the Royal Neighbors of America. In the fall of 1913 she took a much heralded tour of Royal Neighbor organizations in Montana, Idaho, Washington and Oregon, where she visited her sisters Mate and Nellie. In 1917 she was elevated to "Supreme Oracle"- the top position in the national organization. Eva's plans to travel to Oregon in May, 1924 were announced by the *Morning Oregonian* three months in advance. She would be there to help celebrate the silver jubilee of Portland's Royal Neighbor Chapter; but also to visit her sister Nellie.

Philena, known as Nellie or Nell, married her first cousin, Oscar Kendall, son of Jackson's brother Jerome, a union that would be frowned upon today, but was relatively common in America through the 19th century. Neither Nellie nor Eva had children of their own, but would often provide the motherly love to Mate's children when she was too busy to do so herself.

Eva and Nellie were dignified and meticulously attired women who lived in beautifully furnished homes. Mate regularly wore drab, heavy clothing; boots and warm hats; rode horses and camped in tents or huts in sub-zero weather on the wooded hillsides of mining camps. But Mate could dress in the latest fashions if the circumstances called for it, or if she was attempting to impress her sisters or her sisters-in-law. A picture of Mate with her shoulders draped in furs, the heads of dead young foxes dangling across her chest, seems out of place on a woman more likely to eat a fox than wear one. Generally speaking she didn't fuss over clothing, and she didn't dote over children, including her own.

Mate Kendall, by all accounts, was a bit of an enigma. She loved to have fun and could laugh easily, but she was also ornery and bossy. She would ride a horse and camp in the snow, but could also feign helplessness. She loved to travel and lived in many different places, but could also become a prisoner in her own home, hesitant to wander beyond her comfort zone.

Chas. F. Turner,   Janesville, Wis.

Daniel Chipman, the grandfather of Mate Kendall, was a Mayflower descendant and the nephew of U.S. Senator Nathaniel Chipman and U.S. Representative Daniel Chipman.

Mate, right, with her sister Eva in Janesville, Wisconsin circa 1880. The Kendall sisters were from prestigious New England stock. Their mother's line was related to Franklin Delano Roosevelt and could trace its roots to the Mayflower.

Mate Kendall (as Annie Oakley) with the cast of a play, probably in Republic, Michigan. The balding, bearded boy behind her is her young brother-in-law, Patrick Lynch, who would become a founder of the Lynch Brothers Diamond Drilling Company.

Dan Lynch obviously loved Mate. Many pictures reveal his sentimentality toward her during sixty-two years of marriage. He saw something in Mate that many younger members of the family rarely did. While Dan was deeply loved and admired by his children, grandchildren, nieces and nephews, Mate was often feared or tolerated. Suffice to say that Mate was more at ease with adults than she was with children, although photographs in her old age show her clearly pleased to be a great-grandmother.

As a young woman Mate was more like her only brother, Albert, than either of her sisters. "Bert" Kendall moved to the Portland area in October, 1906. Initially he resided in the home of his sister and brother-in-law, Nell & Oscar Kendall, in an area then known variously as Lents, Woodstock or Kendall Station (the train stop named after Oscar) near Portland's Mt. Scott. The *Morning Oregonian* actually announced the October, 1906, arrival of Bert Kendall to the area, as his brother-in-law was by then a famous man in Portland.

"Albert Kendall and family of Belvidere, Illinois, are guests of O.J. Kendall in Woodstock. A. Kendall, who was agent for Chicago & Northern Railway Co. at Belvidere for a number of years, comes to Portland with intention of locating permanently. He thinks Portland is destined to be the railroad center of the West. He said he sold more tickets to Portland and other points in Oregon than to all of the Pacific Coast combined. He expects to enter the company of Northern Pacific."

The article called Albert the brother of Oscar. Actually he was the brother of Nellie Kendall. Perhaps Oscar, who was prominent in the business, political and law enforcement circles of Portland, had never told anyone that he was married to his first cousin.

Albert Kendall settled in Troutdale, a small town located northeast of Portland on the Columbia River, where he was the railroad station agent and raised gladioli. He spent his free time fishing and exploring the woods of the western states. Known for his industry, Bert fashioned special "ice-shoes" out of old tires with heavy tread in order to continue working outdoors during the ice storms so common in the Columbia Gorge.

Sharon Nesbit, writing for the Troutdale Historical Society Newsletter in 2009, reported that, "A.D. Kendall and family arrived in Troutdale on June 14, 1907, and according to his own account, at 6:30 a.m. He *was* a railroad man, after all. He and his wife and four daughters first lived in upstairs quarters of the original Troutdale rail depot, which burned later that summer, resulting in construction of the present depot. Kendall retired from his job as station agent Oct. 16, 1940."

Bert Kendall, along with Troutdale mayor Carrie Larson, was called as a character witness by the defense in the 1914 murder trial of Kendall's neighbor, Joe Mossi. Mossi, a Troutdale rancher, had been arrested on the charge of killing an "unidentified tramp" on his property in November, 1913. A state witness testified that Mossi was known for chasing off vagrants with a shotgun.

Troutdale, Oregon, circa 1910, when Bert Kendall was the depot agent.

Mossi claimed he wasn't home at the time of the shooting and even though a deputy sheriff said that his shotgun had been recently fired, a hung jury meant that Mossi walked away a free man. He was never tried again and the "nameless tramp" remained unidentified.

Bert had four daughters and no sons, but he treated his nephew Fred like a son and a best friend.   Despite a 16 year difference in age between the two, Bert and Fred were "two peas in a pod." Both men were good-natured jokesters who loved to laugh, eat, drink and especially, fish. The two men went on many fishing trips together and Fred never went to the Portland area without visiting Uncle Bert, or without a fishing pole.

After retiring as station agent, Bert Kendall switched his attention to his favorite pastime: raising the gladiolus flower. He'd been doing it as a side job for years. Kendall became the president of the Oregon Gladiolus Society and also served on the board of the Troutdale State Bank.

Fred Lynch jokes with his Uncle Bert Kendall, in straw hat, and Bert's 2nd wife Amanda, at their home in Troutdale, Oregon around 1950.

According to an article on Troutdale history from the town's official website, "In 1928, A.D. Kendall, station agent of the Troutdale Rail Depot, took a custom-made box, filled it with his most prized gladioli, loaded it aboard a refrigerated rail car and set out for the American Gladiolus Society's annual show and competition in Toledo, Ohio. Kendall, his wife and the glads all arrived in fine shape five days later and the Troutdale grown flowers carried numerous awards. His feat of shipping the flowers by rail wowed the other growers."

Kendall and his family moved into a new home in 1928, along the Columbia River Highway. It was built by the Oregon architect Harry Bramhall. According to Nesbit, "The Kendall home is of Arts and Crafts style and unique because it is stucco, embedded with cracked glass. It is unusual in this area, and the few other homes finished in that manner have been painted over."

Evelyn Kendall and Julius Lampert

Bert Kendall's beautiful gladiolus farm, which was directly behind the new home, was inherited by Bert's oldest daughter Evelyn and her husband Julius Lampert. In the 1960s the Lamperts were involved in a landmark case involving pollution. In Lampert v. Reynolds Metal Company, the couple contended that the massive Reynolds Aluminum Plant near Troutdale destroyed their gladioli by releasing fluorides into the air which in turn killed their flowers. The initial court ruled in favor of the Lamperts and awarded them a substantial sum in punitive damages. But Reynolds won on appeal in the district court with the peculiar argument that their company did more good for the general public than the gladiolus farm and therefore should be allowed more flexibility.

On January 19, 1967, the United States Court of Appeals Ninth Circuit dismissed Reynolds's argument and ordered the district court to revisit the issue. But the settlement that the Lamperts eventually received from Reynolds was too late to save the farm. Thanks to the particulates emitted from the Reynolds Plant, the popular Kendall Gladiolus Farm ceased to exist.

The Bert Kendall house still stands at the intersection of Historic Columbia River Highway and Kendall Street, named in his honor. It is the office of the Troutdale Chamber of Commerce. Less than a mile away on the Sandy River is the iconic, and still popular, Tad's Chicken 'n Dumplins' Restaurant, which opened in the 1920s and employed some of Bert's daughters and granddaughters. Members of the Lynch and Kendall clans met there regularly when in the Portland area to visit Albert or other kin.

By all accounts Dan Lynch was well-liked by the Kendall family. He was the son of an Irish-Catholic immigrant and certainly felt the stigma attached to this ethnic group by Protestant Americans during the 19th century. But when he exchanged vows with Mate in 1889 he not only united a prominent Protestant family with a large Catholic clan; he instantly added 246 years to the American roots of his progeny.

Eva Kendall, Supreme Oracle of the Royal Neighbors of America, and sister of Mate Kendall, with husband Fred Childs in Wisconsin. In her final years Eva was cared for by her nephew Frederick Albert Lynch and his wife Molly Wittanen Lynch at her home near Janesville, Wisconsin. She had no children of her own and left much of her property to her nephew.

Three: To Oregon and Back

The newlyweds, Dan and Mate Lynch, initially settled down in Hancock, where Dan had been born in 1867. As the 1890 census was destroyed in a fire it is not known what occupation Dan pursued. Perhaps he was a miner. But after his first child, Frederick Albert Lynch, was born on September 10, 1890, he decided to seek fresh opportunities. Mate's sister Nell lived in Portland, Oregon where her husband Oscar owned the Oregon Steam Dye & Cleaning Works. He also owned the Albany Steam Dye 60 miles south of Portland in the Willamette River town of Albany. Oscar offered his brother-in-law a job running the Albany store. Dan took Mate, who was eight months pregnant, and their two year-old son Fred, on a train to Portland. It was the first time either Mate or Dan had gone west. Though they would return to Michigan for a few years, they would spend most of the rest of their long lives in the Pacific Northwest.

The long train ride was difficult on the pregnant Mate Lynch. On June 15, 1892, shortly after her arrival in Portland, she gave birth to a premature baby girl. Harriet Veronica Lynch, named in honor of Harriet Chipman, would survive, but according to her daughter Fritzi, "She was wrapped in cotton batting, rubbed with oil and laid in a shoe box; the box sat on the open oven door to keep her warm."

Dan and Mate had little Harriet baptized on July 10, 1892, in Portland's Cathedral of the Immaculate Conception. They named Dan's brother Jack as the godfather and Kate Keese, an old friend from Republic, as godmother.

As became the custom in the family, many rosaries were said and it was probably during this trying time that Mate fully embraced her husband's faith. Her family was not happy about the conversion, but she remained a devout Catholic for the rest of her life. That doesn't mean she forgot her roots. Her granddaughter Fritzi recalled that, "She still loved the old Protestant hymns like

'That Old Rugged Cross' and 'He Walks With Me' and sang them at home."

Harriet Lynch in Portland, Oregon circa 1894.

The 1892 Albany, Oregon City Directory lists both the Albany Steam Dye Works and the Dan Lynch family as residing near 2nd and Ferry St. The only surviving photograph linked to their time in Albany is from the famous Crawford & Paxton Studios. Andrew B. Paxton was a respected saddler and a pioneer in western photography. He teamed up with one of his students, James G. Crawford, to form the Paxton & Crawford Studios. Crawford specialized in scenic views and structures, often incorporating people in the scenes. He was also noted for his study of local Native American history.

Fred Lynch, 1893, in Albany, Oregon.

Dan Lynch had his two year-old son Fred sit for a photograph. The innate good nature of Fred Lynch can be seen at this tender age, as he slips one hand in his pocket and rests the other on a fence post, a look of patience on his cherub face. The photograph was sent to Dan's mother in Republic.

A major flood struck Portland in the spring of 1894 and devastated the downtown business district, including Oscar Kendall's business, which had recently been remodeled. A photograph shows Oscar Kendall standing on a plank extending from a back entrance to the Dye Works on West Burnside. Flood water had inundated the building. The damage was likely significant for Kendall's business and might be why he decided to sell the Albany Steam Works to the Magnolia Laundry, which continued to run the company under the name Magnolia on the same location in Albany for another half century.

Mate Kendall Lynch had purchased a piece of property near Mt. Tabor, east of Portland, from her sister Nell for $700. Perhaps it was the intention of the two sisters to settle down near each other. As it turned out, their lives were to take dramatically different routes. Mate followed her husband as he became a diamond driller. Nell's husband would get embroiled in a sensational Portland murder trial, become the bodyguard and trusted assistant to U.S. Attorney Francis J. Heney, and finally die a mysterious death in San Francisco in 1907.

But before his brother-in-law became an unlikely celebrity, Dan returned with his family to Michigan, where he settled in his parent's hometown of Republic and took a job as the bartender for Albert Kittle's Pascoe House Saloon. The Pascoe House still stands and now serves as the Republic Historical Museum. But Dan's stint as a bartender was brief. In 1897 he moved to Dickinson County, Michigan to supervise a diamond drilling crew for Sullivan Brothers Machinery Company, which was headquartered in Chicago. It was the beginning of a long association that Dan Lynch and his brothers would have with the relatively new technology of diamond bit solid core drilling.

Oscar Kendall standing on a plank near the back entry of Kendall's Oregon Steam Dye in Portland following the epic flood of 1894.

The last of Dan and Mate's three children, Kendall Oscar Lynch, was born in Waucedah, Dickinson County, Michigan on May 27, 1897. Naming his son after Oscar Kendall reveals the affection and admiration that Dan Lynch felt for a brother-in-law, who would soon be known as much more than "the steam-dye man."

The Pascoe House in Republic, Michigan, where Dan Lynch served as a bartender in 1897. Courtesy Republic Historical Museum.

Fred & Harriet Lynch, circa 1895.

In 1901, Dan Lynch and his young family were back in Hancock, Michigan where Dan supervised a diamond drilling job for Sullivan Machinery at the Quincy Mine. It was the innocent roots of a company that would be instrumental in the development of the Pacific Northwest. But in the beginning diamond drilling operations set off some of the earliest strikes by miners and union organizers who were dismayed by the switch from hand-operated drills to the "air drills" that included diamond drills. The greatest tragedy in Copper Country history was indirectly related to this fear of change. On Christmas Eve, 1913, 74 people, including 56 children, were trampled to death at the Italian Hall in Red Jacket (now Calumet, Michigan). All of the victims were members of striking mine workers families. The stampede was caused by a false alarm of "Fire" that strikers insisted, but never conclusively proved, was caused by the Citizens Alliance, an organization that supported the mine owners.

Like all improvement in technology, the air drills were inevitable, and as the Lynch Brothers later demonstrated, diamond drill companies employed many people, including men to prepare a site, move equipment and support the drilling crew. Diamond drilling was never a one-man operation.

On September 14, 1901, Jackson Kendall, Mate's father, passed away in Broadhead, Wisconsin and the family took a trip to Hanover to attend his funeral at the Trinity Church. The Civil War veteran was laid to rest next to Mate's mother Harriet in the Plymouth Cemetery.

By the turn of the century all of the Lynch siblings, with the exception of Bridgy and 15 year-old Patrick, had started new lives and careers beyond Republic. Mary Lynch married Dennis McCarthy in Republic on May 20, 1890. Mary was a music teacher. Dennis was a saloon keeper at the time but a few years later he became a section hand for the Chicago and Northwest Railroad office in Republic. In the late 1890s Mary & Dennis moved to Gladstone, Michigan, on the Little Bay de Noc of Lake Michigan, 50 miles south of Ishpeming. They opened a variety store and raised a family of two daughters and six sons.

William "Bill" Lynch became a telephone operator and railroad dispatcher, first in Republic and later in Proctor, Minnesota, just outside of Duluth on Lake Superior. But most of the brothers, like many other Irish from the Upper Peninsula, were lured to the new mining boomtowns of Cripple Creek and Leadville, Colorado; the British Columbia towns of Britannia Beach and Phoenix; and of course, Butte, Montana.

Tim was first to leave, heading to Butte prior to turn of the century. Dick and Con followed him there. But Dan took jobs in Colorado. By 1902 he was a mining engineer for the Isabella Gold Mine in Cripple Creek, Colorado and the following year was working for the Silent Friend Mine of Leadville.

This was a time when Dan seemed to be rushing from one location to another, supervising diamond drill crews for exploratory purposes. Once he satisfied the mine owners that they were on to something he would head off to another job. If two jobs required his attention at the same time he seemed to turn to his apprentice; which just happened to be his youngest brother Pat. Pat turned 18 in 1903, but he was already an experienced diamond driller. And his 35 year-old brother Dan seemed to trust him above all others.

On the back of this photograph Dan Lynch wrote that this was part of the Isabella Mine Co. property where he was a mining engineer.

Dan and Mate Lynch learned how to rough it at remote, mountainous drilling jobs in the early part of the 20th century.

Harriet, Kendall and Fred Lynch during a visit with their grandparents in Republic, Michigan, circa 1904.

Four: The Strange Saga of the Steam Dye Man

Oscar J. Kendall's sudden rise to fame doesn't seem to have been premeditated. In fact, it was probably a bit of a shock to the steam dye man. An accident with an electric street car in 1892 set in motion a wild string of events that made him famous in Portland, but eventually led to his mysterious death in San Francisco.

Born in Michigan in 1858, Oscar Kendall was the third son, and seventh of ten children, to Jerome B. Kendall and Charlotte Abbott. His father was a wagon maker. In 1878 Oscar married his first cousin, Philena "Nellie" Kendall, the daughter of his father's younger brother Jackson Kendall. In the 1880 census he is living with Nellie and her family in Hanover, Wisconsin. His occupation was listed in the census record as "hatter."

Sometime during the 1880s Oscar and Nellie moved west. Death notices about Oscar in 1907, and one letter he received from a friend in 1898, would indicate that the couple first settled in Alaska. The *San Francisco Call* wrote that Kendall, "had spent part of his life in Alaska," and the *Morning Oregonian* reported that Oscar J. Kendall, "was well-known in Portland and equally as well-known in Alaska."

In a personal letter dated August 15, 1898, one James McCloskey of Juneau, Alaska wrote excitedly to Kendall about a recent strike near Tagish Lake, which was on the Klondike trail in the Yukon Territory. "...It is going to be a great thing...They are crazy over the strike...Kendall, it's something grand. I don't see how I can miss it now. When I find out more about the mine I will let you know. Times are very quiet in Juneau but this new strike has them all crazy."

McCloskey also mentions other men who were apparently acquaintances of Oscar Kendall, including Lachie McKennon, Walter Carter, and three men referred to as Staley, Heume and Cruse. The first gold rush to the Juneau area had occurred in the 1880s. It is likely that Oscar Kendall went there with some of these friends. The men are hard to track down but McCloskey was a 38 year-old Irishman who seems to have spent his entire life looking for gold. McKennon was a 31 year-old Scotsman who had a wife and young son at the time of this letter.

But by 1890 prospecting for gold was a thing of the past for Oscar Kendall. He had settled in Portland where he opened the Oregon Steam Dye Works on West Burnside Street between 8th and Park. He advertised regularly in the *Morning Oregonian*. His business "Cleaned, colored and repaired clothing," and also sold women's clothing.

Kendall was remembered as a quiet, unobtrusive man who, along with his wife, was also involved in purchasing real estate, particularly east of the Willamette River, which at the time was not part of the city. In the 1900 census he modestly claims to be a farmer, although he simply raised a few chickens and a garden with Nellie. In reality Kendall's life was not so simple, quiet or unobtrusive.

Oscar Kendall was active in the Portland community the moment he arrived there. Whether it was business or pleasure he kept himself busy. Three days before his life-altering accident he had won the sack race at the annual Scottish celebration known as the Caledonian Games.

As his wealth increased and his business prospered, Kendall invited his brother-in-law, Dan Lynch, to move to Oregon and run a second steam dye company in Albany. But one month after Lynch arrived, and just four days before Lynch's infant daughter Harriet was baptized in a Portland church, Oscar J. Kendall was involved in an accident with an electric streetcar.

Oscar and Nell Kendall tend to their chickens in the backyard of their home on Woodstock Street in Portland, circa 1905.

The Oregon Steam Dye Works in Portland, Oregon, circa 1890. The carriage, and a subsequent photograph taken in 1894 after the store was remodeled, reveals that the exact location of the company was on Portland's Burnside Street between 8th and Park Ave in the downtown district. The individuals in the photograph are not identified but it is likely that the man next to the dog is 32-year old Oscar Kendall. The company's humorous motto is written along the top of the carriage. It says, "We Dye to Live."

On July 6, 1892, the past collided with the future, both literally and figuratively, for 33 year-old Oscar J. Kendall. Driving his horse & buggy down Portland's 2nd Ave. between Oak St. and Pine St. Kendall was struck by an electric streetcar. He was thrown from the buggy and seriously injured. What he could not have known was that his life would never be the same again. Because of the accident he would go from being the unknown owner of a laundry works, to the lead witness in a sensational murder trial; deputy sheriff of Multnomah County; federal secret service agent and finally bodyguard and investigator in both the Oregon Land Fraud Trials and the San Francisco Graft Trials. And he had less than 15 years to live.

Following the streetcar accident, Kendall spent several weeks recovering at home before contacting Portland attorney Xenophon N. Steeves. With the assistance of Steeves he filed suit against the Metropolitan Street Railway Company. He asked for $13,246.40 in damages to his buggy, his horse and himself.

The following June a Portland jury ruled in favor of Kendall but awarded him a mere $1000 for his troubles. While he contemplated an appeal he became a close friend to Steeves. And through Steeves he became acquainted with all sorts of colorful characters from Portland's notorious waterfront, including Joseph "Bunco" Kelly.

Bunco Kelly was a "crimper", which meant he would pinch or "shanghai" unsuspecting men and sell them to ships as forced laborers. Portland was infamous for its Shanghai business which outdid every other west coast city including San Francisco. Much of it took place in taverns, rooms and opium dens beneath the streets of downtown Portland. Kelly admitted to personally Shanghaiing over 2,000 men during his 15-year career. His usual fee was about $50 per head. He became a rich and well-connected man.

One story claimed that Kelly was responsible for stashing away a group of men in the basement of a Portland morgue, making them believe it was the cellar of a tavern. Several of them consumed embalming fluid and died. But Kelly sold them anyway, loading them on to a ship as if they were simply drunk or knocked out. He earned the derogatory nickname "Bunco" for selling a cigar store Indian as a live sailor, but was also known more reverently among waterfront thugs as "King of the Crimpers."

X.N. Steeves allegedly hired Kelly to help him "get rid" of "Uncle George" Washington Sayles, who, along with a business partner Wong Ah Tong, was suing Steeves client, William Allen, following a failed business venture called the Southern Portland Brick Company. Ironically, both Wong and Allen were believed to be involved in Portland's lucrative opium smuggling trade and were well acquainted with Bunco Kelly.

Oscar Kendall was likely familiar with Chinese opium den operators before he became friends with Steeves. As the owner of a laundry business Kendall knew many Chinese men who also operated laundries. In fact, that was the standard business for the Chinese all over the United States in the later part of the 19th century. And the Chinese laundries were often a front for the much more profitable opium dens.

Contrary to popular belief, the opium dens were not the last refuge of the down and out; nor did they simply cater to the Chinese community. In fact, the Chinese populace accounted for a small percentage of opium den patrons. Perhaps the largest clientele, according to historian Timothy J. Gilfoyle in the book *A Pickpocket's Tale* came from "...an American bohemian subculture."

"An ill-defined intellectual proletariat of penniless and carefree writers, journalists, poets, actors, and artists," wrote Gilfoyle, "bohemians challenged a host of Victorian social norms." And that included free-sex and opium. The bohemians shared the dens with rich and poor, black and white, socialite and prostitute. According to Gilfoyle, "The opium den promoted a certain egalitarian ethos." And there was a "loyalty and camaraderie among opium smokers, in which social position accounted for little."

Portland in the 1890s was rivaled only by San Francisco as a cosmopolitan west coast city. It had its bohemian subculture, but it also had wealthy, progressive citizens; some of whom not only tolerated the opium dens but likely visited them.

On the night of September 26, 1894, "Uncle" George Sayles disappeared from his home in the Fulton Park neighborhood of Portland. His body was recovered from the Willamette River ten days later. Uncle George had been bludgeoned to death.

Suspicion immediately fell upon Bunco Kelly and some other crimpers and ex-cons seen hanging around Sayles's home. But as police continued to investigate the crime they came to the conclusion that Kelly acted alone and was hired to kill Sayles by none other than the attorney X.N. Steeves, who wanted to help his client William Allen in the upcoming lawsuit brought against him by Sayles and Wong. Sayles was a popular and generous saloon-keeper and a jury might be sympathetic to him. But Wong was Chinese and his testimony against a white man would not carry the same weight in 1890s Portland or anywhere else in America.

The Morning Oregonian reported that Kelly and his gang planned to shanghai Sayles to keep him from testifying. But Sayles put up a fight and Kelly beat him to death before dumping his body in the Willamette River. Initially the police suspected Oscar J. Kendall as an accomplice to the murder. It was suggested that Kendall was the agent who represented Steeves in negotiations with Kelly to get rid of Sayles.

In the October 12, 1894 issue of the *Morning Oregonian* a headline reads: **Kendall's Vigorous Denial,** with a sub heading of: **He Had No Sort of Connection With the Sayles Case, He Says**
The article reported the following:

"Oscar J. Kendall, proprietor of the Oregon Steam Dye Works, is indignant over the prominence he has attained in the Sayles Murder Case, and the assertion made that he acted as an agent for Steeves. When seen at his place of business yesterday by an Oregonian representative, he was not in the best of humor, and said: 'I know nothing whatsoever about the case, no more than you do. I was subpoenaed as a witness before the grand jury but I could tell them nothing. I was asked a great many questions about things I knew nothing about. The statement published that I apparently first mentioned the scheme to Kelly for the removal of Sayles, or carried out Steeves instructions in any way, is absolutely false. Such statements place a business man in bad light, and injure him to be so misrepresented. I hope it will be corrected.' "

The grand jury was satisfied with Kendall's claims of innocence but Joseph "Bunco" Kelly and Xenophon Steeves were indicted for first degree murder. District Attorney Wilson Theodore Hume would lead the prosecution. Steeves had some reason to believe that Kendall would be a favorable witness. He was soon disabused of that idea. In fact, Oscar Kendall became the star witness for the state in what became the most sensationalized murder trial held in Portland during the rough period of the 1890s. Every word of Kendall's testimony was reported in the *Morning Oregonian* newspaper. The whole affair was great fodder for the press: a respected attorney and a notorious criminal indicted together for a grisly murder.

Under oath Kendall admitted to being on very friendly terms with Steeves and that he was acquainted with Bunco Kelly, but said he never met George Sayles. He also testified that Steeves had sent him to ask Kelly to visit the attorney's office a couple of weeks prior to the disappearance of Sayles. Kendall claimed that the following week, "Steeves told me he had seen Kelly and said that he had a fellow who was an important witness in a lawsuit whom he wanted to get out of town for three or four weeks to prevent him testifying."

District Attorney Hume continued to press Kendall for more details. The witness said that he ran into Kelly the day before the body of Sayles was discovered in the Willamette River. He testified that Kelly told him that, "he had got his man all right, but he was a murderous s---."

The following day, according to Kendall, he went to Steeves office to confront him about what Kelly had said and saw Kelly leaving Steeves's office. Kendall confronted Steeves on the very day that Sayles body was recovered. According to Kendall, Steeves simply admitted, "that he guessed Kelly had done it, as he appeared scratched up." And then, as Kendall related the story, Steeves simply walked out of the office.

John F. Caples served as defense attorney for Steeves and Kelly. Caples was a noted debater and popular in Portland for operating the Sellwood Ferry that took Portlanders across the Willamette to the town of Sellwood prior to the construction of the Sellwood Bridge. Under vigorous cross-examination by Caples, the *Morning Oregonian* reported that Oscar Kendall "was cool and deliberate and gave his evidence clearly and concisely."

However, during the second day of cross-examination Caples revealed that X.N. Steeves had agreed to a deal with Kendall to construct a building on Kendall's property at 8th and Burnside, but that Steeves had failed to put in his share of the money. Caples suggested that this was the reason Kendall had testified against his friend.

Kendall confessed that Steeves had "left him in a bad place" and pressed by Caples, confessed that he had accepted a loan from a law partner of District Attorney Hume after the arrest of Steeves. Caples implied that the loan was made for the purpose of getting Kendall to turn into a state witness. But Kendall steadfastly insisted that Hume was not involved and knew nothing of the loan which was legitimate and amounted to about $200.

John Hall, the attorney who made the loan to Kendall, also testified and confirmed that he had made a loan of $190 to Kendall that was strictly a business transaction without the knowledge of Wilson Hume. But Hume was clearly annoyed by the development.

The *Morning Oregonian* seemed to favor the prosecution, but the defense at least convinced the jury to reduce the charges. Kelly was convicted of second degree murder and sent to the state penitentiary for 15 years. Steeves was convicted of manslaughter, but immediately released on bail pending appeal. The Portland police didn't want to hold him anyway. During his brief incarceration following arrest the jail was inundated with visitors, particularly young women, who wished to see Steeves.

Steeves appealed his manslaughter conviction before the Oregon Supreme Court and on March 2, 1896, the Court threw out his conviction and ordered a retrial. The retrial took place in Hillsboro, just west of Portland, later that year.

Kendall and many of the other witnesses repeated their previous testimony in the Hillsboro trial. But Steeves also submitted to lengthy questioning and his attorney tried to impeach some of the witnesses against him, particularly Kendall. Attorney John Caples produced a note purportedly written by Kendall to Steeves three months prior to the murder of Sayles. It read:

"June 8, 1894 —XN: Please wipe out my gun. I can't come up today. You will find rod in case. Kelly will be the man to look up the Dago. He knows everybody in the North End. O.J.K."

Of course, Caples did not mean to imply that this note had anything to do with the Sayles murder as it would have implicated his man. But it was probably introduced to cast some shadow over Oscar Kendall's reputation.

On December 21, 1896 the Hillsboro jury acquitted Steeves of all charges connected to the Sayles murder. It was sweet relief for Steeves, but too late to restore his reputation in Portland. He continued to practice law in the Portland area for another three years but eventually moved to Arizona where he died in 1927.

Kelly served out his term in the state pen, wrote a book about his experiences in prison and never returned to the crimping business. He also never admitted to killing Sayles. He pinned the blame on a rival crimper by the name of Larry Sullivan, a former prize fighter who had some members of the Portland Police Department on his payroll. Kelly always insisted that Sullivan and the police had framed him for the murder of Sayles.

Only Kendall seemed to have benefited from the scandalous trial. In early June of 1894, Portland and the entire Willamette Valley were inundated with a huge flood. Kendall's business in downtown Portland was nearly destroyed. He sold the Albany Steam Dye Works run by his brother-in-law Dan Lynch, who returned to Michigan. Ironically, it would be Dan Lynch and his brothers who, many years later, as the Lynch Brothers Diamond Drilling Company, would do the core drilling for the Army Corps of Engineers and the Bureau of Reclamation that would determine the locations of the very dams responsible for preventing similar floods to the Portland area, and pave the way for the construction of the dams that created the Bull Run Reservoir, providing drinking water to Portland.

Oscar Kendall was not destroyed by the 1894 flood. His business reopened after the flood. But it would seem that he had made both friends and enemies during the Steeves trial. His name popped up in the *Morning Oregonian* periodically, usually relating to property acquisition or the theft or destruction of property already owned by him or Nellie.

HON. WILSON T. HUME,

Portland, Or.

Wilson Theodore Hume, Multnomah County District Attorney who became a close friend and confidante of Oscar J. Kendall.

Joseph "Bunco" Kelly

In July, 1896, Joseph Richardson, the keeper of a livery stable on 4th and Burnside, was arraigned for larceny of the buggy owned by Oscar Kendall. A year later one J.D. Tiederman, who, like George Sayles, was a Portland saloon-keeper, was arrested for defacing a building owned by Nellie Kendall on Burnside Street. Nellie, according to the *Morning Oregonian*, had asked Tiederman to, "Make good on the damage caused. He refused and was arrested."

Ironically, just two weeks earlier, a P.J. Tiederman had been joined in matrimony by Lillian Cummings. The ceremony took place in the home of Oscar and Nellie Kendall, while they were still living on 10th Street, a couple of blocks from their Burnside property.

But Kendall benefited from friends earned during the Steeves trial more than he suffered from enemies made. In February of '96, he was appointed receiver of the saloon of Thomas Magee on the corner of Sixth & Stark by Judge Stearns on the application of Attorney John H. Hall, the same man who loaned him $190 prior to his testimony in the Steeves trial. But his greatest benefactor seems to have been District Attorney Wilson T. Hume.

Hume appreciated Kendall's honesty and steely character. He also discovered that Kendall was very adept with a revolver; a skill that came in handy during those rough and tumble days in places like Alaska, Seattle and Portland. Hume hired Oscar Kendall to carry the box containing papers from grand jury deliberations to his office and from there his responsibilities grew. Hume and Kendall were kindred spirits. They were the same age and both were active members of the Progressive wing of the Republican Party.

Ironically, it was Hume, not Kendall, that rushed off to Alaska following the letter sent to Kendall by James McCloskey. Hume joined the Klondike Gold Rush in 1899, then moved on to Nome, where he became Deputy U.S. Attorney. In May, 1900, Hume was in Portland briefly on his way back to Nome following a trip to Washington D.C. where he lobbied congressmen on behalf of individual miners against the millionaires trying to tie-up claims in Alaska.

While in Portland he hung out with his old buddy Oscar Kendall. The two men were strolling through downtown Portland on the evening of May 16th when they were accosted on the corner of 4th and Washington by Tom McGrath. McGrath had been convicted of gambling by Hume several years before and when he saw the attorney he began to scream obscenities at him. According to Hume and Kendall, McGrath threatened to kill Hume, but when he tried to throw a punch it was blocked by Kendall who then delivered one knock-down blow to McGrath's face. A large crowd gathered and prevented the fight from escalating until police arrived and arrested all three men on charges of disorderly conduct and in the case of former D.A. Hume, resisting arrest.

The Municipal courtroom was packed the following day for the arraignment. But charges against Hume and Kendall were dismissed by Judge Hennessey, while a furious McGrath was convicted of disorderly conduct.

Nine days later Hume was on a ship bound for Nome, but a year later he was practicing law in San Francisco. He travelled back and forth between Portland and San Francisco over the next few years and was often involved in controversial lawsuits in both cities. Sometime during this period, Oscar Kendall managed to become Deputy Sheriff of Multnomah County. And then, perhaps from a recommendation by Hume, Deputy Kendall caught the attention of U.S. Attorney Francis J. Heney, when he arrived in Portland to prosecute what became known as the Oregon Land Fraud Scandal.

Oscar and Nellie Kendall in front of their home on Woodstock St., circa 1900.

The U.S. Government had decided to sell some federal land to settlers at $2.50 an acre in Oregon. The idea was to help the average American get a start on farming or even timber production. But the big timber barons saw an opportunity and with the help of Oregon's United States senator, John H. Mitchell, and both of Oregon's representatives in Congress, huge chunks of land were handed over to timber companies for a pittance. President Theodore Roosevelt sent Heney to Oregon to put a stop to the land frauds and prosecute Mitchell and his cronies.

Heney got on well with both Hume and Kendall. All three were in their mid-40s, having the distinction of being born a couple of years prior to the Civil War. They had common political views and seemed tireless in their pursuit of political graft. Hume was busy with his own cases up and down the Pacific coast, but Kendall could be of service to Francis J. Heney.

The Oregon Land Fraud Trials were sensational and dangerous. There were numerous threats against Heney's life. Kendall, an expert with a revolver, became his bodyguard. Kendall sat right behind Heney in the courtroom, a loaded revolver inside his suit coat. When not protecting his new boss, Kendall helped with the investigations.

U.S. Attorney Francis J. Heney

Senator Mitchell was found guilty of land fraud and sent to prison; a rarity in American political history. Oregon's two U.S. representatives, John Williamson and Binger Hermann, were also convicted. Only U.S. Senator Charles William Fulton avoided indictment, although Heney had his suspicions about Fulton too. The two would remain bitter political enemies for years to come.

While the trial was underway the city of San Francisco was nearly destroyed by the great earthquake of 1906. Hume was there on the very day it struck, but was not injured. San Francisco, led by Mayor Eugene Schmitz and the good-natured political boss Abe Ruef, was already notorious for graft, including rampant bribery and kick-backs for government contracts. Following the earthquake the city sunk deeper into unmitigated corruption as city officials took advantage of the money, both government and private, pouring in to rebuild the beloved city.

Sugar magnate and philanthropist Rudolph Spreckles urged President Roosevelt to send Heney down from Oregon to clean up San Francisco and offered to put up $200,000 of his own money to help pay expenses. Roosevelt followed through, but San Francisco proved an even tougher nut to crack than Oregon; and much more dangerous.

Heney arrived in San Francisco with Oscar J. Kendall by his side. Kendall was accompanied by his wife Nellie. Now officially part of the federal secret service, Kendall was in San Francisco, not only to protect Heney, but to assist with the investigations. All of Heney's men, including Oscar Kendall, proved an annoyance for Schmitz, Ruef and their cronies.

In December of 1906, attorneys for Ruef tried to dissuade Kendall and other investigators by issuing subpoenas for them to testify in the graft trials. They were trying to expose political motives. Kendall took the stand, but as in the Steeves-Kelly murder trial a decade before, he was unruffled and the defense dropped the tactic.

One month later, on January 8, 1907, Oscar Kendall became violently ill. He was rushed to Lane Hospital, Nellie by his side.

Kendall writhed in pain from convulsions that the hospital spokesman attributed to pneumonia. But when Kendall suddenly died on January 11th his body was removed to the hospital morgue and the press was notified that Heney's trusted bodyguard died of cerebral meningitis.

The San Francisco Call announced the death of Kendall the following day. The article noted that Kendall had been Heney's attendant "since the opening of the graft cases here," and that he was *"adept at handling a revolver."*

"No one would have imagined," wrote *The Call*, "from his quiet and unobtrusive manner that he was a famous shot. He never sought notoriety, and since he came to this city he has avoided any mention of his name in public print."

That desired anonymity would dissipate quickly with his sudden death.

Nellie Kendall accompanied the body of her husband back to Portland, his casket covered with bouquets and "wreaths of green leaves" from Mr. and Mrs. Francis Heney. Upon arrival in Portland the Secret Service ordered an autopsy of Kendall before he could be interred. Dr. Sanford Blanding Whiting (1868 - 1924) was hired to conduct the autopsy. What he found caught the attention of newspapers from Seattle to San Francisco.

The body of Oscar J. Kendall was missing all of its organs. Wadded newspapers filled the voids. Whiting also found high levels of strychnine in the corpse. *The Morning Oregonian* jumped on the news. It came to the conclusion that Oscar J. Kendall had not died from natural causes. He had been murdered.

Kendall was buried on January 15th. His funeral service was held at Dunning's Chapel in downtown Portland with the well-known Presbyterian minister Rev. A. J. Montgomery presiding. The service was well-attended, but only four relatives were mentioned in his brief funeral notice: his wife, two brothers and his sister-in-law, Mrs. Daniel Lynch. But the burial of Oscar J. Kendall did not end the debate over his death; especially between competing newspapers. The *San Francisco Call* published the allegations from the *Morning Oregonian* on the front page of its January 17, 1907, edition. Five successive headlines screamed lurid enticements:

Portland Officials Make Sensational Accusation

SAY HENEY'S GUARD WAS POISONED

Startling Phase of Graft Cases Suggested Declare Kendall Was Victim of Strychnine

Autopsy Reveals the Disappearance of Organs

PORTLAND, Jan. 16.—The Evening Telegram publishes the following:

The family of Oscar J. Kendall, the bodyguard of Francis J. Heney who died suddenly in San Francisco last Friday, suspect that he was poisoned and an autopsy was held here today. Evidence is said to have been found strengthening the belief that Kendall was the victim of foul play. Not only did Dr. Sanford Whiting, who performed the autopsy, find the vital organs missing, but he also discovered strong traces of strychnine poisoning.

Investigation has disclosed the fact that the symptoms manifested by the patient during his brief illness, instead of being those of meningitis, were those of poisoning. All the information which has thus far been secured points so strongly to foul play that a thorough investigation has been started by the authorities.

so strongly to foul play that a thorough investigation has been started by the authorities.

SUSPICIOUS CIRCUMSTANCES

The most suspicious circumstances were furnished through the discovery after the arrival of the body in this city that every vital organ in it had been removed and newspapers stuffed in their place. Where, when or for what purpose these organs were removed constitute the mystery which has aroused the family, friends and authorities to determined action. Their mysterious disappearance, coupled with other strange features of the case, support the suspicion that Kendall was the victim of foul play.

Dr. Whiting, after performing the autopsy, made the statement that all indications point to death by strychnine poisoning. This toxic particularly affects the very organs removed and any one having a motive to remove evidences of poisoning would take these organs for his purpose. With this evidence to work upon an investigation was immediately commenced at San Francisco relative to the circumstances surrounding the sickness and death of Kendall.

Kendall's wife, who was with him in the hospital at San Francisco when he passed away, says that her husband died in convulsions. Physicians here expressed doubt that Kendall died of spinal meningitis when these facts were brought to light. Symptoms which attend that illness are said to have been lacking in the Kendall case.

SYMPTOMS OF POISONING

It is well established in medical science that convulsions are a symptom of poisoning, and strychnine poisoning always causes death by convulsions. It has been learned that with-

in twenty-four hours after the arrival in this city of Mrs. Kendall and the nurse with the body of the deceased, another nurse from San Francisco arrived and registered at a local hotel. The second nurse made an appointment with the one who accompanied the remains and they were in consultation. The authorities sent persons to interview them, but they declined to give any information desired.

The fact that the second nurse followed the first so closely, that they held a conference and then that both declined to talk, leads those who are investigating the matter to believe that the second nurse was hurried here with instructions to warn the first nurse not to give out any information which she might possess about the case.

> A motive for foul play is not lack-
> ing, according to the authorities. It
> is pointed out that Kendall, who was
> the body-guard of Francis J. Heney,
> was also a most active agent in the
> prosecutions which bid fair to send
> several of San Francisco's prominent
> men to prison.

> Oscar J. Kendall died at the Lane
> Hospital on Thursday, January 10,
> after an illness of a few days. His
> death was ascribed to spinal menin-
> gitis, which followed a severe cold
> and an attack of pneumonia. No re-
> port was made here other than that
> Kendall died from natural causes.

The San Francisco Call. (San Francisco [Calif.]), 17 Jan. 1907.
Chronicling America: Historic American Newspapers. Lib. of Congress.

The *Seattle Daily Times* of January 17, 1907, actually added a little
jocularity to their sub-headline:

PAPERS STUFFED INTO BRAIN AND STOMACH
Surgeons, After Holding Post Mortem on Oscar Kendall's Body,
Fill Cavities With News of the Day

"Portland – Some comment has been caused in Portland because
on the arrival here of the body of Oscar Kendall, Francis J. Heney's
body guard, it was discovered that the internal organs, including
the brain, had been removed and the cavity filled with
newspapers."

The Eastern Oregonian in Pendleton also published the story on
January 17th. The Pendleton paper contended that Kendall "was a
victim of poisoning and did not die of natural causes." It went on

to say that "a rigid investigation will be conducted by San Francisco and United States authorities." But *The Oregon Daily Journal*, rival newspaper of the *Morning Oregonian*, was not buying the argument that Kendall had been murdered. In fact, they took digs at the *Morning Oregonian* in their reports on Kendall's sudden death.

The January 17, 1907, issue of *The Oregon Daily Journal,* ran the headline **O.J. Kendall Died a Natural Death** and sub-headline **San Francisco Undertakers Used Embalming Fluid Containing Strychnine Alleged to Have Been Found by Portland Doctors, Who Enter Denial**

The article reported that "Ghastly discoveries in connection with the death of Oscar J. Kendall, a government secret service operative, resulted in a sensational story in one of Portland's daily newspapers yesterday alleging that Kendall may have been poisoned in San Francisco."

The article went on to say that Dr. Sanford Whiting, who performed the autopsy in Portland, had been misquoted. The paper further reported that the two doctors who performed the initial autopsy in San Francisco, Dr. H.C. Moffitt and Dr. G. F. Brackett, confirmed their diagnosis that Kendall had died from meningitis and pneumonia. *The Daily Journal* also reported that both strychnine and arsenic were used during the embalming process.

Finally, the newspaper repeated that Dr. Whiting and his assistant, Dr. Matson, declared "emphatically that they made no assertions that Kendall... came to his death by poisoning."

The following day the *Journal* reported that William J. Burns, the noted San Francisco detective, considered the allegations that Kendall had been poisoned to be "silly." Burns said, according to the *Journal,* but not in quotes, that if "he thought for an instant that Kendall was poisoned he would be the first man to take up the task of hunting down his murderers."

On January 19th *The Journal* increased its attack on the *Morning Oregonian* with the headline **KENDALL CASE IS BADLY GARBLED** and the sub-heading of **Yellow Paper of Portland** (meaning the Oregonian) **Writes False Story in Order to be Sensational.**

The article reiterated the conclusions that Kendall had not been poisoned and explained the missing organs thusly:

"The reason the heart and other internal organs had been removed and not replaced before the body was shipped to Portland was due to the short time elapsing between the autopsy and when the train left for Portland."

On January 20, 1907, *The Daily Journal* reported that Francis J. Heney himself refuted suggestions that his trusted bodyguard had been murdered. The paper claimed to have received a telegram from Heney that read "poison theory absolutely false."

San Francisco in 1907. Photo: San Francisco History Room, San Francisco Public Library, San Francisco, CA. Attribution-Noncommercial-Share Alike 3.0.

Whatever the truth, with his able bodyguard eliminated from the scene, Heney became more vulnerable. Later that year Morris Haas, an ex-con loosely associated with Abe Ruef, walked into a courtroom and shot Francis Heney in the back of the head. Haas was arrested and locked up, pending interrogation. He was found dead in his cell the following day, a bullet through his own head. The police department claimed Haas committed suicide, although an examination found that the gun could not have been close enough for suicide.

Heney miraculously survived his gunshot wound, but could not continue with the trial. His assistant, future California governor and U.S. senator, Hiram Johnson, took over.

Mayor Schmitz and all of the other defendants were exonerated, except for Abe Ruef. Ruef was sentenced to 14 years at San Quentin. The evidence against Ruef was overwhelming, but his Jewish background may have played a role in his conviction. He served four and a half years in prison.

A few months after the attempted assassination of Heney, Portland attorney Charles F. Lord took the federal prosecutor to task for the death of Kendall. In a blistering letter that Lord sent to local papers, the controversial attorney wondered what his fellow citizens would think if their "disemboweled body (was) sent back to your wife, just as the body of Oscar J, Kendall- Heney's bodyguard in San Francisco- came back to her....Poor Kendall knew too much."

Oscar Kendall was initially buried in the Lone Fir Pioneer Cemetery off Stark Street in East Portland. His childless widow Nellie found some solace through her niece Harriet Lynch, who came to live with her. Harriet stayed with her Aunt Nellie for several years while her father supervised drilling operations at far-flung locations. She worked at Meier & Frank Department Store in downtown Portland, not far from where Oscar once ran his steam dye business. After she graduated from Portland's Holmes Business College in 1912 she moved on to Republic, Washington where her father was supervising a drilling operation for a gold mine at Wolf Camp near Curlew.

Also living with Nellie following the death of Oscar was Oscar's older brother Nelson Kendall and his wife Sarah Bennett. Nelson was a veteran of the Civil War, having fought with the 7th Michigan Cavalry under General George Armstrong Custer. When Nellie married an elderly widower named Daniel Llewellyn, Nelson and Sarah moved to Ocean Park, Washington where they died nine days apart in 1917. Nellie Kendall Llewellyn died on March 18, 1929, and is buried in Portland's Mount Calvary Cemetery. Oscar's remains were exhumed from the Lone Fir Cemetery to rest beside her.

Nellie Kendall with niece Harriet Lynch in front of the home she once shared
with Oscar on SE 54th and Woodstock.
The house still stands in its original location.

*The old Holmes Business College on SW 10th & Washington in downtown
Portland where Harriet Lynch went to school while living with Nellie Kendall.
Photo courtesy of Miles Hochstein / PortlandGround.com*

Wilson T. Hume returned to Portland for good a few years after
Kendall's death. On April 7, 1915, he too became the victim of an
assassination attempt. A man named Frank A. Consentino came
to Hume's office and shot him in the back. Hume recovered,
eventually earning a seat in the Oregon Senate. He died of cancer
in 1921.

Francis J. Heney also recovered from the assassination attempt
on his life and ran for governor of California but was defeated.
He died in 1937, little more than a footnote in American history.

Oscar J. Kendall was almost completely forgotten. Even his
namesake, Kendall Oscar Lynch, was unaware of the strange
circumstances of his uncle's death. The fact that the bodyguard
of Francis J. Heney was the very same man who represented the
state as the star witness in the sensational murder trial of X.N.
Steeves and Bunco Kelly over a decade before was never noticed
by the press, including *The Morning Oregonian*.

And no one was ever arrested or charged in the death of the steam dye man.

Nellie Kendall in happier days with brother-in-law Dan Lynch. Circa 1920.

Harriet Lynch with her aunt, Nellie Kendall,
at the O.J. Kendall home in Portland.

Harriet Lynch, left, with two of her cousins from the Harris line, Albert and Mary Horton, camping out in the backyard of Nell & Oscar Kendall's home in Portland, Oregon, circa 1908.

The grave of Oscar and Nellie Kendall,
Mount Calvary Cemetery in Portland.

Five: Nightmares in Montana

Timothy Patrick Lynch, 1875-1908.

As America entered the 20th century there was no more ethnically diverse, culturally colorful or idiosyncratic city within its borders than the western mining town of Butte, Montana. By 1910 the population of the Butte area was near 100,000. Today it is a third of that.

Protestants and Catholics mixed freely with Jews, Muslims, Buddhists, agnostics and atheists. Black, white and Native Americans shared mine shafts, taverns, opium dens and flophouses with Mexicans, Filipinos, Egyptians, Turks, Serbians,

Finns, Poles, Italians and just about every other nationality, including a large population of Chinese.

Some of the Chinese had come to the area for individual claims in the early days of placer mining. But when the big copper companies took over, the Chinese, who were excellent workers, were banned from the shafts. The banishment was racially motivated of course, but in some respects the Chinese were fortunate. They could avoid the dangers of the shafts while making money catering to the needs and desires of workers above ground. Most of the laundries in Butte were Chinese owned, but they were not as profitable as the opium dens. Everything in Butte's Chinatown was strictly, and sometimes ruthlessly, controlled by powerful Chinese "families" that often got their orders from bosses across the Pacific.

The Chinese were an important segment of Butte's population, but, as in the case of the Upper Peninsula, the Cornish and the Irish reigned supreme. Butte, Montana had the highest concentration of Irish Americans in the United States in the early 1900s. In other words, it had the largest percentage of Irish Americans in its demographics. And no state lost more Irish American citizens to Butte than Michigan. The first generation had flocked to the Upper Peninsula from Ireland, and now second generation Irish Americans flocked to Butte from the UP. There were so many transplanted Michigan Irishmen in Butte that the most popular chewing tobacco, the Peerless, was often called "Michigan Hay."

Copper Town, a Works Project Administration history of Butte, states that the Butte Irish, *"Came in by the thousands, bringing with them the Irish flair for politics, a spirit of independence, of broad humor, ambition, superstition and hot temper, which, coupled with an inherent ability for hard work and hard play, complemented perfectly the rugged spirit of the camp."*

These fortune seekers flocked to Montana for three reasons: gold, silver and copper. But copper quickly became king. All three minerals had been discovered in the hills of Montana during the years following the Civil War. Montana, and more specifically the area around Butte, became the epicenter for men who had already exhausted strikes in Michigan, Nevada and California. Among the prospectors who flocked to Montana from California was a 61 year-old man named Jean Baptiste Charbonneau. He didn't make it. He died en route near the town of Jordan Valley, Oregon: the only member of the Lewis & Clark Expedition to die in and be buried in Oregon. Jean Baptiste was "Baby Pomp," the son of Sacagawea.

Those who made it to the Butte area, according to the WPA writers, *"worked like slaves, and played like kings; they asked no quarter, and no quarter did they give; they took their whiskey straight, and they took it often."*

But they would not be working their own claims. The more industrious (and greedy) locked up and consolidated all of the claims. There were the Boston and Montana Consolidated Copper & Silver Mining Company and the Amalgamated Mining Corporation, which became the Anaconda Copper Mining Company, colossal corporate owner of most Butte mines.

When the Lynch brothers lived in Montana, Anaconda became the largest mining company in the world. It didn't just own the mines of Butte, it owned Montana. And as its power grew and its stranglehold over the state's daily newspapers become complete, labor organizers stood no chance. Union leaders were vilified in the press as "socialists and foreign agitators." When World War I exploded, they were "anti-American Bolsheviks."

Pollution from the Anaconda smelter chimneys was so extreme that it was said "Not a blade of grass grew in Butte," and that Butte, "was ugly as sin."

Most of the men worked in deep, dangerous underground mine shafts. They shared the shafts with mules and horses that pulled train cars full of ore. Some of the unfortunate animals spent most, or all, of their lives underground. Small pens were carved out of the tunnels where they would rest and eat before the next shift. They were kept relatively content with oats and hay.

Miners were kept relatively content with booze. Despite the dangerous nature of the work, which sometimes took place in dark tunnels 3,000 feet below the surface of Butte, men regularly packed beer or harder drinks in their lunch buckets. Some went all the way to the surface at lunch time to purchase beer. Booze in Butte was cheap and plentiful.

Hundreds of taverns catered to the men, who consumed Cornish pasties and washed them down with a "Shawn O'Farrell"- a whiskey with a beer chaser, almost immediately after emerging from a hard day's labor in the mines. Most saloons offered a variety of foods for free, as long as the patron bought a beer. The biggest saloon was *The Atlantic*. It had a bar the length of a city block. Fifteen bartenders kept the drinks flowing at *The Atlantic* and flow they did. 12,000 beers were served on a typical Saturday night. Some bars had very colorful names, like *The Cesspool* and *Bucket of Blood*. There was even a *Lynch Brothers Saloon* in Butte around 1900, but it cannot be determined if it was owned by Tim, Dick and Con, the three Lynch brothers who lived there at the time.

If beer was popular in the Lynch clan, then so were the Cornish pasties. According to Fritzi Bernazani, granddaughter of Dan Lynch, "Every Lynch woman competed for who made the best pasties and that's extended down through the family even today."

But Jack Lynch, grandson of Dan Lynch, claims it was not an Irish Lynch who made the best pasties in the family, nor was it a Cornish Lynch, like Tillie Trenerry, the wife of Timothy Lynch. It was Mollie Wittanen Lynch, the daughter-in-law of Dan (and wife of his son Fred). Mollie's father was from Finland and her mother was from Sweden, but Jack savored her pasties most of all. "They were big and delicious," recalled Jack. "She only used the best meat and one pasty was enough for a full meal." His cousin Fritzi disputes Jack's claim. "My mother, (Harriet Lynch Biner)," insisted Fritzi, "made the best pasties!"

Suffice to say that the title of "best pasties" was something strived for in virtually every Irish and Cornish kitchen in America.

When the miners weren't packing pasties in their dinner buckets they were toting what they called "stirabout." Stirabout was simply a thick oatmeal mush. Down in the mines many Irishmen would add some tea and a pinch of salt to their mush for a hearty, belly-filling meal.

Tim, Con, Jack and Dick Lynch all moved to Montana. Dan and Pat would visit between jobs of their own in Michigan and Colorado. While Tim and Con worked the Butte mines, Dick, who had his own barber shop in Republic by age 16, opened a new shop on Butte's North Main Street near the Miner's Union Hall. When Dan and Pat visited they may have been scouting the situation for Sullivan Machinery; perhaps looking for workers to pull away for various drilling operations that Sullivan was bidding on, or at least to educate their brothers on the bright future of diamond drilling.

Butte, Montana was initially the focus of gold and silver speculation, until an Irish immigrant named Marcus Daly sank a shaft for silver and hit copper ore instead - a lot of it. Daly and his backers reaped millions in profit with the Anaconda Mine and thousands of Irish and Cornish miners broke their backs helping them do it. That included several of the Lynch brothers as well as the families of the women they would love.

Tim Lynch seemed to settle into to the Big Sky Country the best. He already had plenty of mining experience having worked for the Republic Iron Company back in Michigan during most of the 1890s. Like his brother Dan, Tim was not afraid of crossing cultural lines. Tim wooed and married Mary Matilda Trenerry, the young daughter of a Cornish miner. Such personal confidence earned him a job as shift boss at the Rarus Mine and he found a home on Pennsylvania Avenue, behind the livery stables on Copper Street.

Before his career with the Lynch Brothers Diamond Drilling Company, Dick Lynch, left, was a barber in Republic, Michigan and then in Butte, Montana.

Tim is mentioned in Butte newspapers for his involvement in the Miners Union and as a member of a committee assigned to dole out a $10,000 reward for information leading to the arrest and conviction of the men who murdered John J. Daly on November 9, 1898. Daly, an elections clerk, was about to count ballots from an area known as Dublin Gulch when two masked men entered the precinct office and tried to steal the ballot box. Deputy Sheriff Dennis O'Leary prevented the theft, but not before the bandits shot him and killed Daly. The murderers escaped into the night. The Irish community, suspecting the murder was the result of an attempt to prevent the Irish-supported Democratic legislative slate from winning the election, banded together to post the reward. But no one cashed in as the assassins were never found.

Four of the Lynch Brothers in Butte, MT, circa 1905. L to R in darker suits, Tim, Dick & Con. The brother in the lighter suit is Pat.

Tim Lynch, in Butte, Montana, circa 1900.

Not all of Tim's duties were so serious. In the summer of 1903 he helped organize the annual Miners Union Picnic to be held at Mountain View Park in Anaconda on August 16th. The event offered food, music, speeches, a baseball game and other sporting events, and of course, plenty of booze. One of the responsibilities for the committee was to arrange transportation for miners and their families from Butte to Anaconda. This was easily accomplished on the Butte, Anaconda and Pacific Rarus Railway, which linked the Anaconda Smelter Plant in Butte to another smelter plant in Anaconda, a distance of about 25 miles.

Whenever he was mentioned in the newspaper, Tim gave his name as Timothy P. Lynch. It is likely he did not want to be confused with another Tim Lynch in the area. That Tim Lynch, originally from North Dakota, was a notorious horse thief.

Timothy's wife Tillie, as Matilda Trenerry was affectionately known, gave birth to three beautiful children during their brief marriage; daughter Florence Irene in 1903; son Raymond Cornelius in 1905, and daughter Montana Mary in 1907. Tim's parents, Cornelius and Bridget, took a train from Republic in the summer of 1907 to visit their sons Tim and Dick and meet their new grandchildren. While in Butte, Bridget sent a postcard to her youngest son Pat, who was working for his big brother Dan at the Britannia Beach Mine in British Columbia. All of her sons were gainfully employed and the future looked particularly bright for Tim and his young family. But then a series of unspeakable tragedies shattered everything.

On February 5, 1908, Tim and two friends, Edward Dwyer and James Shea, were walking to work, as so many miners often did, along the railroad tracks. What happened as they approached the mine was graphically reported by a local newspaper, *The Anaconda Standard Record.*

"Timothy P. Lynch, a young and popular miner of Butte and of a family of miners from Republic, Mich., was instantly killed, his body horribly mangled, by being struck and ground under the drive wheels of Great Northern locomotive No. 2 on the main line 200 feet west of the West Course mine, at 5:26 o'clock last evening. The body was picked up in fragments strewn for 20 feet along the track. The body was severed just below the chest. The accident occurred in a cloud of steam from the Gambetta shaft, which hid the approaching engine from sight."

But the grisly sensationalism that was typical of the time was not finished. *The Standard Record* elaborated.

"A horrible sight met the eyes of those who gathered on the track. Lynch's body had not only been virtually chopped in two, but the left arm was torn from its socket, the head badly crushed and the feet were a pulp.... The investigation that followed made clear the reason, for the accident. In hoisting, the exhaust from the Gambetta shaft completely covers the track. The hissing sound practically drowns all others. The three miners were just entering this cloud of steam which the engine came upon them. It was then still light, but sight and sound of the approaching locomotive were nevertheless cut off. For the same reason the engineer and fireman were unable to see the men on the track. The locomotive was running down grade, heading west, at the time, and accordingly gave little warning of its approach."

Dwyer and Shea escaped with minor injuries by diving out of harm's way at the last second. But Tim Lynch had been walking between his two friends down the middle of the tracks.

Jack Lynch was operating a general store in Loretto, Michigan when he learned of his brother's death. His first thought was to console his aging parents in Republic. Jack wrote to them the day after Tim died, on their 44th wedding anniversary. The letterhead was inscribed *M. Josephine Lynch, General Merchandise*, suggesting that Jack's wife, Mary Josephine "Phene" Bartlett Lynch, was either the owner or co-owner of their store. She was also a school teacher.

Dear Mother and Father,

I write to sympathize with you in the loss of your beloved son and my dear brother. We certainly will suffer pain for a short time on his account but we must also remember that his physical sufferings have left him and that he has gone where all good people go, to Heaven. He was a man who never harmed a person, was always honest and was good to his wife and children.

So Mother if God is merciful Tim is surely in Heaven and we ought to be thankful instead of sorry. My tears are dropping so fast that I must quit and hope you see it in the light that it is God's Will and for the best.

Your loving son, Jack

In May, 1908, Tillie Lynch filed a lawsuit against the Great Northern Railway and the Boston & Montana Consolidated Copper and Silver Mining Company, owners of the Gambetta Mine. Tillie contended that at least 500 miners walked the tracks daily. Great Northern and Boston & Montana knew that the exhaust from the Gambetta shaft obscured the tracks but took no precautionary measures to protect the miners. Tillie asked for $24,188 in damages. The figure was based on the fact that Tim was paid $1,277.50 annually and an insurance policy to continue the annual payments to his widow and children would cost $24, 188. Tillie was represented by the Butte law firm of Breen & Hogevoll. A lower court denied Tillie Lynch a settlement and her attorneys appealed to the Supreme Court of Montana.

The appeal reached the Montana Supreme Court and a decision was rendered on March 27, 1909. In the appeal Breen & Hogevoll contended that both the mining company and the railroad not only knew that the men used the tracks as a path to work but approved it. They further contended that Lynch was near a railroad crossing, that the railroad company was pushing a caboose in front of the engine and went through the crossing, which was obscured by steam from the mine shaft, without even blowing a warning whistle.

John "Jack" Lynch with his wife, Phene Bartlett.

Nevertheless, and perhaps not surprisingly for the times, the Montana Supreme Court upheld the lower court and Tillie Lynch received no compensation from the multi-million dollar companies. In fact, the court went so far as to suggest that Tim Lynch himself may have been guilty of "gross negligence" for walking into the steam.

It is easy to imagine how Tim's death affected his young wife Tillie. His shockingly sensational death was the talk of Butte. But how did Tillie explain to her three young children, ages five, three and one, that their daddy would never come home again? She found some comfort and support from Tim's brother Dick and his wife Sabina Norman, the daughter of Swedish immigrants, who was also Tillie's best friend. Tillie and her three children would move in with Dick and Sabina on West Copper Street. She would need their love and support more than she could possibly imagine.

In the summer of 1910, just two and a half years after her husband's death, all three of Tillie's little children became deathly ill. As their fevers rose and their lungs filled with fluid, Tillie, Dick and Sabina did everything they could to comfort them. But on June 29th the youngest child, three year-old Montana Mary Lynch, expired. The heartbroken Tillie scarcely had time to bury her little girl next to the grave of her husband when her beautiful older daughter, Florence Irene, with her long curly hair, took her last precious breath.

An obituary in the local newspaper captured the intense sadness that the entire mining community shared with the grief-stricken Tillie Lynch.

LITTLE GIRLS BEARERS OF BODY OF PLAYMATE

"The funeral of little Florence Lynch, 7 year-old daughter of Mrs. Tim Lynch, of 30 West Copper Street, was held yesterday afternoon at the home. The body was taken to St. Patrick's Church where services were conducted by Rev. Follett. The journey of the little white hearse through the streets was a pathetic one. The white casket rested upon a bank of white and heaped about it was a wealth of white flowers. Six little girls, all playmates and all dressed in white, walked beside the hearse as pallbearers. The burial was beside the father and another sister in the Catholic cemetery."

"Mrs. Lynch has had more than her share of sorrow to bear. About two years ago her husband was killed by a train while he was going to work. Only a week ago, another daughter, Montana Mary, four years old, died and Saturday little Florence was taken. Mrs. Lynch has the sympathy of all who know her and her friends are doing all in their power to make her affliction less hard to bear."

Montana Mary Lynch, 1907-1910.

Florence Irene Lynch, 1903-1910.

But Tillie Lynch had something else to focus on - her surviving son Raymond. As Raymond's condition worsened, Dick Lynch made a desperate move. He took the young boy to the nearest mine and held him in the steam to help clear his lungs. It may have been the very steam shaft that had obscured the track on the day his father was killed. But what contributed to the death of the father may have saved the son. Little Raymond slowly recovered. The experience would bond him to his Uncle Dick for life. After Tillie married a man named Moses Aubrey, a French-Canadian miner, Dick and Sabina adopted Raymond Lynch and raised him as their own.   Raymond become an important member of the Lynch Brothers Diamond Drilling Company and invented several diamond bits that the company used in their drilling operations at Grand Coulee and other sites. He also became an owner of the company after his uncles had died.

Raymond Lynch would marry Juanita Leafdahl, a graduate of the University of Oregon and native of Nebraska. Together they had five children of which the two youngest, Tim and Mike survive.

In 1915, Raymond's mother, Tillie Lynch Aubrey, gave birth to a daughter, Marjorie, and two years later a second daughter, Catherine. It seemed as if her life had started over. But the joy would not last long. Tillie died in 1924 at the age of 44, leaving seven year-old Catherine and nine year-old Marjorie motherless. Once again remarkable Aunt Sabina stepped in, acting as a surrogate mother to the two girls for the rest of her life.

The graves of Tim Lynch and his daughters in Butte's St. Patrick's Cemetery.
The V. after Timothy should be a P.

Tillie Trenerry Lynch Aubrey, wife of Timothy Lynch, who lost her husband and two daughters in the space of two and a half years.

The saintly Sabina Norman Lynch, wife of Dick Lynch, and best friend to Tillie, took in Tillie's surviving son Raymond, and later, after Tillie's untimely death, Tillie's two daughters by her second marriage to Moses Aubrey, and raised them as her own.

Tillie's grave in Seattle's Calvary Cemetery.

Raymond Lynch, the only child of Tim and Tillie to survive childhood, went on to invent diamond drill bits for the Lynch Brothers Diamond Drilling Company and became co-owner of the company in its final years. Note the now infamous insignia at the bottom of this picture, taken some 30 years before the Nazi's adopted it. The next page shows Raymond Lynch with big sister Irene.

Richard "Dick" Lynch, helped save the life of Tillie's surviving child Raymond by holding the young boy near a steam shaft so that his lungs would open. Dick and his wife Sabina, who had no children of their own, would raise Raymond as their son. Dick was a barber in his early years but become a founder and owner of the Lynch Brothers Diamond Drilling Company.

John Michael "Jack" Lynch, 1871-1913

Following Tim's death, Jack Lynch wanted to be closer to his other brothers. He and his wife Phene sold their general store in Loretto, Michigan and moved to Great Falls, Montana with their young son John Harris Lynch. Jack's intention was to open a store similar to the one he and Phene had in Loretto, but there is no indication that it ever happened. By 1910 Jack was working for the Great Northern Railroad Express Office, possibly through the recommendation of his brother Bill, who was the train dispatcher for the Great Northern in Superior, Wisconsin. Newspapers said Jack was a supervisor. But the 1910 census says he was a baggage man.

Phene Lynch became the bookkeeper for the new National Laundry Company when it opened in 1910 (the company is still in operation 104 years later). Sometime thereafter Jack either quit or was fired from his job at Great Northern. Desperate to help support his wife and son he resorted to the old family trade and went to work at the Barker Mine a few miles south of Great Falls. Barker, Montana and nearby Highland are listed as ghost towns today but from 1880 through 1930 they were bustling mining towns that produced silver, lead and copper. It is unlikely that Jack wanted to be a miner. In 1913, with his wife still working for National Laundry Company, Jack moved out. Whether it was a real separation or just a matter of access to job sites, no one knows for sure. It seems apparent that they always loved one another, but in this case love did not seem to be enough.

On December 9, 1913, Jack took a room at the Keystone Hotel in the southern end of Great Falls. An article in the *Great Falls Daily Tribune* on December 22, 1913 contended that Jack "had been complaining of being sick for some time and it is stated that he was afflicted with a trouble of chronic character that frequently caused him terrible suffering."

It is unclear what the *Tribune* reporter meant by the term "chronic character." It could have been any sort of infirmity of the mind or body, but it was most likely a case of severe depression.

Carbolic acid is an aromatic organic compound that was originally derived from coal tar. Also known as Phenol, it is highly volatile and causes severe burns. A poisonous ingredient used in many products, from plastics to detergents,   it was easily acquired in the early 20th century and became an all-too-common tool for suicide, especially among women, despite the fact that its consumption caused severe burning of the lips and mouth, followed by excruciating pain in the stomach and intestines. For one who felt the need to be tortured, carbolic acid certainly proved a suitable agent.

The *Tribune* reported that a bottle of carbolic acid was already in the room that Jack Lynch rented in December of 1913. As he dwelled on the failures of his life, and the disappointment he felt he had become to his beautiful wife Phene, Jack Lynch decided to swallow carbolic acid.

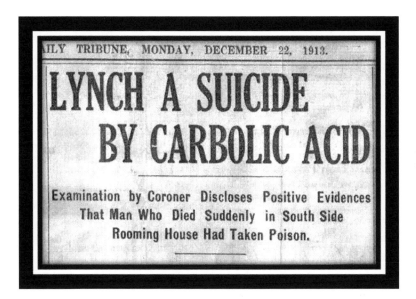

ILY TRIBUNE, MONDAY, DECEMBER 22, 1913.

LYNCH A SUICIDE BY CARBOLIC ACID

Examination by Coroner Discloses Positive Evidences That Man Who Died Suddenly in South Side Rooming House Had Taken Poison.

"His screams were heard for some distance," reported the *Tribune* under the sensational bold headline **LYNCH A SUICIDE BY CARBOLIC ACID,** *"And persons hurried to the door of the room from which they emanated. They found it locked and while Lynch was still writhing in the agonies of a horrible death they forced their way into the room."*

But it was too late. 42 year-old Jack Lynch, shirtless and wearing only his trousers, was taking his last desperate breath. It was Saturday afternoon, December 20, 1913. Four of his brothers (Dan, Cornelius, Dick and Pat) were working mines in British Columbia and had to be tracked down to receive the awful news. Had Jack resisted the temptation to end it all on that cold day in Montana, he might have joined his brothers in the highly successful family business formed less than a year later in Alaska.

Jack Lynch left no suicide note and the county undertaker, T. F. O'Conner, was a bit astonished to find no burn marks on his lips or mouth. And yet, the unmistakable odor of carbolic acid permeated the autopsy room. O'Connor suspected that Jack wanted to conceal his own suicide by carefully pouring the acid down his throat.

Jack was buried on December 23rd in Great Falls' Calvary Cemetery. It was less than 43 years after the death of the first born brother he unwittingly replaced, and whom he was destined to honor with his own middle name: Michael. Jack's tombstone reads simply "J.M. Lynch."

Jack's parents, back in Republic, Michigan, received a telegram with great distress. According to the Republic newspaper the elderly couple, "Did not even know that Jack had been ill." Perhaps they never learned the truth.

Judy Heinrich, the granddaughter of Jack Lynch, revealed the painful story in a 2012 letter.

As an adult Judy was visiting her mom and dad when they began to talk about the Lynch family, of which she knew little about. Judy asked her father how his dad had died.

"There was a long awkward silence," recalls Judy, "And then my mom said, 'Oh, Harris, tell her.'

"He told me that his dad had committed suicide and he had never talked about it to anyone but my mom. Apparently it was a source of great shame in his family. Phene must have loved him very much because she was devastated (and would) sometimes lock herself in the closet and weep. She once told mom (Grazel Lynch, her daughter-in-law and the wife of John Harris Lynch) that it was because she missed Jack so much."

John Harris Lynch, the only child of Jack and Phene Lynch, was born in Michigan in 1901. After his father's death, Harris moved to a boarding school. By 1920 he was back with his mother who had remarried a man many years her junior. In fact, Joseph "Mac" McNeil was only four years older than his stepson Harris. Census records and her tombstone both indicate that Phene told her young husband she was born in 1886. That would have made her eleven years older than Mac. In fact, she was born in 1870, 26 years before Mac. Yet Phene retained her youthful looks and beauty. Mac and Phene remained together until her death on June 4, 1939. By then her son John Harris had moved to Seattle where he earned his law degree and married Grazel White, the gregarious, good-natured daughter of an Irish miner and a native of Republic, Michigan. In fact, the White and Lynch families had followed one another from Republic to Butte to Alaska and finally Seattle.

Phene Bartlett Lynch with son John Harris Lynch.

According to Judy Heinrich, daughter of Harris and Grazel Lynch, her father, "Served in the Judge Advocate Core in the Army. We were sent over to Germany after the war and the original assignment was to participate in the Nuremberg trials. His orders changed after we arrived and he and our family were sent to

Frankfurt where he was involved with the relocation of Germans. It was a great disappointment to him to miss that opportunity (prosecuting in the Nuremberg trials)."

Joan Egan, the late daughter of Harris and Grazel Lynch, recalled that her father "Was cerebral, serious, and intellectual. (He was) a fly fisherman and a loner, and he loved to take his wife up into the wilds of British Columbia for fishing trips. She didn't like it much, because there weren't enough people around to suit her."

John Harris Lynch would author the book, *Digest of Leading Washington Cases on Workmen's Compensation Law*. His son Patrick was an NCAA All-American in skiing and all three of Harris and Grazel's children (Patrick, Joan and Judy) inherited their parent's insatiable love of learning and life. John Harris Lynch died in 1980 at the age of 79. Grazel lived to be 97.

Joan Lynch (1930-2012) married Harold Egan and was the mother of Maureen, Timothy, Kevin, Mary, Colleen, Kelly and Daniel Egan. Patrick Lynch (1931-2010) married Margaret Whyte and was the father of John Christopher and Jennifer Lynch. Judy Lynch married Gary Heinrich and is the mother of Michael, Thomas, David and Kathleen Heinrich. Many of John and Grazel's grandchildren have children of their own. In fact, the number of descendants from the only child of Jack and Phene is now at thirty and will certainly grow: a surprisingly large legacy for Jack Lynch, who in an injudicious moment of despair took his own life nearly two decades before his first grandchild was born.

On the following page is a picture of John Harris "Harrie" Lynch in uniform when he served in the Judge Advocate Core of the U.S. Army following World War II.

The youthful Phene Lynch with her niece, Harriet Lynch, the daughter of Dan Lynch & Mate Kendall, several years before Jack's suicide. The photograph seems to convey a mature understanding between the young Harriet and her Aunt Phene. Jack Lynch was Harriet's godfather.

Six: Aiming High, Drilling Deep

Following the tragic deaths of Tim and Jack Lynch, the five surviving Lynch brothers; Dan, Con, Dick, Bill and Pat, gravitated toward the mining industry if they hadn't already been gainfully employed through it. None of the brothers had more experience than Dan. Dan continued to work for Sullivan Machinery, learning the ins and outs of diamond drilling and supervising crews throughout the country and overseas.

An article about the Lynch Brothers written in the 1930s revealed that the brothers had drilled in Finland, Brazil and Cuba. Pat was diamond drilling in the Helena area in 1910 and it seems likely that he supervised some drilling at the Panama Canal, which was completed in 1913. Dan, as the most experienced driller, never stayed in one place for long and he cannot be found in the 1910 census. He was probably in Africa.

For a few months in 1907, Dan and Mate Lynch (and presumably young Kendall Lynch) were in Jerome, Arizona where Dan was supervising a drilling operation for the United Verde Works. Like Hancock, Michigan, and Butte, Montana, Jerome was a copper mining boomtown. It was also, in the words of a reporter for the *New York Times*, "The wickedest city in the West." At the very least it was almost as culturally diverse as Butte, with a smorgasbord of nationalities from Irish to Chinese to Mexicans and Italians. Saloons and whorehouses were plentiful. Gunfights and price gouging were routine. It was not a place for the weak-kneed. Dan and Mate Lynch could handle it.

Like all mining boomtowns, Jerome, situated on a 5000 ft. mountain, was destined to die. Today it is one of the smallest towns in Arizona with a population of about 350; a far cry from the days when it boasted 15,000 with 31 hotels and more saloons and brothels than a typical western town three times its size.

United Verde Works, Jerome, Arizona.

Mate sent her son Fred a postcard from Jerome, Arizona.

Dan & Mate Lynch in Jerome, Arizona, 1907.

Kendall Lynch, center, and Harriet Lynch, dark skirt, at mining camp.

Harriet Lynch Biner recalled living briefly in Tombstone, Arizona as a young girl. Perhaps she was just visiting her uncle, Con Lynch. But the picture on the following page would suggest that she did spend some time in the arid Southwest.

This much seems to be certain: while Dan was in Jerome he sent word to his brothers of other mining opportunities in Arizona. Only Cornelius Jr. took the bait. He did move to legendary Tombstone, the silver-mining town most famous for the gunfight at the O.K. Corral. Con looked like he belonged in Tombstone. Tall and handsome, with dark eyes and a thick mustache, he presented the very image of the Wild West man. Looks sometimes deceive. Con was anything but wild. His wife Jane McKenna was the more domineering figure and his granddaughter Susan remembers Con as a gentle, quiet man, fond of smoking his pipe and sitting in silent contemplation.

Harriet Lynch talks with a young boy probably in Arizona. Her mother Mate stands directly behind her. Below is her uncle, Con Lynch.

According to family oral history, Jane McKenna Lynch was the great-granddaughter of Thomas McKenna and Jane Foulkes, two genuine heroes from the Irish uprising of 1798. Lady Jane Foulkes, the daughter of English gentry, fell in love with the Irishman McKenna while her father, a British military officer, was stationed in Ireland. Thomas McKenna was part of the United Irishmen, a revolutionary organization seeking Irish autonomy. Legend has it that Jane donned men's clothing in order to fight alongside her Irish husband in the ill-fated rebellion. The couple avoided the mass executions and slaughtering by British troops, possibly due to intervention by Jane's father, and fled to the hills of County Kerry where they raised a large family near Listowel.

A man named Patrick McKenna, said to be the son of Thomas and Lady Jane, immigrated to Michigan's Upper Peninsula, where his granddaughter Jane was born in 1879.

Jane McKenna and Con Lynch with their children
Howard, Doll and Neil.

Tragedy struck the family of Con and Jane Lynch during their time in Arizona. On August 11, 1908 Jane gave birth to their 4th child, a boy named Thomas McKenna, in honor of her Irish clan. Eleven months later the little boy died of pneumonia in Courtland,

Arizona: almost a year to the day before the two young daughters of Con's brother Tim would die from the same ailment.

In 1911 Con took his young family, which now consisted of Jane and three children; Howard, Philothea (Doll), and Cornelius III (Neil), and crossed the border into Mexico where he worked mines near San Pedro, Chihuahua, Mexico and a year later in Cananea, Sonora, Mexico. From there he moved briefly to Pocatello, Idaho, and then took a short-term job working for his brother Dan in Republic, Washington. He eventually returned to Butte and was the last Lynch brother to leave that famous mining town. He moved to California from Butte in 1924.

After the Jerome job, 40 year-old Dan began a long-term contract to supervise diamond-drill crews at the big Britannia Beach Mine near Vancouver, British Columbia. For the first time Dan's son Fred went to work for him and would do so, off and on at Britannia Beach, over the next seven years. During the school year Fred lived in Portland and attended Columbia University, a Catholic college later renamed the University of Portland.

Dan also secured a job for his youngest brother Pat, just five years older than Fred, with Sullivan Machinery, and in the summer of 1907 22 year-old Pat was working a drill crew in Iron River, Michigan. Later that year he joined Dan on the job at Britannia Beach. Then he drilled briefly in Montana. Three years later at the age of 25, Pat was supervising a crew in far off Chile.

Around 1910, while Fred was finishing up school and his sister Harriet was working in downtown Portland at the Meier & Frank Department Store, Dan slipped off to West Africa to lead a drilling operation for Sullivan Brothers Diamond Drilling Company. He knew that Mate would not approve of the idea so he intentionally kept it from her until a day or two prior to his departure.

Mate was livid, especially since her husband would be gone for the better part of a year. Determined not to let him pull such a stunt again she kept him in sight after his return and accompanied him on most of his jobs, sometimes serving as cook for the smaller drill crews.

From 1912 to 1915, Dan Lynch worked on projects for Sullivan Machinery Company and Boyles Brothers Drilling, which had major interests in northeast Washington and southern British Columbia. One extensive job, at a place called Wolf Camp, above Curlew Lake, a few miles north of the nearest post office in Republic, Washington, made for an interesting exchange of cards to his parents in Republic, Michigan. Pat had returned from the job in Chile and Dick had sold his barber shop in Butte to join Dan on a job. When Pat and Dick left to seek new opportunities in Alaska, Con arrived in Republic to help Dan finish the job at Curlew Lake.

Juneau, Alaska was in the middle of a mining boom when Dick and Pat arrived with their nephew Fred to check things out. Perhaps at Dan's urging, Dick and Pat scouted out drilling needs in Alaska. While he waited to hear back from his younger brothers and son, Dan continued to supervise drilling operations for Boyles Brothers in eastern Washington, southern British Columbia and Alberta. But instead of turning over information on opportunities in Alaska to Sullivan Machinery or Boyles Brothers, Dan agreed with his brothers' decision to form a drilling company of their own.

Dick and Pat turned to their brother Bill (sometimes called Will); still working in Proctor, Minnesota, for financial assistance and in 1914 started the Lynch Brothers Diamond Drilling Company in Juneau, Alaska. Because the diamond drill was still relatively new in Alaska and because it was more cost-effective than the heavier cable-tool and rotary drills, the new company was an instant success. The brothers took on jobs and hired crews throughout the Alaskan panhandle. They drilled for some of the largest private mining companies and for the U.S. Bureau of Mines. Fred Lynch returned to Portland, but after graduating from Columbia College, he quickly rejoined his uncles in Juneau.

Dan, Ken, Fred and Mate Lynch at mining camp in Okanogan County, Washington in 1911.

Britannia crew. Fred Lynch is sitting in the snow, third from right.

Dan and Mate Lynch roughing it at another mining camp.

Top: Wolf Camp, Curlew Lake near Republic, Washington.
Bottom: Mate stands next to Dan, sitting, at Wolf Camp.

Dan Lynch in a diamond drill workshop circa 1910.

Pat and Dick Lynch were accepting a flurry of job offers for the new company when word reached them from Republic, Michigan that on February 25, 1915, Bridget Harris Lynch, the matriarch of the clan, had died at the age of 73, leaving her deaf daughter by the same name to care for their father. It is not known which, if any, of the Lynch Brothers were able to return for her funeral. She was buried beside her mother, Bridget Longe Harris, in the Republic Cemetery.

The first big contract that the new diamond drilling company secured was with the Perseverance Gold Mine in the mountains east of Juneau. During the term of the contract at Perseverance the brothers completed over 75,000 ft. of diamond-drill holes. When the contract ended in 1917 the drills were moved to the massive Kennecott copper mine, in the Wrangell Mountains of the Alaskan panhandle. At the time Kennecott was the largest copper mine in the world. The ore mined in the Wrangell had an average grade of 13% copper, with some mines producing grades as high as 70%. And Kennecott was looking to expand.

At picturesque Latouche Island, in the Prince William Sound, the Beatson-Bonanza Mine would produce over 100 million pounds of copper, even though the ore had an average grade of only 2.4%. In 1915, the Kennecott Copper Company purchased the Beatson mines and constructed a huge concentrating mill on the island that crushed and processed the ore before it went on to smelters.

Kennecott hired the new Lynch Brothers Diamond Drilling Company to drill at Latouche. The brothers set up an office in a small building on the waterfront and brought nephew Fred Lynch over from Juneau to set drill bits. The company was there in 1918 when Latouche experienced its biggest year, with 435,826 tons of ore extracted.

The mines at Latouche continued to yield copper until they were shut down permanently in 1930 and with that came an end to the long-term contracts that the Lynch brothers had secured with the Kennecott Copper Company. Most of the picturesque little town of Latouche, including the Lynch Brothers office, was destroyed in the monstrous 9.2 earthquake that struck Alaska on Good Friday in 1964.

Fred Lynch canoes in front of the Lynch Brothers headquarters (smaller house-shaped building in the middle) on Latouche Island, Alaska.

While drilling at Latouche, the brothers continued operations in other parts of Alaska. Lynch drill crews operated at the Jualin gold mine north of Juneau and the Ellamar copper mines near Valdez. Fred Lynch would supervise a drilling operation at the El Capitan marble quarries on Prince of Wales Island. Eventually the men would drill for petroleum and coal exploration as well.

During the treacherous winter of 1915-16, most drilling operations in the panhandle were postponed due to heavy snow and avalanches. When the weather improved the Lynch Brothers made up for lost time by drilling a 1,680 foot horizontal hole for Alaska Gold Belt Co. near Juneau. It was a record for Alaska and was thought to be the deepest horizontal hole ever drilled anywhere in the world. But after mining newsletters reported it as such, word came from none other than Hancock, Michigan that a slightly deeper hole had been drilled earlier that year by E.J. Longyear Co. at, ironically, Hancock's Quincy Mine, where the Lynch family first mined in America!

Prior to 1920 the Lynch brothers were using Sullivan drills on their jobs. In fact, the Sullivan "Champion" was the drill that set the Alaskan record. The drill had a rating capacity of 1500 feet. The Lynch brothers exceeded that capacity by 180 feet. Eventually they would patent their own drills with diamond bits designed by their nephew, Raymond Lynch, son of their dead brother Tim.

In 1918 the brothers drilled for the Gould & Curry Company and the ill-fated Alaska Treadwell Gold Mining Company on Douglas Island. Fred Lynch was at the Treadwell Gold Mine in April, 1917, when a huge cave-in destroyed the mine. On the back of a postcard he sent to his sister Harriet, Fred explained the resulting devastation:

"This is where the old swimming tank was before the cave in. This large cave in damaged and destroyed three of the large gold mines here. Millions of dollars was lost. All families of those houses had to move out because earth was cracking all over."

The Treadwell mine had been dug some 500 feet below sea level and beneath the Gastineau Channel. Serious leakage warned mine owners of an impending disaster and the mines were evacuated before the massive cave-in. A few mules and horses perished below, but all of the miners reached the surface before the cave-in.

The *Morning Oregonian* reported on April 24, 1917 that the Treadwell disaster resulted in a $10,000,000 loss of machinery and other equipment. But the paper went on to report that "Explorations had shown that the whole of Douglas Island was under-laid by low-grade ore, which had already yielded $60,000,000 of gold." The Alaska United Gold Mining Company intended to abandon the shafts and open "a completely new mine at a greater depth." This strategy was adopted because drilling by the Lynch Brothers "Had shown the presence of sufficient ore to warrant the enormous expenditure entailed in this plan."

Treadwell Mine after the cave-in.

The dangers associated with mining may have played a role in what became a major shift in focus for the Lynch Brothers. More likely it was a realization that greater opportunities existed in the Pacific Northwest, where the expansion of electricity to cities like Seattle and Portland called for new generating sources. And the Northwest had those sources in a multitude of wild rivers.

In 1917, while still involved in at least five operations in Alaska, the Lynch Brothers began a string of high profile jobs conducting the foundation exploration for hydroelectric dams in the Pacific Northwest. They would soon become a critical cog in the wheel that not only brought electric energy to the Pacific Northwest, but drinking water for urban areas; irrigation for rural areas; a near end to annual floods and hundreds of thousands of jobs for a nation that would suffer through a Great Depression and a second World War.

From 1917 through the 1960s the construction of virtually every major dam in Oregon, Washington, and Idaho was initiated by the core drilling of the Lynch Brothers Diamond Drilling Company. They were the unsung heroes that brought what remained of the "Wild West" into the 21st century.

A Lynch Brothers crew shows off a drill in Alaska.

Fred Lynch sent this beautiful picture from the Britannia Mines to his Aunt Eva Kendall Child in 1909 while working there with his father, Dan, and his uncle, Pat Lynch.

Switching much of their efforts to drilling for dam location did not decrease the dangers that the Lynch Brothers' workers faced in the mines. It simply changed the nature of the dangers. Now drowning became a real possibility as many of the rivers they would drill on were untamed, wild rivers with raging rapids and deep gorges. At least one worker would drown during their first dam project on the Skagit River.

There are no records and no way to know how many workers were killed or injured during the 50 years of the Lynch Brothers Diamond Drilling Company. But Raymond Lynch, the last owner of the company, told his son Tim that "Lots of guys were missing fingers and eyes."

Britannia Mines, B. C.

A crew at Britannia Beach, British Columbia, where Dan Lynch supervised diamond drilling off and on for several years.

Dan Lynch clowns around with an unidentified woman in this photograph circa 1912. The wherabouts of his wife Mate is unknown!

Seven: The Skagit River Project

Dick and Pat Lynch moved the company to Seattle in 1918, but maintained an office in Juneau for their Alaskan operations. In Seattle, oldest brother Dan was hired on as a supervisor for drilling operations and Bill moved out from Minnesota to become president of the company. The first big job the brothers landed after the move was the historic Skagit River Project in the North Cascades. Seattle City Light wanted to tame the wild Upper Skagit and build a series of dams to provide electricity for its growing metropolis. It was a major undertaking and the Lynch Brothers scored a huge victory by underbidding more established diamond drilling outfits. This became their introduction into the booming business of hydroelectric power, which would dominate their efforts over the next 40 years.

The December 1, 1919, issue of "Engineering World" explained the work and the compensation for the Lynch Brothers on the Skagit project.

Diamond Drill Operations on Skagit River Project

"Lynch Brothers, who have the contract for diamond-drilling operations on Seattle's Skagit River hydroelectric project, have been running three gasoline-driven drilling outfits of their own and two outfits belonging to the city, receiving $1 per ft. for holes drilled. The city, however, pays cost of transportation, pays the cost of operating, including renewals and repairs, the wages of men employed, and for loss in weight of diamonds used. Up to Oct. 1st, according to A. H. Dimock, city engineer, the drilling on Gorge Creek amounted to 8804 ft. of holes, which cost the city $8.94 per ft. Similar drilling operations on Ruby Creek, for the same project, amounted to 3343 ft. of holes, which cost $10.67 per ft. The character of the drilling is considered very difficult on account of a heavy overburden of boulders. The contract let to Lynch Brothers constitutes a cost-plus arrangement. The drilling is in the nature of tests of the rock formation preparatory to dam construction."

The October 19, 1919 copy of the *Seattle Times* announced that the Shipyards Laborers, Riggers and Stevedores Union of Seattle filed a request with the City Council for a detailed statement on the amount of money spent on the Skagit project and information on the drilling operations. The outcome of that request is unknown, as is the nature of the request. What seems relatively obvious is that many men not only worked for the Lynch Brothers on the Skagit project, but that most of them enjoyed the experience enough to continue working with the company on future projects. And many of them were strong union men.

Without question it was the Skagit River Project that firmly established the Lynch Brothers as a major player in the diamond drilling business and opened many doors, especially in the Pacific Northwest. Fortunately one member of the 40 man crew on the Skagit project kept a journal. It remains the only personal, anecdotal record of a Lynch Brothers project known to exist.

Will D. "Bob" Jenkins was born in Olympia, Washington in 1899, during the time that his grandfather, the first W.D. Jenkins, was Washington's Secretary of State. But the younger Jenkins spent very little time in the state's capital city. Instead he grew up in a rustic log cabin with his diminutive mother and his brother Sidney, near the town of Rockport in the North Cascades.

Jenkins became intimately familiar with the rugged Upper Skagit and was working for the Forest Service when the Lynch Brothers arrived to determine the sites of the proposed Diablo, Gorge and Ruby (later Ross) dams. The adventurous 20 year-old signed on to the crew, eager to do whatever he was instructed to do. He proved to be a fast learner. He ingratiated himself with the Lynch brothers and other crew members by his willingness to do anything, and amused them with his witty observations and constant note-taking.

Jenkins went on to become a journalist. His wife, Mildred Hunley, was also a writer and authored the popular book *Before the White Man Came: Pacific Northwest Indian Culture:* illustrated by her multi-talented husband.

In 1984, at the age of 85, Jenkins published his first book, the informative and amusing *Last Frontier in the North Cascades, Tales of the Wild Upper Skagit,* in which he recounted several stories from his days with the Lynch Brothers. At the age of 98, shortly before his death, Jenkins published another book, *Chilcotin Diary,* about the forty years that he and Mildred spent in an even more remote and rugged wilderness in northern British Columbia.

Last Frontier in the North Cascades: Tales of the Wild Upper Skagit was published by the Skagit County Historical Society and is no longer in print. It is also difficult to find; a shame because it is a very entertaining book written by a true storyteller of the Pacific Northwest. The author of this history was fortunate enough to read much of it at the archives in the North Cascades National Park Visitors Center, thanks to ranger Laura Humes, and later found a copy at the Oregon State University Library.

It is clear from Jenkins' book that the young man not only enjoyed working for the Lynch Brothers, but that he had a great deal of respect for them as well. He was particularly fond of Pat Lynch, for reasons which will become obvious as his great stories are retold here.

Jenkins joined the drilling company in August, 1920. Ironically, Cornelius Lynch, the Lynch family patriarch, died in August, 1920, and both Dan and Dick Lynch left the Skagit project temporarily to attend their father's funeral and wrap up his affairs in Michigan. Pat Lynch stayed behind to run the Skagit project in his brothers' absence. Consequently, it is not surprising that Jenkins attached himself to this youngest Lynch brother.

Pat assigned Jenkins as a helper for drill runner Earle D. "Dusty" Rhoades. "Drill Runner" was the title held by workers who actually operated the expensive drills. They were expensive because they were loaded with up to $5000 worth of black bort diamonds from Brazil: equivalent to about $60,000 in 2014 dollars. Only the most trusted workers could be drill runners and Rhoades fit the bill. He continued working for the Lynch Brothers long after the Skagit project and was a drill foreman at the Grand Coulee Dam, the biggest project in the history of the company.

HEADQUARTERS FOR GORGE CREEK DRILLING. Seattle City Light's hydro-electric project on the Upper Skagit began with core drilling for the first dam at Gorge Creek. Here the Lynch brothers, Dan, Dick, and Pat, had headquarters for their diamond drilling crew of forty men in March of 1919. The log building housed offices, a big dining room, and kitchen. All supplies, including tons of food, machinery, and hardware, came in by packtrain from Marblemount.

Jenkins Collection

Photograph and caption from the Jenkins Collection, originally published in the book Last Frontier in the North Cascades **by Lynch Brothers' crew member Will D. "Bob" Jenkins.**

According to Jenkins, the forty man crew at Skagit *"camped in new tents set up among giant boulders at the river's edge, and in a big log building that served as cookhouse, dining room and office."*

Equipment for the drilling operations and supplies for the crew came by pack train over rugged trails from the town of Marblemount. Seasoned packers brought in tons of supplies on mules and horses. Jenkins reported that the supplies *"included the stripped down Model T Ford engines that furnished power on the drills; the angle-iron frames on which the motors were mounted; the "worm" drive shafts and gears; thousands of lineal feet of hollow steel rods to which the diamond-studded drill bits were attached; hundreds of feet of four-inch cast iron casing pipe, and tons of miscellaneous hardware, tools and grub for the camp."*

None of the packed-in supplies was more eagerly awaited than the "grub." Naturally, the camp cook, cranky old Jack Henry, was a respected member of the crew. The strenuous and dangerous work that these men did led to powerful appetites and it was Henry's job to satisfy them. The Lynch Brothers spared no expense making sure he did.

Lunch break for a Lynch Brothers crew on the Skagit Project.

While men were ravenously gulping down food in the dining room they tried to keep up conversations, but it wasn't easy. Jenkins remembered that *"The vibrating roar of the Skagit was so loud"* that he found it *"difficult to make conversation without shouting."* So he learned to read lips. Men of many nationalities worked on the crew, but the Lynch Brothers didn't overlook their Irish friends, including some who had worked the mines in Butte. And while they might have shown some favoritism to the Irish in hiring, they were clearly fair and considerate of all of their workers.

Jenkins wrote, *"Dan, Dick and Pat Lynch ran this outfit. You seldom saw a workman at the bottom of a timber-cribbed test pit in unstable ground that one of the Lynches was not also down in the hole. They had come up in the rugged profession of diamond drillers the hard way."*

Perhaps the most trusted member of the crew was tough Jim Miller, the diamond setter. Jenkins recalled that Miller *"carried a king's ransom in smoky black stones in a rawhide poke laced to his belt. The fortune in Nature's hardest substance that swung on Jim's belt was balanced by a long-barreled Parabellum Luger on his opposite hip whenever Miller was on the trail."*

It took a full day for the pack train to travel the eighteen miles from Marblemount to the Lynch Camp on Gorge Creek. The last six were particularly dangerous as they followed the narrow "Goat Trail" carved into a cliff high above Gorge Creek. A wooden foot bridge at a spot known as Devil's Elbow connected the Goat Trail to the Lynch Camp. A year before Jenkins took a job with the crew, and while he was still with the Forest Service, there was an unfortunate incident involving the bridge. Jenkins recounted the mishap in a chapter called *"The Devil's Elbow."*

"This place was known as The Devil's Elbow, or sometimes it was called Devil's Corner. Passing up-river, you came to the Elbow and some of the most rugged trail the Northwest has ever known; crooked, winding, often steep as it twisted among huge chunks of granite the ages had tossed into the Skagit gorge from high and snow-crested summits. And just before you came onto the actual bend of the Elbow, you crossed a sheer-sided chasm on fifty feet of puncheon footbridge which hung above the seething river."

"This little bridge, a vital link in the chain of miles known as The Goat Trail, was destroyed by fire in June of 1919. The fire marooned the Gorge Creek camp of the Lynch Brothers' Diamond Drilling Company, containing more than fifty men, the Davis family at Cedar Bar, and the Forest Service crews on the Upper Skagit, all of whom depended on pack train supplies. I was stationed at the Bar that year and helped rebuild the bridge. The job was no small feat. The little span was still standing (forgotten and bypassed by the tunnel route) when last I visited some of my old haunts in 1970. The story of the rebuilding of the span should be of interest to anyone with affection for mountain country trails and an appreciation for the labor of building them."

"Lynch Brothers were operating half a dozen drills in the Gorge Creek area. Cause of the fire was never actually proved, but two youths who had been discharged and compelled to make the long walk out to Marblemount on a warm summer day were suspected of firing the bridge to spite Dick Lynch, who had canned them for goldbricking on the job. Within two hours of their departure down-trail, smoke boiling up through the gorge caused general alarm in the camp and several in the crew got down to Devil's

Elbow in time to see the flaming stringers collapse into the chasm of the Skagit."

It was up to Jenkins and some co-workers to find the timber to replace the bridge.

"I had worked with Art Newby on Baker River in 1917 and the two of us were assigned by Ranger Tommy Thompson to rig a cable go-devil across the chasm. Windy Luke Hendrickson and a gang of helpers from the Lynch Brothers' camp set to work on a timbered flat a mile upstream, cutting out cedar stringers and puncheon for a new span."

"Finding old-growth cedar of sufficient size to make good stringers fifty feet long was a problem but Windy eventually located two good trees which he broad axed on the flat above Gorge Creek. I do not recall the number of days we spent on this project but it was less than a week, Dick Lynch giving us any and all help needed. Cedar puncheons were also cut on the flat. To move the fifty-foot stringers over a mile of steep and crooked trail was no small task. With ten to twelve men shouldering each of the heavy timbers, they were thus carried over the full distance, and at times it was necessary to rope the big sills to snub them around sharp bends or to drag them manually where the trail among the rocks was so crooked it was impossible to shoulder the heavy timbers. In like fashion the thick cedar puncheons were transported from the flat to the new span, Lynch's men carrying the big slabs one at a time, shoulders padded with gunny sacks."

Today a few ragged timbers hanging from the cliff is all that remains of the bridge the Lynch Brothers rebuilt in 1919. It is directly beneath what is called Tunnel #1 on scenic Highway 20, just east of the town of Newhalem.

Will Jenkins' sidekick during his time with the Lynch Brothers was *"A little Irishman named Tommy Walsh, an ex-Montana copper miner from Butte, who called me his cousin Jake, and who never permitted me to go down a test pit without his company."*

"The geology at Gorge Camp," wrote Jenkins *"was badly shattered and irregular as the result of ancient upheavals. To clear away loose rock in order to get the cutting bits on solid stone, for test boring, it was often necessary to sink a shaft, cribbing with timbers as we dug down through loose talus. Then would follow the four-inch heavy iron standpipe, the chopping bits and water pressure to flush out the hole, and finally the clean cutting diamond drills, to bring up solid core for study."*

Bridge over Gorge Creek at Devil's Elbow in 1921. Photo courtesy Noel V. Bourasaw, Editor, Skagit River Journal of History & Folklore, www.skagitriverjournal.com

The federal government required a minimum of 250 feet of solid core bedrock before a dam could be built. 249 feet and the men had to try again at another spot. Jenkins recalled that three sizes of diamond bits were attached to rotary drills and powered by the Model T engines packed in by mules. He described the bits as, *"the small "E" bit, which cut a core seven-eighths of an inch in diameter; an "A" casing bit, which was large by half an inch; and what was known as the big Masabe bit, which cut core to a diameter of approximately two inches."*

Jenkins and another Lynch crew member named Bill Patton were assigned the first job on what was then known as Ruby Dam. They were to descend to the Rip Raps above Ruby Creek and blast out a ledge for the drilling rig. 300 feet of rope and long pole ladders were needed to reach the area where they would hand-drill holes to place highly explosive gelatin sticks.

"To drill the shot holes, Bill and I sat on a plank slung on blocks and tackle with our dangling feet scant inches above the white water of the Rip Raps. It was cool there, with spray from the river soaking our backs and legs as we single-jacked the holes with three-quarter steel and short hammers."

After the long fuses were lit, Jenkins and Patton scampered up the long pole ladders and ropes to safety before the blast that initiated the Lynch Brothers work on the site of the future Ross Dam; a dam that would change the face of the North Cascades forever by creating the 23-mile long Ross Lake.

It is hard to find the names of men, outside of Lynch family members, who worked on crews for the Lynch Brothers Diamond Drilling Company. Besides Miller, Rhoades, Patton, Henry and Walsh, Jenkins also refers to Ed and Dave O'Conner; Rocky Wilson; Howard Paul; and a man he literally looked up to: the drill runner "Big Bill" Bazinet.

Jenkins described Bazinet as, *"260 pounds of good nature always looking at the funny side of life."*

The younger Jenkins endeared himself to Bazinet by trying to make their mid-river perches, known to diamond-drillers as "doghouses", as dry, warm and comfortable as possible. He even installed an old wood heater and stove pipe on one doghouse, much to the delight of Big Bill. But such considerations did not make Jenkins immune to Big Bill's pranks.

The Lynch Brothers' drills ran continuously (24 hours per day) and Jenkins worked a night shift with Big Bill. *"One cold and stormy night as we were huddled by the stove listening to the drone of the rods deep in the bedrock, Bill muttered, 'I sure hate to do it, but we'll have to pull the rods'."*

Rods would be pulled quickly if the drills hit a split or open seam causing the cooling water to drop away from the diamond drill. Then the intense heat caused by the friction of the drill could disintegrate the bit, potentially losing thousands of dollars' worth of diamonds. So when an experienced drill runner like Bazinet told a young gopher like Jenkins to pull the rods there were few questions asked, regardless of the conditions.

Jenkins put a coal lantern on his elbow and climbed the pole tripod to the steel pulley at the peak.

"The wind was howling up-river that night and rain was cold and continuous. Reaching my high perch I hung the lantern on its nail and waited for the signal to lower the hook for the first gang of rods. And waited. In the dim light below I could see Bill Bazinet sitting on his powder box, one ear close to the rods. He was humped over, unmoving. I waited. And got cold, and the rain was finding the inside of my collar. And waited!"

"I noticed Bill looking around as if he was searching for something. Finally he looked up, and feigned great surprise at seeing me at the top of the tripod with my arms wrapped around the pole."

"Hey! What'n hell you doin' up there?" Bill yelled above the roar of the Skagit."

"You said we had to pull the rods, I shouted back."

"Oh yeah. We will, son. Not yet, though. We pull 'em just before we get off shift at four. Come on down where it's warm."

Jenkins concluded, *"Bill's roaring laughter shook the drill stand."*

"I climbed down, and he slapped me on the back of my wet slicker, laughing in his high joy of what Bazinet would recount as a good joke on his ambitious new helper."

Bazinet's prank was harmless enough, but most joking around happened when a shift crew was not working. Diamond drilling was dangerous and expensive work. Nevertheless, serious efforts to keep the drills moving could sometimes lead to unexpected amusement.

Mate Lynch and some crew members enjoy down time on the river.

If diamonds were lost in a split or seam deep in the bedrock, they could sometimes be fished out by lowering a line with tallow inserted into the open end of a piece of iron pipe. Jenkins wrote that, *"After much fishing the diamonds might be raised up, stuck in the tallow."*

But if diamonds were not lost then a small split or seam could be overcome with plaster of Paris. Gallons of plaster of Paris would be poured into holes where it would settle into the seams and harden after an hour or two, allowing drilling to resume. There were times when the crew ran out of plaster of Paris; but that was no problem, according to Jenkins.

"Here I learned an old driller's trick from Pat Lynch. His inventive mind had come up with the fact that a dry hole in a rock seam could be effectively sealed off with dry manure."

One day Dusty Rhoades hit a dry hole at 244 feet. Rhoades was quick about shutting down the drills and managed to save all of the diamonds.

"Pat Lynch was on the platform that day," Jenkins recounted many years later. *"He studied the bit raised from the hole when the gang of rods had been pulled up, then turned to me, saying, 'Bob, we're fresh out of plaster of Paris, so you go down to the horse corral and see if you can get us about a gunny sack full of horse shit, the real dry, grainy kind where the pack trains have been fed. And hustle it up!'* "

Jenkins crossed the river in the Lynches go-devil, ran off to the horse corral and brought back, *"A sack full of the driest, most grainy big turds I could find."*

Pat Lynch pulverized the horse dung with his hands and Dusty Rhoades poured it into the rod hole, flushing it down with water. Jenkins continued the story. *"The dry manure, heavy with undigested oats, wheat and corn, quickly swelled when the water hit it and soon we had the break tightly sealed off. We resumed drilling."*

About this time some "inspector" came knocking around asking dumb questions. These inspectors were not part of the Lynch Brothers crew. They were political appointments from Seattle trying to get in on the big money that was being spent on the Skagit project by walking around with note pads and asking questions they thought sounded important, like, "How deep are you men?"

Jenkins job during the horse shit adventure was to remove the core samples and place them into the core box. They were placed in such a way that geologists could study the chronology of the rock formation. The Seattle inspector was standing next to

Jenkins when he removed the core sample that included the compacted horse manure, which had been, *"tightly compressed under the great weight of nearly 260 feet of steel rods during the last hour of operation."*

Jenkins carefully placed the core sample in its correct channel in the core box. *"Nearly two feet of sand, grit, cracked corn, oats and wheat – a highly conglomerate mixture of ancient stone and recent manure."*

Rhoades saw an opportunity and shouted to Jenkins, *"Be careful you don't scratch any of that core. The geologists are very concerned about this hole."*

That caught the attention of the inspector, who started examining the sample with his pencil. Jenkins wrote that the inspector *"opened a gold penknife dangling from his watch chain, and with the fine point of the little blade dug out a kernel of grain. His amazement was profound!"*

The clueless inspector shouted, *"Look at this whole grain, men! Wheat, and oats and yes, corn, too, if I'm not mistaken. Yes, that's what it is...At what? 248 feet, you say? Well now. Amazing! Do you fellows realize the significance of this? What it really proves?"*

"Oh, we've hit stuff like that before," responded Rhoades. *"Seems like it's all around in this strata."*

The inspector requested a tiny piece of the core, which Rhoades gave to him, feigning reluctance.

"The inspector folded it carefully in his handkerchief and tucked it into a pocket of his shirt. He was still saying something about an amazing discovery when he left the rig and headed for the City (Seattle Lights Lights) office on Gorge Creek."
A couple of weeks later a Seattle newspaper arrived at the camp via the pack train and told the remarkable story of *"positive evidence of a prehistoric civilization"* buried 248 feet below the foaming rapids of the Skagit. C.F.Uhden, the chief engineer for

Seattle City Lights read the article to the great amusement of the Lynch crew eating their dinner at the cookhouse. It just so happened that the inspector was eating there too, and according to Jenkins, *"He left the table in deep embarrassment, and soon thereafter left Gorge Camp for good."*

Jenkins wrote that *"The Lynch crew had its share of good-natured pranksters, such as you'd expect in almost any similar camp, but horseplay was strictly forbidden the moment we went to work. There was no tolerance for risky foolishness. Out on the river you were not only your own safety man; you were also your brother's keeper and constantly reminded of that fact by the roar of the Skagit sweeping under the skimpy platforms."*

It was dangerous work, and the Lynch Brothers took every precaution to protect their workers. So when a worker proved negligent he was not long for the company.

Jenkins tells the tale of a young University of Washington student named Jimmy who took a summer job with the diamond drill crew during the Skagit project. It was Jimmy's first day on the job when the crew he was assigned to hit a pocket of loose rock about 100 feet below Gorge Creek and decided to use dynamite to clear it out. Pat Lynch, Dusty Rhoades, Jim Miller and Jenkins fashioned a torpedo tube from salvaged sheet metal and discarded gasoline cans.

"Into the tube we pressed and carefully packed the soft, mushy contents of thirty-five sticks of gelatin powder, a type of dynamite of very high potency."

Miller inserted four blasting caps and carefully inserted a water-proof plug and smeared it all with grease.

"As you might appreciate," recounted Jenkins, *"our attention was focused on the bomb, fully aware of the deadly charge held in the cylinder, and no one was talking."*

Except Jimmy who was overheard saying, *"I'm ready when you are."* That caught Jenkins's attention and he looked over to see a smiling Jimmy *"seated with the little oak box of electric firing device between his knees. The plunger on the box was raised full length, its thrusting handle gripped in Jimmy's hands. The long electric wires attached to the caps in the torpedo he had already fastened to the terminals in the box. All that was needed at that moment to explode thirty-five sticks of high gelatin was a downward push on the handle!"*

Jenkins quickly grabbed the shank of the plunger with all of his strength and told Jimmy to let go, which he did, *"looking puzzled and disappointed."*

Miller was holding the torpedo during all of this and after Jenkins pulled the wires he let out his breath and whispered, *"Holy Jesus!"*

Dusty Rhoades did not say a word. He just shook his head in disbelief and walked away. But Jenkins recalled that Pat Lynch exploded!

"Pat's Irish vocabulary, studded with colorful adjectives learned in over thirty years of hard rock drilling in the four corners of the world, now burst above the roar of the river; and I'm certain the likes of what he had to say had never been equaled by any man at Gorge Creek."

Jimmy's first day with the Lynch Brothers was also his last day. Jenkins wrote this account some 60 years after it occurred and it is possible that he is confusing one Lynch brother with another in this particular story. Pat Lynch was the youngest of the brothers and had been diamond drilling for about 15 years, not 30. Perhaps it was the oldest brother, Dan Lynch, who unleashed the torrent of verbal abuse on the hapless Jimmy. Regardless, it is an excellent illustration of the fact that diamond drilling was dangerous, not just because of Mother Nature, but because of the occasional knucklehead too. And it further illustrated the importance that the Lynch Brothers placed on the safety of their crew.

Safety and happiness: the Lynch Brothers valued both. In fact, they were willing to lose money if it meant their valued workers were happy. Jenkins experienced this first hand in the saga of Tony, his beloved sidekick who happened to be an Airedale dog. Jenkins remembers getting the dog from one Melvin Lynch, no relation to the brothers, but a crew member just the same. Lynch couldn't take care for Tony, so passed him on to Jenkins, who had always been an animal lover. Tony followed Jenkins everywhere. He took on bears and cougars, made away with meat that didn't belong to him and was simply a good-natured mischievous pup.

Jenkins was working for the Lynch Brothers in Newhalem, moving iron pipes across the Skagit in a go-devil, *"when Tony, riding the cable carriage with me as usual, fell through the bottom of the bucket to be swept down the white water crest of the Skagit."*

Tony's wiry head bounced along the rapids and then disappeared at a bend in the river. A heart-broken Jenkins told Pat Lynch what had happened and Lynch felt confident that the dog might still be alive. He shut down three drills and sent all of the workers off in an all-out search for Tony.

"I cite this incident," wrote Jenkins in 1984, *"because it revealed the real measure of the man. Lynch Brothers' drills were all in solid bedrock on the power site flat at Newhalem. There was no loose overburden, and at a premium rate being paid by City Light for every foot of core, those drills were making money fast for Pat and his brothers. The profits stopped when drills were idled, but it was Pat Lynch's own doing – and nine men spent the next three hours searching for a lost dog."*

A crew member named Vic Wilson finally found Tony, *"howling mournfully from a narrow ledge where he had crawled from the charitable mercy of an eddy."*

"I think Pat Lynch was as happy as I was, though the past three hours had been expensive for his company. The feeling of gratitude to my employer I felt that day has never diminished."

Will Jenkins and Tony in the go-devil. Photo courtesy Noel V. Bourasaw, Editor,
Skagit River Journal of History & Folklore, www.skagitriverjournal.com

In 1996 the Skagit River & Newhalem Creek Hydroelectric Project, including the three dams where the Lynch Brothers conducted the core drilling (Gorge, Diablo and Ross), was officially added to the National Register of Historic Places by the National Park Service. The 129 page document on the history of the project included this reference to the Lynch Brothers:

"By the spring of 1918, the City of Seattle had survey and drilling crews exploring possible dam sites for hydroelectric development on the Skagit. By March of 1919, the Diamond Drilling Company, operated by three brothers—Dick, Dan and Pat Lynch--was under contract with the city to bore cores for bedrock analysis at various sites along the river. Their crew of forty was housed in tents above Gorge Creek. The first structure built in connection with the Skagit Hydroelectric Project was a two-story rectangular log building which served as the company office, dining room, kitchen and warehouse, located near Gorge Creek. Workers for the company referred to the building and tents as Gorge Camp.

The camp was abandoned when the drilling crew finished their work in the early 1920s; the log building lasted until the late 1930s, gradually falling into ruin."

Dr. Jesse Kennedy III, historian for North Cascades National Park Service in Marblemount summed up the Lynch Brothers contribution to the Skagit River Project when he wrote, *"Dick, Dan, and Pat Lynch and their company did some incredible work."*

The Diablo, Gorge and Ross Dams continue to provide energy for the city of Seattle. The beautiful structures, now part of the North Cascades National Park, stand as a lasting monument to all of the workers who risked life and limb to see the project through. And it was all started by the Lynch Brothers Diamond Drilling Company.

Will D. "Bob" Jenkins and his wife Mildred. Jenkins wrote the only known anecdotes of the Lynch Brothers on the Skagit River Project. Photo courtesy Noel V. Bourasaw, Editor, Skagit River Journal of History & Folklore, www.skagitriverjournal.com

Pat Lynch on the Go-Devil during the Skagit Project.

Dan Lynch, far right, with a drill crew on Skagit River Project.

On the back of this photograph from the Skagit project one of the Lynch brothers wrote: "Same drill on another hole in the river bed. One of our boys drowned here. It is a very bad river. And the water is always ice cold."

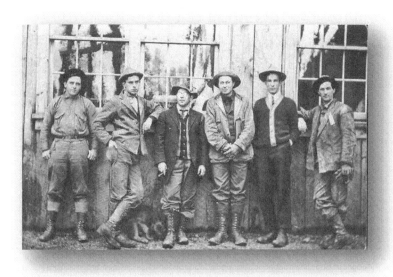

Lynch Brothers' diamond drilling crews faced death by drowning or falling from craggy, slippery cliffs during the historic Skagit Project.

Pat Lynch, left, and Dick Lynch, right, flank older brother Dan during the days of the great Skagit River project.

Above: Lynch Brothers set two drills at a dam project in Washington. Next page: Four drill rigs testing on the Skagit River. The Lynch camp is in the background.

A Lynch Brothers drill crew.

Dan Lynch led this crew at the copper boomtown of Phoenix, British Columbia, where his daughter Harriet met her future husband, the boxing brewmaster Billy Biner.

A little levity was welcome relief after a hard day's work with a diamond drill crew. Dan Lynch was a practical joker who kept his brothers and crew members laughing. Here a "heavily-armed" Dan poses with Mate in the North Cascades.

On August 22, 1920, during the busy Skagit project, Cornelius Lynch, Sr., the patriarch of the family, died at his home in Republic, Michigan. He was 84. Dan and Dick Lynch made the trip back to Michigan to attend his funeral and reunite with their sisters, Mary and Bridget. Mary and her husband Dennis McCarthy had eight children and seemed to be doing well in Gladstone, Michigan. Nevertheless, they would join the Lynch brothers in Seattle off and on over the next 15 years. Bridget, however, was now alone. The ever welcoming Sabina Lynch, wife of her brother Dick, invited her to live with them in Seattle.

Finally, the younger generation of the Lynch clan would get to know their personable, loving, deaf-mute aunt from Michigan. And while the Harris clan remained in the Upper Peninsula, the Lynch clan was now a family of the Pacific Northwest.

Cornelius Lynch as an old man, with his daughter Bridget,
in front of the Lynch home in Republic, Michigan.

Dan and Dick Lynch, 2ⁿᵈ and 3ʳᵈ from left, at the family home in Republic, Michigan following the funeral of their father, Cornelius Lynch, in 1920. With them are their sisters Mary Lynch McCarthy and Bridget Lynch. Sitting on the railing is Mary's son, Raymond McCarthy.

Mary McCarthy (far left) and Bridgy Lynch (far right) at the Lynch home in Republic, Michigan, following the death of their father.

Eight: Fred Lynch, the Singing Policeman of KOMO

Frederick Albert Lynch, 1890-1982.

Fred Lynch, the first child of Dan and Mate, had a mobile existence during the first twenty-five years of his life. Fred always said he was born in Hancock, Michigan, the very town where his father was born 23 years earlier. But the Michigan births and christening index indicates that Fred was born on September 10, 1890, about 100 miles down the road from Hancock, in Iron Mountain, Michigan. Regardless, he didn't stay long. By age two he was off to Oregon with his father and pregnant mother. They settled in Albany, Oregon where his father worked for the soon-to-be famous Oscar Kendall. But after a flood shut down the business in 1894, Dan, Mate, Fred and now little Harriet returned to Michigan. Over the next five years they moved from Republic, where Fred's grandparents lived, to Waucedah, where his little brother Kendall was born, and finally back to Hancock. During this period, Dan Lynch returned to the mining industry, and discovered diamond drilling.

As Dan Lynch accepted jobs supervising drill operations for Sullivan Machinery, he and Mate shipped Fred and Harriet off to Mate's sisters and kept little Kendall with them. This was probably because it was time for Fred and Harriet to earn an education and moving from mining towns to far-flung mining camps would disrupt that necessity.

In 1905, Fred moved to Hanover, Wisconsin, to live with his childless aunt, Eva Kendall Child. It was during this time that Fred, for reasons unknown, acquired the nickname of "Jerry." Aunt Eva was busy with her DAR and Royal Neighbors of America duties and was on the road, at times accompanied by her husband Fred Child, the local railroad station agent. Ironically, when Eva and Fred Child were away, Fred lived in their home with a young female servant, the daughter of German immigrants. Her name was Tillie Dolghner, and she was only two years older than Fred. A 1905 special state census shows 16 year-old Tillie living with 14 year-old Fred Lynch. They were still living under the same roof two years later at age 18 and 16 respectively, and one could easily imagine that if there was any physical attraction between Tillie and the lanky, charming Fred, then a crush (or perhaps more) could have developed.

Fred came close to losing his Aunt Eva on January 19, 1907, during his final year of high school. Eva was on her way home, possibly from the funeral of her brother-in-law and first cousin,

Oscar Kendall. Kendall had died on January 10th and was buried in Portland on January 15th.   On the night of January 19th Eva was in Chicago where she boarded the eastbound Queen City Special No. 38 of the Cleveland, Cincinnati, Chicago and St. Louis Railway, also known as the Big Four Railroad.

As the train approached the town of Fowler, Indiana at a speed of 50 mph through dense fog, the engineer failed to see the stoplight of a semaphore, warning that a westbound freight train was approaching. A train dispatcher fired shots from a revolver and waved a lantern but it was too late. The Queen City Special collided with the freight train. Twenty-five people were crushed to death, or burned alive when engine coals set most of the cars on fire.

Only two cars escaped serious damage, including the sleeper car Eva occupied with several other passengers. Upon her return home to Hanover, Wisconsin, the *Janesville Daily Gazette* conducted an interview.   On January 21, 1907 the *Gazette* published this report:

BARELY ESCAPED DEATH IN WRECK
MRS. EVA CHILDS IN THE BIG FOUR WRECK SATURDAY TELLS OF HARROWING SCENES

Was Awakened by the Shock of Collision—Saw the Mangled Bodies of Victims

"Among the passengers on the ill-fated Queen City Special on the Big Four road that was wrecked early Saturday morning was Mrs. F. B. Childs of Hanover. Mrs. Childs was in the Indianapolis Sleeper, the only regular sleeper that was not destroyed by fire, and saw all the horrors of the dreadful accident. She reached Janesville Sunday morning; and went immediately to her home in Hanover. In speaking of her experience this morning, Mrs. Childs said: "We were all awakened by a tremendous bump about two-thirty, but did not know what was the matter until a half hour later. We were all in our berths when the conductor came through and told us to get up; that there had been a little accident and we would be delayed for some time, and might have to look after ourselves. ...We dressed hurriedly and all left the car.

The sight that met our eyes was horrible. Our car was only slightly off the track; the front trucks being derailed; the sleeper from Cincinnati lying on its side and the combination car on top of the engine. On one side of the road were laying many of the injured and the dead that had been taken from the wreckage. Arms and legs were scattered about. It was horrible. The majority of the passengers in our car were sent back into the sleeper immediately and then they began to bring in the injured and the equipment of the other sleeper. We did everything we could do for the suffering, but there was not much we could do. Two of the injured died before they reached the hospital. Meanwhile an engine had come and pulled our car onto the tracks and away from the wreckage which was now burning ...then they began to load the special car of Mr. Schaff (*Charles E. Schaff was a vice-president of the Big Four and the car was occupied by his wife, Leila White Schaff*). Mrs. Schaff refused to allow her car to be used and the negro porter stood on guard at the door. It took some time to arrange that some of the injured should be placed in there, (but) only the part of the car where no beds were was opened for the use of the injured and they were forced to lie on the floor."

It is interesting to note that Eva Childs, herself a woman of distinction, showed no mercy for the insensitive Mrs. Schaff in her interview with the *Gazette*. But one of the railroad industry trade journals, The *Locomotive Fireman's and Engineers Magazine*, in its 1907 issue, turned Mrs. Schaff into the heroine of the train tragedy.

The magazine absolutely gushed with praise for Mrs. Schaff under the heading: **A True Heroine**

"History affords no instance wherein the spirit of gentle charity mingled with that of true heroism has been more fully or generously displayed by woman than when during the awful scenes immediately following the recent wreck on the Big Four railroad at Fowler, Indiana. Mrs. Schaff, wife of the vice-president of that system, arose to the occasion and by her noble deeds of bravery and mercy brought relief and comfort to so many of the unfortunate victims of that awful catastrophe."

"It was on the night of January 19, 1907, passenger train No. 38, the Queen City Special, eastbound, while going at a rate of 50 miles per hour, collided with a westbound freight. The passenger train consisted of a combination baggage and day coach, three sleeping cars and vice-president Schaff's private car, in which his wife was travelling from Chicago to Cincinnati, Mr. Schaff not being on board."

"When the crash came, Mrs. Schaff, arising from her comfortable berth, promptly assisted in the work of rescue: she directed that the injured be taken to her car, and personally assisted in dressing their wounds and looking after their comfort. Amidst all the turmoil incident to such an occasion, she quietly, earnestly and sympathetically carried on the work of relief. Everything that a true woman could do to mitigate suffering and console the afflicted was done by Mrs. Schaff in the midst of scenes calculated to quail the stoutest heart and shake the strongest nerves."

The writer for the trade journal can be excused for his hyperbole. It was a common style of the times; and it is unlikely that he was aware of Eva Childs' chilling interview in the *Janesville Daily Gazette.* But it does seem that Mrs. Schaff (or perhaps her worried husband) parlayed shameful conduct into underserved praise.

On June 7, 1907 Fred Lynch was awarded what today would be called a high school diploma from the State Graded School in Hanover, Wisconsin. Two months later he was in British Columbia, working for his father at the Britannia Beach Mine. On his 17th birthday he received a postcard from Aunt Eva that read in part, "Dear Fred, why don't you send Tillie a card? She wonders at not hearing from you. Don't forget it…"

Fred eventually got around to sending Tillie a card. She wrote him back and sounded as if she was trying to make him jealous, but also exposed either a lack of education or a difficulty with the English language. The card is difficult to decipher, but perhaps she was wondering if things were the same between them. Tillie wrote: *"Hello Fred must answer your postcard. I hope you are well. Must tell you that Fred* (last name is unreadable) *is marry. I went to a dance hear a week ago and I am going to one in Foothill tonight. I thought I wood hear from you be fore dont we as at all as that agen. Mr. & Mrs. Child are well. Hope to hear from you soon agen. Tillie Dolgner."*

Tillie wrote Fred again a few months later about another friend who had married and wondered what he thought about that. Perhaps she was trying to suggest something to him.

Tillie's real name was Ottilie, a feminine version of the German name Otto. She remained a maid most of her long life, did a bit of travelling, and likely saw Fred when he returned to Janesville many years later to care for his ailing Aunt Eva. Tillie Dolgner never married and died at the age of 99 in 1988. She is buried in the Bethel Cemetery in Janesville, Wisconsin, not far from three of Fred's relatives from the Chipman line.

In October, 1907, Fred had moved to Woodstock, Oregon, (now part of Portland) to live with his aunt, Nell Kendall, just nine months after his uncle's mysterious death in San Francisco. Fred's sister Harriet was already living with Aunt Nell. Fred was in Portland to look at Columbia University (now the University of Portland) but in January, 1908, Aunt Eva wrote him to see if he would be interested in taking over her husband's job as railroad agent in Hanover. It was quite an offer for a 17 year-old man, but Fred turned it down. He also heard regularly from his uncle, Pat Lynch, only five years his senior, who was living in Norway, Michigan at the time. Pat engaged in small talk in his postcards to Fred. Fred was more like a cousin than a nephew to Pat Lynch. They had no way of knowing that in a few years they would be working together in the Alaska Territory for a company that Pat would start with his brother Dick.

The following summer Fred was back in British Columbia where he worked on and off for his father, but also took up temporary residence in Vancouver, BC, before returning to Portland to attend Columbia University. During this time he had numerous postcards from Aunt Eva, from his cousins Loretta and Mary McCarthy (the daughters of Mary Lynch), and from a young female admirer named Florence Ehrlinger.

Florence was a month younger than Fred and from the town of Belvidere, Illinois, just 40 miles down the line from Hanover. It's likely Fred got to know Florence when he visited his Uncle Albert Kendall, who was station agent in Belvidere when Fred was living with Eva Kendall. Florence tried to keep in touch after Fred moved away, but eventually gave up and married a younger boy from Hanover by the name of Carl W. Grinke. She bore him two children; daughter Norma and son Donald, who became a corporal in the U.S. Marines and saw action in the South Pacific during WW II.

One of Fred's early girlfriends, Florence Ehrlinger (1890-1965).

While attending Columbia, Fred lived at 802 N. Cleveland Street in Portland. His sister Harriet lived with him for a while as she worked in downtown Portland's Meier & Frank Department Store. Fred kept in touch with family members, including 2nd cousin Oscar J. Kendall, not to be confused with his dead uncle by the same name. The younger Oscar was a nephew of Uncle Oscar, and the son of Oscar's brother William. He lived in Spokane at the time and would write to Fred about the lack of job prospects. That didn't seem to be a problem for Fred, who worked for his father whenever he was out of school, whether at Britannia Beach or in Republic, Washington, which was just a few miles from Spokane. It is not known if Fred secured a job for Oscar in Republic.

Harriet Lynch at her brother's house in Portland, circa 1911.

Fred Lynch, third from left, on early drill crew in northern Washington.

Harriet Lynch on horse at northern Cascades mining camp.

Fred Lynch likely knew from an early age that he was a gifted singer. Ballads were an important part of many Irish families. While in Portland, Fred attempted to improve on his gift. He took voice lessons from Leo Charles Sparks (1867-1957) and would follow Sparks to Los Angeles several years later when the music teacher relocated there.

Fred's cousin, Loretta McCarthy, the daughter of Mary Lynch, kept in close contact with Fred throughout her life.

Silent films were the rage in the early years of the 20th century. It proved to be a good time for Fred Lynch to begin his professional career as a singer. Radio would not become widely used until the Roaring Twenties and "Talkies" wouldn't replace silent films until the 193Television was not a household fixture until the fifties.

And so it was in 1913, when Fred burst onto the music scene, that most people looking for entertainment were turning to silent films.

Theatres sprung up in big cities like Portland and drew large crowds. But there was down time as reels were switched out, and of course, too much silence. Theatre owners quickly discovered that the best way to keep the crowds engaged and in their seats was through live entertainment between films. That is how Fred Lynch got his start in the music industry; and it was one of the mainstays of his career for twenty years.

The July 27, 1913 issue of the *Morning Oregonian* announced that Fred Lynch, the recent graduate of Columbia University, would be performing at the Arcade Theatre in downtown Portland on Washington Street between 6th and Broadway. Interestingly, his first few appearances were as a baritone. Fred would discover that he was more gifted as a tenor and would become regionally famous as an "Irish tenor." But in the beginning he was a baritone.

It is ironic how many family events occurred on a six-block stretch of Washington Street in downtown Portland. It was on 4th and Washington, 13 years earlier, where Fred's Uncle Oscar Kendall got into a fist fight with Tom McGrath while defending former district attorney Wilson Hume. In 1912 Fred's sister Harriet graduated from Holmes Business College, located on 10th and Washington. And In the summer of 1927, 14 years after Fred's performance, the Honeyman Building, located on Washington and Broadway next to the Arcade Theater, collapsed. Fred's cousin Nora Horton, the daughter of Anthony Harris, who was the brother of Fred's Grandmother Bridget Harris Lynch, fell into a hole created by the collapsed building! She was injured and filed suit against the owners of the building, Lorenz Brothers & Honeyman Investment Co., for $15,000.

It is not known if Nora Horton won her lawsuit; but she could have used the money. After raising two children of her own with husband Charles Horton (Mary and Albert), she raised the eight sons of her deceased brother and sister-in-law Thomas and Adelaide Harris. When Nora had her accident she was 60 years old and at least four of her nephews were still living with her and Charles, who worked in a Portland saw mill. Nora also had eight grandchildren; six by her daughter Mary who was married to Valentine Prentice. Mary Horton Prentice (1892-1974) was the life-long best friend of her 2nd cousin Harriet Lynch Biner.

At the Arcade Theatre Fred kept the audience entertained between the showings of the Danish film, *"The Governor's Daughter,"* a comedy called *"Their Lucky Day,"* and one of the first animated shorts: *"In Cartoonland"* by Hy Mayer. And while the *Oregonian* complemented the films, it also found praise for young Fred Lynch saying he offered, "Some pleasing new songs."
In August, 1913, Portland's new Sunnyside Theatre, on SE 35th and Belmont celebrated its one year anniversary with a movie and musical extravaganza. Five films were featured along with performances by the Peoples Amusement Company, which included violinist Marie Chapman; banjoist "Musical" Stanley, and baritone Fred Lynch.

Fred performed regularly in Portland and had his first studio photograph as a musician taken there in the Davies Studio. That photograph would be used ten years later in the *Los Angeles Examiner*. But Fred must have realized (or been told) that there was little chance of making a living with his voice, so he continued to work for his father, learning the trade of diamond drilling.

Sometime during 1911, Fred went briefly to Alaska for the first time, perhaps on a job with his father or one of his uncles. He would return for a much longer period between 1915 and 1922 when he would become one of the first members of the Lynch Brothers Diamond Drilling Company; find the love of his life, and discover that he really wanted to be a singer.

Early promotional picture of the singer Fred Lynch taken at Davies Studio in Portland, Oregon.

Harriet Lynch (below with her widowed Aunt Nell Kendall in Portland).

Between 1912 and 1914, when not performing in Portland, Fred worked at several mining camps, including the Wolf Camp above Curlew Lake near Republic, Washington, where his father supervised diamond drilling at gold mines, and at various mines in British Columbia and Alberta, including Phoenix, British Columbia, the site of a spectacular copper boom. His sister Harriet would meet her future husband, Billy Biner, the boxing brewmaster, in Phoenix.

The wedding picture of Billy Biner and Harriet Lynch, 1914.

Harriet Lynch remained close to her older brother Fred throughout her life. He became the cherished uncle to her children and grandchildren.

In 1915, Fred moved to Juneau, Alaska to work for the newly created Lynch Brothers Diamond Drilling Company. But he also became one-half of the two-person police force for Juneau. He started singing and performing in plays. And he met and wooed a vivacious teenager from nearby Douglas named Mollie Wiitanen. In 1916 Mollie was named "Queen" of the biggest event in Douglas, the annual Eagles Carnival. She was 17 years old. A year later she would marry the 27 year-old Fred Lynch.

At first sight they seemed an unlikely pair. Mollie was petite, a bit temperamental and from a Scandinavian Lutheran background. Fred was tall, gregarious, and even-keeled; and from an Irish Catholic background. But both of their families had immigrated to Michigan's Upper Peninsula and both of them were fun-loving social creatures who enjoyed their friends, good food, drinking, smoking and entertaining. Fred was already gaining a reputation as the singing policeman of Juneau when he met Mollie, who had to cross the Gastineau Channel from Douglas Island on a boat, but did so regularly to party in the bigger town of Juneau with her equally bohemian friends. Policeman Fred walked the wharfs of Juneau, cajoling drunks and miscreants to behave, and it is probably there that he first met Mollie. By all accounts, it was love at first sight.

Policeman Fred Lynch is sitting right behind his young bride.

In 1916, Fred joined Mollie and a cast of eight in the play *"The Heart of a Shamrock."* It was performed at the Lyric Theatre in Douglas. Hailed as the "Fireman's Show" it was likely a presentation to thank firefighters for saving the Lyric when a fire destroyed much of downtown Douglas a few years earlier. The Lyric Theatre was damaged, but not beyond repair. *The Daily Alaska Dispatch*, Juneau, AK, of March 10, 1911, described the fire in a vivid article. The fire apparently started in the upstairs apartment of the cook at an eating establishment known as The Grill and quickly spread.

"Those who saw the fire first say it suddenly burst into flame from the Grill, appearing to set fire to the Island Hotel and Lyric Theatre buildings simultaneously, jumping the street so quickly that the barbers in the Day buildings were barely able to escape without saving anything. The barber shop was directly across from the Grill."

Later in the article the firefighters were acknowledged. "The Juneau fire department sent forty men to the fire, all being experienced and energetic firemen, and today Douglas expresses the deepest appreciation of their work."

"When the flames were seen in Juneau orders were immediately issued to the electric light station to cut out all the Douglas lights, which allowed the firemen to work around the network of fallen wires without fear of injury."

In *"The Heart of a Shamrock"* Fred played the part of Grizzly Adams, a cattleman, and young Mollie was Gad, a city waif.

On February 19, 1917, in the Roman Catholic Church of Douglas, Grizzly Adams and the city waif were married. For some unknown reason the marriage certificate has Fred as Albert H. Lynch, when it was actually Frederick Albert Lynch. But no one seemed to contest the certificate over the next 63 years of marriage.

From the relatively modest Lyric Theatre, Fred moved on to preform regularly at Juneau's popular Spickett's Palace. Opened by John Spickett in 1916, as a vaudeville theatre, the Palace was the place to perform in Juneau's mining heyday. In fact, it continued to offer shows until the year 2001, and was a scene in the 1999 John Sayles film, *Limbo*. It now stands deserted and condemned as unsafe on Juneau's Franklin Street. In a sign of the times one of the last performances that Fred Lynch participated in while living in Alaska was a blackface comedy at Spickett's Palace called *Moose Minstrels*.

The 1916 cast of "The Heart of a Shamrock" at Lyric Theatre in Douglas, Alaska. Fred Lynch is the cattleman, 4th from left. Mollie Wiitanen is 3rd from right. Fred & Mollie Lynch Collection.

FIREMEN'S SHOW

LYRIC THEATRE

MONDAY AND TUESDAY
NOVEMBER 20-21

PROGRAM

THE HEART OF A SHAMROCK

CAST OF CHARACTERS

Father O'Neil, the Pastor	Roy Noland
Bob, "the Sheriff," his brother	H. E. Murray
Larkin, the youngest brother	Pat McGuire
Grundy Adams, a cattleman	P. A. Lynch
May, an Irish rose	Miss Jessie Koss
Vird, a city waif	Miss Mollie Williams
Mrs. Donovan, the housekeeper	Miss Stella MacLeod
Jean, a ranchman's daughter	Mrs. H. T. Prock

ACT I
Sitting Room in Father O'Neil's home. Evening, about
7 o'clock.

ACT II
The same. About 11 o'clock.

ACT III
The same. One hour later.
The action of the play takes place at Wild Cat, Arizona.

SPECIALTIES WILL BE GIVEN BY
THE PITTMAN SINGING QUARTETTE.
Miss JESSIE KOSS.
Mr. P. A. LYNCH.

Admission to All Parts of the House .... 50 Cts.
Tickets on Sale All Over Town ...... Curtain at 8:15

Fred Lynch is in this picture, it is just impossible to know which one he is as all the white performers are wearing blackface in the waning years of the now shameful minstrel show era.
Courtesy of the Alaska State Library, Winter & Pond Collection. Image ID No. P87-1180

When America entered World War I Fred registered for the draft. On the day he registered, July 12, 1917, in Spokane, Washington, he was employed by the Lynch Brothers at the Perseverance Mine near Juneau. Yet he listed his address as 802 Cleveland Avenue in Portland. That is where he had lived during his college days. The draft registration card recorded Fred as tall and stout, with blue eyes and light brown hair. He was nearing his 27th birthday at the time and was never called to duty. But the following month his 20 year-old brother Kendall would enlist.

Fred returned to Alaska and spent the next five years drilling for his uncles, but continued to perform in concerts and plays. He appeared on the March, 1922 Spickett's Palace bill that included a production by the soon-to-be-famous Hal Roach (1892-1992), who spent some of his early years in Alaska, before producing such comedy acts as Laurel & Hardy and The Little Rascals.

As he reached the age of 30 Fred decided it was make or break time for his musical career. And so in the fall of 1922, Fred and Mollie Lynch moved to Los Angeles, California, where Fred's old voice coach Leo Sparks had relocated. Newspaper accounts in Juneau said that Lynch planned to study in LA for two years before returning to Alaska.

It took little time for Fred to get established in Los Angeles. In January, 1923 he signed with the legendary showman Sid Grauman (1879-1950) to perform as the regular Irish tenor in the new Grauman's Egyptian Theatre. The more famous Grauman's Chinese Theatre would open in 1926. Grauman also made Lynch available to perform live on two brand new Los Angeles radio stations, KWH (owned by the *Los Angeles Examiner*) and KFI (owned by Earle C. Anthony). It was a turning point in his career.

The radio frequencies could occasionally be picked up as far away as Alaska. A 1923 Juneau newspaper reported under the banner **Fred Lynch Heard in Songs at Douglas**:

"Fred Lynch, popular tenor soloist who made his home in Juneau for several years, until last fall when he went to Los Angeles to study voice culture, has not been lost to his Gastineau Channel fans. Although hundreds of miles away Lynch's tenor voice has traveled through the air from sunny California to the Northland and his songs have been heard in Douglas by Robert Caughlin, through his radio receiving set. "

"Mr. Caughlin said he heard Mr. Lynch from KFI, the Earl C. Anthony Broadcasting Station, and chief station of Los Angeles. Mr. Lynch was announced and shortly after his songs came to his audience and old friends in the Caughlin home."

Caughlin was the same age as Fred. He worked as a mechanic at a gold mine, quite possibly on a job for the Lynch Brothers, who despite relocating their headquarters in Seattle had many ongoing jobs in the Juneau area.

The January 9, 1923, issue of the *Los Angeles Examiner* featured a photograph of a young Fred Lynch under the headline *80 Minutes of Radio Melody Today's Treat.*   The article included the following:

"An artist of exceptional attainment is Fred Lynch, who possesses a natural tenor voice of clear tone and sympathetic sweetness, and is gifted with a magnetic personality which carries itself to the audience through his beautiful voice. Although a newcomer to this city, Mr. Lynch already has won countless admirers and his popularity was attested to by the storm of applause that greeted his efforts at Grauman's theatre last Sunday morning when he appeared at the regular morning concert. He will present the numbers he used at Grauman's Sunday morning, including *"Once in a Thousand Years"* and *"First Rose of Summer."*

The good-natured Fred was deadly serious about his career while in Los Angeles. In addition to Sparkes' tutelage, Fred studied voice culture under the respected teacher William J. Chick (1867-1957). But what he really desired, and ultimately earned, was an audition with the international opera star, Rosa Ponselle.

Mollie Lynch in Los Angeles, 1923.

Fred Lynch, lower right corner, featured in the Los Angeles Examiner, January 9, 1923. The photograph was ten years old. Los Angeles fans were probably surprised to see Fred with so much hair.

Rosa Ponselle (1897-1981) was widely regarded as the greatest soprano in America during the 1920s and 30s. Geraldine Farrar, herself a noted soprano opera singer, once said, "There are two singers you must put aside, one is Enrico Caruso, the other is Rosa Ponselle. Then you may begin to discuss all the others." And the renowned soprano Maria Callas said, "I think we all know that Ponselle was simply the greatest singer of us all."

When Ponselle appeared in Los Angeles for a performance in May, 1924, Fred and Mollie were in attendance. Having read that Miss Ponselle would be staying at the LA Biltmore, Fred was bold enough to send her a note asking for a voice trial. He was elated when he heard back from her devoted secretary, Edith Prilek.

"My dear Mr. Lynch: Miss Ponselle will give you a voice trial at five P.M. May 16th at hotel Biltmore Room 642-644. Yours very Truly, E. Prilek (sec)."

There is no written account of Fred's meeting with Ponselle. One can only imagine how nervous he must have been when he sang, presumably alone, to arguably the greatest female singer in the world. The letter he received from Ponselle the day after his audience with her was certainly a prized possession. It was kept in its original envelope in a scrapbook put together by his wife, Mollie. It was clearly written in Ponselle's own handwriting and not by Miss Prilek.

"May 17th 1924

My dear Mr. Lynch,

I enjoyed hearing your voice yesterday – particularly the resonant qualities of your upper tones.
With proper development and guidance I can see no reason why you couldn't make a field for yourself either in light opera or concerts – this is of course a matter entirely dependent upon the effort and intelligence shown upon your part. With every wish for your success, believe me.

Cordially yours – Rosa Ponselle"

Although Fred Lynch cherished this letter, it was not enough to keep him in Los Angeles. It remains a point of conjecture as to how successful and perhaps famous Fred Lynch might have become had he remained in Los Angeles. Certainly he had a successful career as a tenor, mostly for KOMO Radio in Seattle. But Los Angeles offered more opportunities, which he decided to pass on. He kept his promise and returned to Alaska after two years in Los Angeles.

One of the reasons that Fred Lynch wanted to return to the "Northland" was the fact that the Lynch Brothers Diamond Drilling Company was doing so well. He knew that if he could not make ends meet as a singer he could always have a job with the company. Fred was also fond of his relations. He was the one member of the Dan Lynch and Mate Kendall union who went out of his way to stay in touch with every branch of his family. He visited and communicated with many members of the Lynch and

Harris clans, as well as the more Americanized Kendall's and Chipman's on his mother's side.

Fred's sister Harriet was about 250 miles southeast of LA in the border town of Calexico during the early 1920s. At the time her husband, Billy Biner, was the brewmaster for the Mexicali Brewery across the border, which he operated with some of his brothers. Fred indirectly helped the brewery with his rendition of a particular song. The song was *"Mexicali Rose,"* written in 1923 by Jack Tenney and Helen Stone. Fred was one of the first to sing the song and make it popular. In fact it was Fred Lynch who introduced the song to the people of Mexicali when visiting his sister and brother-in-law in 1923. Needless to say, the song became wildly popular in the Mexican border town.

Harriet and her family would eventually return to British Columbia in 1928. But Fred was ready to move back north by the summer of 1924. He said goodbye to his new friends and fans, to the city of Los Angeles, and the potential stardom it offered, and returned to tiny Juneau, Alaska.

It was a pretty big deal when Fred returned to Juneau. *The Express* happily reported under the heading:
LYNCHES BACK IN JUNEAU

"Mr. and Mrs. Fred Lynch who left Juneau in the summer of 1922 and who have since resided in California returned on the steamer Princess Mary Tuesday night and will probably make Juneau their home. Mr. Lynch is remembered as an accomplished vocalist and during his residence in the south he not only continued voice culture but held many engagements as a singer. The Lynches are warmly welcomed back to Alaska and opportunities for hearing the popular singer will probably be given in the near future."

A few days later the paper announced in bold print:
FRED LYNCH TO APPEAR TONIGHT –
Will Make First Appearance at Entertainment Since His Return North.

Fred introduced the sunny Mexican hit for his fans in chilly Alaska.

NEW WALTZ BALLAD IS SUNG BY FRED LYNCH

"Fred Lynch made his third big hit at the Palace last night in tenor solos. Perhaps of the two selections, *"Mexicali Rose"* heard here for the first time, proved the most popular. This was written by Jack B. Tenney, director of one of the large orchestras now playing in California. Fred Lynch was one of the first soloists to sing the waltz ballad in Mexicali, from which the title gets its name, and it instantly proved one of the big hits and is now all of the rage. That it will prove popular in Juneau, as was attested last night at the Palace, goes almost without saying. Mr. Lynch's illustrated song was *"Take Me Back to Our Heart"* and it also proved popular."

Fred did solos in musicals and took comedy roles in plays, including *"Jazz Marriages"* and *"Sittin' Pretty,"* a popular 1924 Broadway musical. As venues like Spickett's Palace began to show more silent films, Fred and other musicians were hired to entertain the crowd between reels, in what became known as the theatrical circuit. It was similar to what he had done with Portland's Peoples Amusement Company a decade earlier. Sometimes the live performers would steal the show at the movie houses.

The Juneau Express reported:

Concerts Appealing at the Movie Theaters

"Fred Lynch and the musical trio Woofter, Burford and Beery, draw an added clientele to the Palace on Sunday and Monday nights. The programs are always good. Fred Lynch is now singing solos by request and it is astonishing the wide demand made upon this popular tenor. Many of those submitting requests are disappointed that their choice should be put off so long, but the management of the Palace and also Mr. Lynch are trying to oblige in the order of the receipt of the requests. Again the requests are so many that it would take almost an entire evening if all requests were complied with at once."

Fred also starred in the musical *"The Alaskans"* and was backed up by The Princess Charlotte Orchestra. The highlight of the show was Fred's rendition of *"La Golondrina,"* a traditional Mexican ballad that he probably learned in Los Angeles, which became one of his signature songs.

As a regular at Spickett's Palace, Fred occasionally received top billing over the featured film. He was a particular hit during the showing of George Beban's critically acclaimed *"One Man in a Million"*. A newspaper account of the performance stated that, "In keeping with the picture, Fred Lynch, dressed as an Italian, made a distinct hit in one song, sung in Italian, and then in that popular song everybody knows, which is something about 'the shores of Sunny Italy.' So well did the audience last night like the song that Lynch was forced to respond to three encores at the first show."

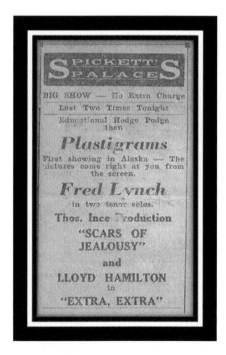

Advertisements for Spickett's Palace silent films featuring Fred Lynch,
"The Big Man with the Quality Voice," in solos.
Fred & Mollie Lynch Collection.

Richard Bathelmess
and
Dorothy Gish

IN

The
BRIGHT
SHAWL

e of the Year's Big Feature

HAROLD LLOYD
IN
HE LOVES NOT

EXTRA
ATTRACTION

Fred Lynch

in Prologue

Singing the big success

"CORAL GABLES"

SPICKETT'S PALACES

AST TWO TIMES TONIGHT

Hodge Podge and Kinograms

Fred Lynch

he Big Man with the Quality
Voice will sing

"Dear Little Mother
of Mine"

"Wandering Husbands"

Featuring LILA LEE
and
JAMES KIRKWOOD

It's Some Comedy

JACK WHITE COMEDY
"UNCLE SAM"

With Lee Moran and Co.

2 Shows—7:30 and 9:20

It couldn't last. The little compensation and personal pleasure that Fred sustained while entertaining the good people of Juneau and Douglas, Alaska was not enough. He had tasted the bright lights of Los Angeles and yearned for a larger venue. Within a year of his return he would leave Alaska again, this time for good. The Lynch Brothers Diamond Drilling Company had already relocated to Seattle and that's where he would start. He was still undecided about his future and only knew that he wanted professional singing to be part of it. *The Juneau Express* bid a final adieu to the "Singing Policeman."

FRED LYNCH LEAVES FOR STATES TONIGHT

"Fred Lynch, one of Juneau's most popular tenors, who has been active in all musical affairs in this vicinity for years, accompanied by Mrs. Lynch, leaves for the states tonight on the Princess Mary. Mr. Lynch has several propositions in sight, one to work diamond drilling with his father, who has a large contract on the Skagit River in Washington, another with the Lyceum Circuit, on the concert stage, and a third proposal to appear in a Seattle theater as special singer."

Although Fred Lynch would never live in Alaska again; the North Country never left his heart. He took a cue from his little brother Kendall and wrote a poem about his connection to the North.

I'm From the North by Fred Lynch

Let us gather around for a ballad or two
Let us sing to our loves whether fickle or true
Let us sing to the friends we meet on the trail way;
Let us sing to a dear Mother of Gray.
I'm from the North where the wild wind is blowing.
From the North where the pine tree is growing.
From the North with the soul of a Viking.
From a land that is more to my liking.
The land that is fair and the land that is mine,
The North, where the air is like glorious wine.
You can sing of the West, and the South, and so-forth.
I'll sing to the North land, for I'm from the North.

Fred would work for his father and his uncles on several projects in Washington, but the job he made a career out of would be at Seattle's KOMO Studios, as an Irish tenor and studio director. Fred's final performances in Alaska took place at the A.B. Hall in Juneau and at Ketchikan's historic Coliseum Theater where he shared the stage with singer-songwriter Laszlo Schwartz. *The Juneau Express* reviewed the show.

"Fred Lynch, the second number of the program, received a regular ovation when he appeared on the stage and this popular tenor was given meritorious recognition following his rendition of *"Phantoms"* and *"Moon Radio"* both lyrics and music by Mr. Schwartz. Mr. Lynch appeared perfectly at ease in the two selections and made his usual hit as was attested by the audience."

As soon as Fred arrived in Seattle his uncles sent him to Port Angeles to be in charge of core drilling operations for the proposed Glines Canyon Dam on Washington's beautiful Elwha River. A lower dam, named for the river, had been built a decade before, primarily to support industry in Port Angeles. Glines Canyon Dam was built further up the river in 1926-27 by Northwest Power and Light Company to generate power for a big Crown Zellerback mill. The dam had an elegant design, but like the Elwha Dam downstream it proved to be an ecological nightmare, especially for salmon runs on the Elwha. Both dams have since been removed and the Elwha is slowly returning to its natural state.

Fred would put in a hard day's work as a diamond driller at Glines Canyon followed by an equally demanding, yet more pleasurable, evening as an entertainer down in Port Angeles. He joined a local theatre troupe and starred in a presentation of the musical-comedy *"Pickles."*

Construction of the Glines Canyon Dam when Fred Lynch led the drilling crew for the Lynch Brothers. Photo courtesy of Nippon Paper Industries Corp.

Newspaper accounts of the play praised Lynch for his performances. Under the headline **"Pickles is Tuneful and Full of Fun,"** the *Port Angeles Evening News* reported that "The singing of Fred Lynch, of Glines Canyon, as Arthur Crefoni, one of the leading parts, was perhaps the outstanding hit of the show. Lynch, with a beautiful tenor voice, sang several numbers, the first solo number being *"Why Do I Always Remember"* being especially good."

Another article about the play, held at the Olympian Theater in Port Angeles, reported that "The leading part in the show is taken by Fred Lynch of Glines Canyon, known as the John McCormack of Alaska. Lynch, who is a lyric tenor, will give the people a great musical treat." Any vocalist in the 1920s, and particularly an Irishman like Fred, would have been honored to be compared with John Frances McCormack (1884-1945), a world famous Irish tenor.

Like his father Dan, the humorous Fred Lynch knew how to strike a pose at an otherwise serious drilling project.

Following the rave reviews of *"Pickles,"* Fred and his fellow singers from Port Angeles were invited to sing live on CFTC Radio in Victoria, British Columbia. *The Evening News* reported that "A fine feature of the broadcast was Fred Lynch, robust tenor soloist, who sang *"Roses of Picardy,"* *"Lay My Head Beneath a Rose,"* *"Why Do I Always Remember"* and a fourth number besides singing a solo part in *"Mystical Pool."*

When the Glines Canyon project was finished, Fred and Mollie settled in Seattle where Fred auditioned for the new KOMO radio station. It is not a stretch to say that KOMO was built on the illegal sale of liquor.

The good-natured Roy Olmstead was the king of Seattle's bootlegging empire during the early years of Prohibition. In 1924 he formed the American Radio Telephone Company with a radio engineer named Alfred Hubbard. Together they operated station KCTL. Olmstead was one of the good guys in the bootlegging business. He didn't resort to murder or blackmail to make his fortune. Consequently he was a safe "bad guy" for federal authorities to target. His arrest in 1925 and subsequent conviction in 1926 proved to be the biggest liquor violations trial during all of Prohibition.

KCTL became KOMO under new owner Bill Fisher in 1926, who was worried that the KCTL letters were too closely linked to bootlegging. He claimed that KOMO had no meaning; he just enjoyed the sound of the name. The new studios were located at the 303 Westlake Square Building and the first broadcast hit the airwaves on December 31, 1926. One of the first stars Fisher signed with KOMO was the popular Irish tenor Fred Lynch.

According to radio historian John Schneider, "The new KOMO's inaugural broadcast was an all-day radio extravaganza involving over 250 people, including music performed by the station's new full-time staff orchestra. KOMO was soon broadcasting an unheard-of 14 hours a day to Seattle audiences. All of KOMO's programs were live from the start, and the station was reported to be the largest employer of musicians in the state."

A year later KOMO expanded its operations into the Cobb Building on 4th and University St. in downtown Seattle. "The station quickly became the most popular in Seattle," wrote Schneider, "With a staff of 65 producing fourteen hours of live programs a day."

And no live performer was more popular than Fred Lynch.

The KOMO Orchestra, 1928. Fred Lynch is third from right, back row, next to microphone.

In 1927 Bill Fisher formed the Totem Corporation, which included business leaders from around the Seattle area who would sponsor, promote and profit from KOMO Radio. The musicians, who backed up singers like Fred Lynch, became the Totem Concert Orchestra. By February 1927, the National Broadcasting Company (NBC) out of New York, signed KOMO as an affiliate and soon the golden voice of Fred Lynch was heard on NBC stations up and down the west coast.

The first big KOMO concert heard live on the west coast NBC radio stations, known as The Pacific Coast Network, was held on June 1, 1927. It was so popular that a second show, originating from the KOMO studios in Seattle, was broadcast on October 1, 1927. *The Seattle Times* mentioned four of the featured vocalists, including Fred Lynch. One month later Fred was the star of a KOMO tribute to Spanish music. He joined Italian tenor Aurelio Sciaqua and the Totem Spanish Orchestra for a lively evening of song that included some of Fred's favorites, like "La Golondrina" and "La Paloma."

On February 13, 1928, Seattle fans got the opportunity to see the singers they could only hear on the radio when KOMO stars Fred Lynch and Rhena Marshall performed with the popular Wayne Anderson Orchestra at the University of Washington's Athletic Pavilion. *The Seattle Times* expected a big crowd because, as it reported on Feb. 12th, "...when a group of KOMO artists went to Victoria (Canada) to present a concert, it was necessary to give two concerts in one evening to satisfy the thousands of Victorians who clamored to see and hear the KOMO artists."

KOMO manager Bill Fisher saw more than just a singer in Lynch, who continued his association with the Lynch Brothers Diamond Drilling Company as a drill supervisor throughout his radio career. By 1928 Fisher promoted Fred to KOMO Studio Director. It's difficult to imagine how Fred was able to do live performances, go on tour, supervise drilling operations and run the KOMO studios at the same time, but that seems to be the case.

Of the many acts and performers coordinated by Fred as KOMO studio director, none was more colorful or unique than Victor Aloysius Meyers.

Meyers got his start in music as a drummer for a ten-piece band in Seaside, Oregon. By the time he moved to Seattle he was a popular bandleader known for his outrageous behavior. He would promote his band during the Roaring 20s by driving a beer wagon around Seattle blasting the anti-prohibition song *"Happy Days Are Here Again."* And Fred Lynch was happy to have Meyers perform at KOMO even if the shows were few and far between.

Vic Meyers and his Columbia Recording Orchestra became popular across the country and KOMO was too small a venue for the bandleader. It might be said that everything was too small for Meyers and his thirst for the limelight. A self-proclaimed champion of the downtrodden, he threw his hat in the ring as a tongue-in-cheek candidate for mayor of Seattle. He added all sorts of colorful stunts to his campaign, such as leading a goat around town while dressed like Mahatma Gandhi with a top hat. It was not surprising that he lost the race, although he did finish sixth out of ten candidates.

Meyers enjoyed the added spotlight that politics gave to his musical career. In 1932 he considered running for governor of Washington, but he didn't want to pay the $60 filing fee so opted instead to file for lieutenant governor at a cost of $12. "I don't know how to spell it," joked Meyers, "but I'll take it." He also promised not to lie about his opponents if they promised not to tell the truth about him.

Much to the chagrin of his own party, Meyers was elected lieutenant governor of Washington in the FDR Democratic landslide of 1932. He led his orchestra in a performance at his own inaugural ball. Meyers was so popular with the people that he later served as Washington's secretary of state. More conventional candidates were outraged. "To the Victor goes the spoils," retorted Meyers, "And I'm Victor."

Victor Aloysius Meyers (1897-1991)
Courtesy Washington State Digital Archives, Susan Parish Collection
(Image No. AR25501080-ph002136)

Continuing with his musical career throughout his political career, Meyers would disappear for weeks at a time; to perform, go on fishing trips or travel overseas, without even notifying his staff in Olympia. The Seattle newspapers regularly noted that the search was on for Vic Meyers. In short, despite his sterling liberal convictions, fondness for the common man, and great sense of humor, the bandleader that Fred Lynch briefly directed at KOMO became one of the greatest political hoaxes in American history. Vic Meyers, the "Clown Prince of Politics" died in 1991 at the age of 93.

In May, 1928, the *Seattle Post-Intelligencer* column *"Stars of the Mike"* featured Fred Lynch.

"A policeman who can bank on the power of a good tenor over the more deadly "billy," on a tough beat in a tough town, he is just too good to be a copper. That's why Fred Lynch is on the KOMO staff."

"Fred was a policeman and had such a beat- the waterfront-at Juneau, Alaska. He's Irish, and congenial, and the voice - it won every time. But then came the chance at KOMO fourteen months ago. The same combination has made him a permanent fixture there, much to the joy of thousands of fans. And incidentally, fan mail from Juneau is heaviest if all."

The article goes on to give a little bio of Fred, including his roots in Michigan's Upper Peninsula and his Los Angeles performance for the great Rosa Ponselle.

Fred Lynch was a prime time performer for KOMO. Fans often waited until the evening hours between 7 PM and 11 PM to hear their favorite Irish tenor. For most it was well worth the wait. For one listener, in the spring of 1927, it was a life saver. On July 9th a letter arrived from Tacoma to *Station KOMO, Seattle, Washington.* It read:

Dear KOMO:

I read in the Seattle Post-Intelligencer this morning of how your station saved the life of a young boy who was very sick and was not expected to live, but some announcements made during the kiddies program for his special benefit gave him renewed interest in life and saved his life. Had it not been for reading this in the paper, I would never permit myself to tell you the story that I am now going to tell. I feel, however, that it is only in justice to those who have saved my life to tell my story, hoping that you will understand why I do not care to sign my name.

It is not necessary to tell you of the misunderstandings, the shattered dreams, the false friends and the loss of those nearest and dearest that brought me one spring evening a few months ago to the shores of American Lake, ready to take the step that would deliver me from an existence devoid of any happiness or hope.

As I stood on the dock I heard a song coming from a radio in a confectionary store nearby. Momentarily this song drew my interest and I hesitated. It was Fred Lynch singing "My Buddy." Somehow, I don't know how to explain it, it seemed that the black world behind me and the rippling waters in front of me that were beckoning me, vanished and it seemed that a voice of a friend was calling me back from what I had planned to do. For some time I sat there on the end of the dock listening, not only to the songs of Fred Lynch, but by Donald Gray and others on your staff. Out of the air had come the voices of friends and with a renewed hope, I turned back to tackle my own little life problems, and since that time new hopes and new ambitions have come my way.

Some of my former dreams, which seemed utterly crushed, now seem ready to be fulfilled. It may be that this life will still give me the happiness that I have always sought. Always, however, I will remember the voices that came out of the air, calling me back from the waters of American Lake when all hope seemed dead. You know now why I cannot sign my name.

From an ardent KOMO listener.

Fred Lynch was a devout Catholic and he also saved and cherished letters from nuns and priests who were fans. One big fan was the Rev. Father G. Taylor Griffith, the Episcopalian chaplain of Good Samaritan Hospital in Portland, who listened to Fred regularly on both KOMO and Portland's KGW Radio. On Sept. 25, 1929, Father Griffith wrote the following fan letter, in stylistic but hard to read cursive, to Fred Lynch.

"My dear Mr. Lynch:

I cannot refrain from telling you how thoroughly we all enjoyed your glorious voice and artistic singing last night. I'd rather hear you than Caruso. I've heard all the tenors in Europe & America.
Do you know I'd like to have a picture of you to add to my collection of my favorite artists – Lynch an Irish name! I'm ½ Welsh and ½ Irish and enjoy McCormack and Fred Lynch. The Irish are a brilliant people. I hear the Blessing of God from them.

God Bless You,

Father Griffith
P.S. Send a picture- and autograph it too please!"

Fred was kind enough to send Father Griffith the autographed portrait and even promised to pay him a visit during his next trip to Portland, since he visited Portland regularly to see his uncle, Albert Kendall. Father Griffith was ecstatic and wrote back to explain in great detail how to contact him since the switchboards at the hospital were unreliable. He promised to take Fred to lunch at the Portland Hotel. He thanked Fred profusely; called him generous and kind and lamented over the fact that KGW radio did not feature him enough.

Since Fred saved the letters it is very likely that Father Griffith had that lunch date with the singer he rated above the great Caruso!
The Totem Broadcasters 1927-28 Yearbook, a glossy 80-page tribute to KOMO, featured a full-page promotional portrait of Fred (see page 191). Another picture, seen on the next page, shows three KOMO stars; Fred, violinist Zita Dillon and baritone Bob Nichols, preparing to lead a group of children on a train ride.

Fred, who had no children of his own, loved kids and was always quick to volunteer his services to bring happiness to young people.

FRED LYNCH—ZITA DILLON—BOB NICHOLS

Every Wednesday afternoon the Davidson Bread Train pulls out from the K O M O depot with its merry load of children to visit by radio interesting places in the Pacific Northwest. Here is the train crew getting ready for its trip. Left to right: Engineer, Fred Lynch; Nursemaid, Zita Dillon; Conductor, Bob Nichols.

Fred & Mollie Lynch Collection.

In the summer of 1928 Fred Lynch did a tour of Canada performing in at least six provinces. It is likely that he also visited some of the Lynch Brothers' on-going projects in Canada. As he had done in Alaska, Fred shared the stage with vaudeville acts and the showing of popular silent films. He sang during the presentation of the Colleen Moore farce, *"Oh Kay!"* at several theatres in Canada, including the Colonial Theatre in Port Arthur, Ontario. The Port Arthur newspaper gushed about the comedy,

FRED LYNCH

Fred Lynch, tenor soloist on the Totem staff, is the pride of all Alaska listeners, who remember him as Juneau's famous golden-voiced tenor.

Thirty-three

Fred is at the far left. Fred & Mollie Lynch Collection.

starring the popular American actor Alan Hale Sr. (1892-1950), father of Alan Hale Jr. (1921-1990), who would gain fame as the Skipper on the television series *Gilligan's Island*.

The Port Arthur paper, after praising the film, wrote that second only to the film, and first among the live performers during the two-night engagement, was "Fred Lynch, the Singing Policeman." The paper reported that Fred "has a pleasing voice that appeals to everyone. His popularity as a radio star is surpassed on the stage, due to his engaging personality."

At the Capital Theatre in Calgary, Alberta, Fred performed for audiences during showings of *"The Cardboard Lover;"* Clara Bow's *"The Fleet's In;"* and one of the first talking films, *"The Air Circus."* He repeated his performances in Winnipeg and Brandon, Manitoba. The *Manitoba Free Press* of October 8, 1928 wrote that, "Fred Lynch, radio star of KOMO, draws a fine ovation, his numbers being exceptionally well-rendered." The Brandon newspaper reported on October, 23, 1928 that, "Fred Lynch, the singing policeman, added to the program last night with several selections that were of real merit. He has an excellent voice and presents some popular and classic numbers in an impressive style."

In Trail, B.C., where his brother-in-law Billy Biner had recently become brewmaster for the Kootenay Brewery, Fred performed at the Rialto and Daylight Theatres as the added attraction to movies like *"Glorious Betsy,"* and *"The Waterhole,"* based on a popular Zane Gray book.

Phone 551 | # RIALTO | Continuous 6 to 11

The House of Better Entertainment

ADDED ATTRACTION
ON the Stage
FRED LYNCH, tenor soloist of Radio Station K. O. M. O.

Today and Tomorrow
DOLORES COSTELLO And CONRAD NAGEL
— In —

"Glorious Betsy"

Glamorous romance of two lovers who defied

the world! Heart history of Jerome Bonaparte, brother of Napoleon, and Mistress Betsy Patterson of Baltimore..

Dashing Drama of Danger, Daring and Devotion

ALSO—COMEDY, SCENIC, FABLES, TOPICS

MATINEE SATURDAY, 2:30

$45.00 overcoat, ladies' or gents' will be given away next Monday. Save the coupons you get at box office.

When Fred returned to Seattle in December, 1928, it was announced in the *Post-Intelligencer* under the heading **LYNCH COMES BACK TO KOMO**, with an accompanying photograph and caption that read **"Fred Lynch Returns."**

"Fred Lynch is coming back tomorrow. That's KOMO's answer to 9,999 queries from fans who wondered where he disappeared to so suddenly some months ago. Lynch has been touring through Canada on the same theatrical circuit which has captured so many local stars of the "mike" the past few years. He started at Vancouver, B.C., swung East through all the principal towns as far as Toronto, then back again."

"Lynch is known to thousands of Pacific Northwest listeners as "The Golden-Voiced Tenor." His first appearance following his return will be on the 9 to 11 o'clock broadcast. He will sing "When Irish Eyes Are Smiling," "All the World is Waiting for the Sunrise," "Were to Call You," and "Estrelilita.""

During Fred's tour of Canada, *Sunset,* the western lifestyle magazine first published in 1898, and still going strong in the 21st century, featured a story about some of the western radio stars, including Fred Lynch. The top story, seen on the cover below, was titled:

"In Person!" Pictures and Pertinent Paragraphs About the Leading Radio Stars of the Far Western Stations.

People are queer. They do such weird, contradictory things. I know a football player who tats and crochets when he thinks nobody can see him; and a little 94-pound woman who just *loves* to drive trucks and tractors; and a bank president who adores cooking so much that he does it professionally three evenings a week in a little joint he owns under cover; and a butcher who has a passion for rare perfumes.

And there is Fred Lynch. By profession and preference, Fred, besides being Irish, is a hard-rock driller whose bit has gouged into gneiss and granite from Panama to Alaska. It happened that the last nice drilling job petered out when he was in Alaska, so he turned from hard rock to harder, tougher characters, handling them gently but firmly on the waterfront of Juneau, capital of our northern territory, where Fred represented the city police department. He was half of it.

When drilling jobs were not to be held and the majesty of the law required no upholding, Fred Lynch used his tenor for making a living. It was a good tenor, so good that Rosa Ponselle urged him to study the art of tone production profes-

sionally, but Fred, being Irish, preferred to roam, to drill, to wander and drift— until the Juneau admirers of the melodious manhandler almost compelled him to give the KOMO audiences a sample of his vocal wares.

They liked that sample so well that Fred Lynch came to anchor in Puget Sound, a permanent fixture on the station staff. And Mrs. Fred, an Alaskan native daughter, heaved a sigh of relief. Tune in on KOMO some night and listen to the cheerful tenor; you'll like the voice and the personality that comes to your antenna.

From the Fred & Mollie Lynch Collection.

Fred's human fans were not the only ones pleased about his return to Seattle, as the following picture, sent across the country by the *International Newsreel*, and saved by Fred's wife, Mollie, charmingly reveals.

HIS MASTER'S VOICE!—Tige is shown singing an accompaniment to a song that his master, Fred Lynch, of Station KOMO, in Seattle, is singing over the radio on the other side of town. Even a big steak couldn't lure Tige from the loudspeaker when his master is singing. —International Newsreel photo.

Fred really hit his stride in late December, 1928, when *Broadcast Weekly*, the radio magazine published in San Francisco, featured the Irish tenor on its cover and in its lead story.

Fred Lynch of KOMO

By Monroe R. Upton

HERE'S a radio tenor who not only dislikes being pedestaled by worshipful maidens but admits it. "Feminine hero worshipers" he does not like, although he receives a normal amount of stimulation from the approval of radio listeners of any sex. Other of his dislikes are also interesting. Conversation immediately preceding a microphone appearance. Temperamental orchestra leaders. And jazz! On the other hand, he is fond of action, color, art displays, outdoor scenery and symphony concerts, attending the last named as often as possible. Outside of the realm of music, however, his tastes can scarcely be said to verge on the "high-brow." Richard Dix and Thomas Meigham command his respect and interest on the silver sheet while Rex Beach, Cooper and Winston Churchill have written the books he likes best.

Fred Lynch, contrary to the usual rule, is a popular tenor who is active, athletic, robust and fond of the outdoors. In addition, he has a jovial, Irish nature. When he tells his story in song his affection for people, coupled with his sympathy for streams, forests, mountains and all of the great out of doors lend a masculine quality to his voice which perhaps accounts for much of his unusual success.

This Irish tenor did a deal of living himself before he became ambitious for a career which, to be successful, must put life into the hearts of others. His grandfather had been a blacksmith and his father a diamond driller. Fred followed in his father's footsteps. He worked as a diamond driller in Alaskan mines. He was a policeman in Juneau, Alaska. They presented the genial Irishman with the toughest beat in town and he not only held it down but he held it down with credit and glory. Mining and policing weren't the only chances he took in Alaska: he got married when he was there, to an Alaskan born white girl. He was twenty-five at the time. They say that when Fred sings he thinks of Alaska and his extreme popularity in the Northland indicates that Alaska thinks considerably well of him, in return.

He was born and raised in Michigan and

Southern Wisconsin, coming to the northwest when a young man. That music was destined to become his life's work was presaged by his reaction to Il Trovatore at the age of ten in Milwaukee. It made an impression upon him that still lingers in his consciousness. He wasn't the type that grew up with music, however. It wasn't until he was fully matured that he felt the need for some sort of artistic expression and then he thanked his lucky stars for the fact that in school he had been required to learn to sing. Some praise from a chance meeting with Rosa Ponselle helped to focus his ambitions. At twenty-one he made his first appearance in public, and was successful enough to try again. There followed a number of years in musical comedy and stage presentations, principally on the Pacific Coast and over the Canadian Paramount circuit. Previous to his stage work he had graduated from Columbia University in Portland, Oregon.

About two and one-half years ago Fred invaded the land of the broadcasting studio and has since sung over stations KOMO, KFI, KHJ, KHQ, CNRV, CNRW and CNRR. He was nervous and shaky at first, in spite of his long stage appearance, and he was reminded of his first footlights experience, which left him nervous and sick. His ambitions are to please the largest number of listeners and to this end he puts in three hours of hard work practicing every day. He enjoys it, however, so perhaps we shouldn't call it hard work. His teachers have been Charles Sporks of Portland, F. X. Arens of Los Angeles and Clifford Kantner of Seattle. He likes the radio better than the stage and so, God and the public willing, he is on the air for keeps.

Approval of the public for a radio entertainer cannot be as spontaneous, nor as obvious as for the stage artist, but it's there just the same. Sometimes a radio singer's voice accomplishes some rather unusual things. A letter came to KOMO's popular tenor telling the story of a young man's disappointment in life and despair of the future, which had led him to the shores of a lake with the determination

(Continued on Page 20)

8

Fred & Mollie Lynch Collection.

FRED LYNCH OF KOMO
(Continued from Page 8)

---

to end it all. Apparently the letter was from an ex-service man, possibly from the veterans' hospital at Fort Lewis, for the lake mentioned was American Lake, located at the edge of Fort Lewis, an army base in Washington. The letter said, in part: "As I reached the edge of the lake and prepared to thrust myself in, a song caught my ear. It came from a radio set in a nearby confectionery store. It was not just Mr. Lynch's voice that caused me to hesitate(but the beautiful words and melody of "My Buddy" which he was singing, coming out of that clear cold night, and it seemed that a friendly hand reached out to encourage me to carry on. With a new determination I turned my back on the lake and resolved to make the tangled mixup of my life resolve itself. That was weeks ago, and now things have happened that have made me glad that your voice caused me to hesitate when on the verge of eternity. I do not care to even sign my name to this letter, but I credit my life to your ability to sing."

Of course, life saving can hardly be said to be the usual thing for radio tenors, but his popular and semi-classical ballads do add much to the joy and savor of living of thousands of KOMO listeners almost daily. When he is not singing or practicing he likes best of all to go duck hunting or salmon trolling. His other hobbies are handball, mountain climbing and swimming. He is still interested in mining. There is no indication yet that she's "deep enough" around KOMO for Fred Lynch. He joined the staff in January, 1927, and his popularity has increased steadily ever since.

Fred also made the *Citizens Radio Call Book Magazine*, a popular hobbyist magazine with worldwide readership from Chicago, Illinois. Although the magazine focused on radio technology it occasionally featured a "poster page" of radio stars. Fred appeared in one along with ten other stars from around the country.

Fred & Mollie Lynch Collection.

Fred continued with his daily live radio performances through the first half of 1929. By late spring he had accepted a job offer from the Lynch Brothers to lead a drilling operation at an exploratory gold mine in southern Oregon. The job kept him off the airwaves for several months, but as usual the Seattle papers heralded his return. On August 11, 1929, the *Seattle Post-Intelligencer* ran the headline, **LYNCH COMES BACK TO KOMO**. But 12 days later he was in San Francisco, auditioning for NBC and his last chance at national stardom. No records exist as to what happened at the audition, but it is safe to say that Fred had reached his professional peak. He returned to Seattle where he continued to perform for KOMO and go on tours.

On the exact day that Fred auditioned for NBC in San Francisco, KOMO received a charming letter, written to Fred Lynch by a 70 year-old widow named Ella Campbell Holt (1859-1949). Mrs. Holt, in exquisite cursive, wrote:

"Mr. Fred Lynch,
Dear Sir:

Yesterday I had pen and paper in my hands, ready to send you a request to sing La Golondrina. As I passed the radio, I tuned in and just in time to hear you sing it. To me it is one of the sweetest things ever sang, and though I have heard Mexicans and Spaniards sing it, no one of them ever, to me, quite equaled your rendition."

"I love your voice just a little more than any other which comes over the air. You are the only tenor I have ever heard (and I have heard scores) that has the Chauncey Olcott lilt." (Olcott, 1858-1932, was a world famous Irish tenor from New York).

"For years I timed my visits to Chicago so that I could be there while he was playing and singing there. I heard him sing "The Wild Irish Rose" there and he was called back until the manager came out and said the audience must allow the play to proceed. This of course is not of much interest except to show you what a compliment I am paying you."

Mrs. Holt went on to complain about the musicians who accompanied the KOMO singers and often drowned them out. It was her opinion that the accompanists tried to monopolize the whole broadcast.

"I would like to furnish chloroform, ether, morphine or what not, if it would dampen their zeal."

But Mrs. Holt, with a heavy dose of humor, asked Fred not to share those feelings with the musicians.

"Please don't let any of them learn my name, for I am a woman seventy years old and if they used the muscular ability on me, which they display on their accompaniments, I fear I would not survive. Again, telling you what a source of pleasure your singing is to a lonely "old lady."

I am Sincerely,
Ella C. Holt"

Mrs. Holt added a postscript. *"No publicity to this please."*

Fred honored her wish. The letter was neatly tucked away in Fred and Mollie's scrapbook for the rest of his life. It is reprinted here for the first time since it was written, 85 years ago and 65 years since the death of Mrs. Holt.

The 1930 census shows Fred and Mollie living with Dan and Mate Lynch, at their home near Green Lake. Dan is listed as a diamond driller, but Fred is listed as a radio artist. He would remain so for a few more years, but the entertainment world was rapidly changing and Fred was a star of a time gone by. By the 1940 census he was listed as a diamond driller.

In 1931 Fred left on a Northwest Concert Tour. A highlight would be a series of performances in Victoria that featured the Russian cellist Nicholas "Kolia" Levienne, who was married to the ballerina Lila Zali. The program also featured soprano Ve Ona Socolofsky and pianist Frank Leon in a mostly classical presentation. The foursome performed at the Royal Victoria Theatre, sponsored by The Victoria Musical Art Society. In attendance at the December 5th show was the premier of British Columbia, Simon Fraser Tolmie; Lt. Governor Fordham Johnson and Victoria's mayor, Herbert Anscomb. *The Daily Colonist,*

Victoria's newspaper, had high praise for Levienne in its December 6th edition, but also found some worthiness in Lynch.

"Fred Lynch, the tenor, has a voice which is resonant and flexible, and his articulation was good....The little Irish song, "Open the Door Softly," had a thoroughly delightful national character and spontaneity which, in the matter of singing alone, merited it first place in his groups on the programme."

During the rest of the tour Fred continued to sing his more popular and contemporary songs, those his radio fans could sing along with. But the days of the theatrical circuit and vaudeville acts had been replaced by the talkies. Fred's singing career was ready for another, and more parochial, direction.

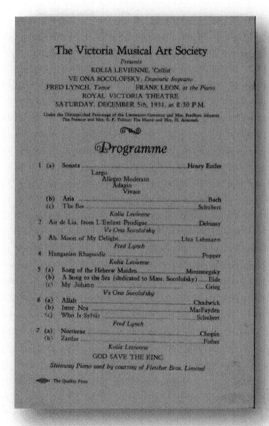

On January 18, 1932, John McCormack gave a recital at the Fox Theatre in Seattle. McCormack (1884-1945) was considered by many to be the greatest Irish tenor in the world. Fred and Mollie were in attendance at McCormack's rare Seattle appearance. Fred took a few notes in his program; things he might try to incorporate in his own rendition of particular Irish ballads. But he may also have been faced with his own shortcomings on that night.

POPULAR
IRISH
TENOR

KOMO
Staff
Artist

FRED
LYNCH

...In Concert

Northwest Concert Tour

1931 - 1932
October to January

William Moyes (1894-1975) was a native of Lawrence, Massachusetts and a graduate of Yale. While teaching journalism at the University of Washington in the 1920s Moyes became a radio junkie and certainly knew of the popular KOMO tenor Fred Lynch.

In 1931 Bill Moyes moved to Portland and took a job with the *Oregonian* as the radio critic. His column was called "Behind the Mike," and it was so popular that it ran for 62 years; although Moyes himself left the newspaper in 1952 to work for the rival *Oregon Journal* and later *The Portland Reporter*. 1952 was the same year that Portland got its first television station (KPTV) and the *Oregonian* might have thought that columns catering strictly to radio listeners were PASSÉ. Moyes had become nationally famous for his column, which combined news with gossip and often biting opinion. *TIME Magazine* wrote a piece on Moyes in its Nov. 4, 1946 issue. It reported that Moyes, "went radio-crazy during college days at Yale, (and) has never gotten over it."

Moyes was also featured in *Newsweek,* which called him "radio's most vitriolic professional critic," and he was regularly quoted in *Variety*. Following his death in 1975 the Oregonian admitted that Moyes "perceptive and caustic comments on prominent radio personalities gained him national recognition."

But he spared those caustic comments when it came to Fred Lynch.

In his May 11, 1932 "Behind The Mike" column Moyes wrote that one of his "spies", Laure McCormick, spotted KOMO radio star Fred Lynch in town and thought that he might be planning to join a Portland radio station. Moyes went on to "guess" that "Fred has tied up with KOIN." The column featured Fred's latest studio portrait with the caption, "**FRED LYNCH...?**" Moyes called the portrait "A beautiful photo."

Fred was back in Portland two weeks later to perform for the Society of Oregon Composers at a fundraiser for the YWCA. It was simply a prelude to his new job. Moyes was correct. On June 11, 1932 Fred became a regular feature on KOIN Radio in

Portland. KOIN, founded in 1926, was purchased by *The Oregon Journal* newspaper in 1931, and broadcast its radio shows live from Portland's elegant Heathman Hotel.

In addition to his solo shows Fred joined the KOIN-Journal Quartet in Portland and performed on Columbia Northwest Stations three times a week. But he did not forget his obligations to the Roman Catholic Church. On January 1, 1933 *The Oregonian* reported that Fred Lynch would be performing a religious recital at Portland's Immaculate Conception Cathedral – the same cathedral where his little sister Harriet had been baptized 41 years earlier.

Jimmy Riddell (left), first tenor of the KOIN-The Journal quartet and vocal director at the station, was telling a "big one" when this shot was taken. Other quartet members (from left) with broad smile— Fred Lynch, second tenor; Gail Young, baritone, highly amused, and Gene Baker, basso, somewhat skeptical. This group presents the "Serenaders" program through KOIN-The Journal and the North-west Columbia system stations three times a week.

Fred & Mollie Lynch Collection.

His days with KOIN would be short-lived. By then a middle-aged man, and with the Lynch Brothers landing the biggest drilling jobs in the Pacific Northwest, it was time for Fred to face the music. He could make a better living in the diamond-drilling business. In his spare time Fred contributed his musical energies to the Catholic Church he loved so much, and was in constant demand for weddings, funerals, high masses and other religious functions.

Fred Lynch strolls down the street during the 1950s.
The popular KOMO live radio star of the 20s and 30s was by then just
another pedestrian in busy Seattle.

Fred returned to Seattle and when he wasn't supervising jobs for the Lynch Brothers, he worked for Seattle's Bonney-Watson

Funeral Home. He sang at funerals but also drove a hearse! A practical joker with a knack for dark humor, Fred had a habit of surprising family and friends, including his aging parents, by driving a hearse to their homes unannounced.

Fred performed regularly at the imposing St. Joseph Church in Seattle and was a favorite of the Carmelite Monastery. According to his niece Fritzi, "The nuns loved his singing and he was a good friend of the Mother Superior who he teased constantly with his sly humor. When she was ailing her doctor prescribed daily beer for her and Uncle Fred got Dad (Billy Biner) to provide cases delivered to her."

Fred Lynch was a devout Catholic and a leader of Seattle's Knights of Columbus, a Roman Catholic philanthropic and fraternal organization, and a member of the Maryknoll's Catholic Foreign Mission Society of America. He had a particular fascination with "The Miraculous Infant Jesus of Prague": a 16th century wooden icon revered by the Carmelite nuns. One of the many powers attributed to the Miraculous Infant was helping women during pregnancy. Perhaps the Mother Superior sought divine intervention for the childless Fred and Mollie Lynch. Fred carried holy cards and prayers to the Miraculous Infant in a leather billfold until his death at the age of 92, but there would be no infants in his life, save the many nieces and nephews who adored their great-uncle, a man who would have been a magical, if not miraculous, father.

Fred's billfold was full of prayers and holy cards, not just for the Miraculous Infant of Prague, but for the many friends he helped "send on to heaven" with his mournful funeral songs. And yet, despite his devout faith, Fred Lynch was never overtly pious or reverent.

Fritzi Bernazani recalled an event that was typical Fred Lynch. Charlene Fulton (granddaughter of Fred's sister Harriet) married Charles Collora in a 1970s Oregon outdoor counter-culture wedding, presided over by a popular priest, Father Jack Morris, founder of the Jesuit Volunteer Corps, who, like Fred, was a devotee of Alaska. When the "hip" Father Morris asked those in attendance to offer each other a handshake or kiss of peace, Fred, by then an octogenarian, turned to those around him and said, with a twinkle in his eyes, "Peace on you."

This was similar to the times he took the Fulton kids to the Portland Zoo or Tad Chicken n' Dumplins. Before the kids piled into his big car he would bellow, "Go now, or forever hold your pee."

Fred called his wife Mollie "the Finn" and he was an endless reservoir of Scandinavian jokes. Mollie's dad was from Finland, while her mother was from Sweden.

Although Fred and Mollie continued to live with Fred's parents during the 1940s and early 1950s, (unless in Wisconsin caring for Aunt Eva), they had plenty of reason to travel back and forth between Seattle and Portland. Fred's good-natured uncle, Albert Kendall, was still running his gladioli farm in Troutdale. Mollie had moved her mother, Mary Wiitanen from Douglas, Alaska to Portland, where she was hospitalized with a mental illness until her death in 1961.

Fred's brother Kendall Lynch and his sister Harriet Biner, both moved to Portland in the early 1950s. Kendall was the proprietor of the Barrel Inn Tavern while Harriet's husband Billy Biner, owned the popular Leipzig Tavern in Portland's historic Sellwood district. After World War II, Harriet's daughter, Betty Biner Fulton, produced a Portland "Baby Boomer" family of ten children. These became the children that Fred never had. The gentle giant would serenade the Fulton kids with Irish ballads and a rousing rendition of *"Seattle,"* the Hugo Montenegro song made famous by Perry Como. As the Fulton siblings fondly remember, Uncle Fred would nearly break the windows with his powerful voice, and then nearly break them again after he fell asleep on an easy chair and started to snore.

The early 1950s were emotional times for Fred Lynch. His father, Dan Lynch, passed away on November 27, 1951, which was, ironically, his mother's 81st birthday. Mate Lynch didn't care much for the birthday surprise. She died 45 days later. But when word reached Seattle that Mate's sister, the childless Eva Kendall Childs, was also dying, Fred and Mollie rushed back to Wisconsin to care for her.

Eva Childs, who raised Fred during his teenage years, died on May 9, 1953, in Janesville, Wisconsin and she did not forget her "honorary son" in her will. Fred and Mollie inherited most of Eva's estate, making it possible for them to live a comfortable life for the next thirty years.

During his days in Janesville Fred became close friends with Monsignor Ewald J. Beck (1895-1971) of St. Mary's Catholic Church. Beck was just five years younger than Fred and the two had much in common, not the least being a high regard for Eva Childs. Fred helped celebrate Beck's elevation to Monsignor the year after Aunt Eva died and carried a card commemorating the event in his "holy" billfold for the rest of his life.

Fred spent much of his retirement keeping in touch with every side of his extended Lynch-Kendall clan. He seems to be the only one who did. He regularly visited cousins from both the Lynch and Harris lines, on his father's side, and from the Kendall and Chipman lines on his mother's side. It is accurate to say that when Fred Lynch died the Lynch-Kendall family that he loved so much ceased to exist as an extended family unit. Cousins who knew little or nothing of each other went their separate ways when the glue that held their parents together was gone.

In his later years Fred remained an avid outdoorsman and spent many a leisurely day fishing alone, or with his Uncle Bert and nephew Bob Biner. After his brother-in-law Billy Biner died, Fred and Mollie moved to Fullerton, California to be near his sister Harriet. But when Harriet began to spend more time with her daughter Betty's growing family in Portland, they returned to Seattle.

Big Fred Lynch in Buena Vista, Colorado on Labor Day, 1936.

Fred strikes a pose at Mesa Verde National Park.

On February 19, 1967, Fred and Mollie Lynch celebrated their 50th wedding anniversary at the home of their niece, Betty Biner Fulton, in Portland. They stayed in Portland to help celebrate Betty's 49th birthday, with her ten children, the following day.

Fred displays his catch after a fishing trip in the Pacific Northwest.

On November 8, 1969, 78 year-old Fred Lynch gave one of his final concerts, performing for the Alaska Yukon Pioneers Annual Banquet at Seattle's Arctic Club. He would continue to sing well into his eighties, mostly at church events, and more informally for his adoring nieces and nephews in Portland, who had no idea that their great uncle was once the most popular singer in Seattle.

Fred & Mollie's golden wedding anniversary, Feb 19, 1967.

In the late 1970s Fred Lynch slipped into the abyss of dementia. He slowly withered away in a Seattle nursing home, oblivious to the visits of friends and relatives, and his faithful wife Mollie, or to weekly letters from his niece Mary Bernazani. Ironically, it was the lonely Mollie who died first, on April 5, 1981. She was 82 years old. Fred hung on for another 14 months. He died on June 20, 1982; two months shy of his 92nd birthday. His passing went unnoticed by the Seattle papers that once lavished praise upon "The Singing Policeman of KOMO."

Although Fred Lynch had no children of his own, and most of his friends, family and fans had preceded him in death, more than 100 people attended his funeral. His godchild, the author of this book, was honored to deliver the eulogy, knowing Fred as a loving uncle, but unaware of how important he had been to so many people during the heyday of live radio.

At the age of 83, Fred Lynch gives one of his final performances in Seattle. At his left is Seattle's mayor, Wes Uhlman

Top: Fred Lynch, the gentle giant, in a familiar pose. Below: Mollie with nephews Dan and Joe Fulton in Portland.

Nine: The Boom

While the Lynch Brothers continued several operations in Alaska, they also scored a series of contracts for work in British Columbia, Oregon, and the state of Washington, where they decided to relocate permanently. In 1920 they won a contract with Spider & Northern Light Groups to drill for copper deposits near Prince Rupert, British Columbia. The following year they were hired by a Belgium mining syndicate to drill for gold at the Premier Mines near Stewart, BC.

The Ashland (Oregon) *Daily Tidings* of November 9, 1921 reported on a Lynch Brothers job in southern Oregon. "The work of drilling oil well No. 1 at the Southern Oregon Development and Exploratory Co. was begun Tuesday (Nov. 8) on the Westerland Orchards lease. Rotary drills took 15 minutes per four feet."

The Evening Herald of Klamath Falls, Oregon elaborated in its Dec. 6, 1921 issue: "The Western Oil Company which is drilling a well near this city (Medford, Oregon) has made a contract with Lynch Brothers of Seattle, who are now sinking a well for the Southern Oregon Exploration Company, which stipulates that the Brothers shall finish the well started by the private rig of the Western Oil Company with a diamond drill to production or 2000 feet. The well is already at 1,100 feet and gas on top of the bailer has been noted for some time past."

The brothers were soon regarded as leading experts in diamond drilling for dam foundation and oil exploration. In "The Diamond Drill in Oil Exploration" from a 1922 issue of *American Association of Petroleum Geologists Bulletin*, author Robert Davis Longyear wrote: "The writer is indebted to the Lynch Bros., diamond drill contractors of Seattle." He then proceeded to make the case for the use of diamond drills in the field of oil exploration.

Longyear had good reason to promote the diamond drills. He was the son of Edmund Joseph Longyear, a pioneer in the use of diamond drills. Edmund was three years older than Dan Lynch and like the Lynch Brothers grew up in Michigan's Upper

Peninsula. In 1911 he formed the E.J. Longyear Co. which became a major manufacturer and contractor of diamond drills. The Lynch Brothers purchased Longyear drills in the early days of their own company. Like Longyear, the Lynches knew that diamond drills would soon out-perform the cable-tool and conventional rotary drills.

Cable-tool drilling had been around in one form or another for centuries. Originally used to drill for brine, it became the primary method for drilling oil, gas and water wells. A spring pole brought a heavy bit up and down to smash rock with repeated blows. It was called cable tool drilling because the rods and drilling tools were suspended by steel cables (and by hemp rope in earlier days). Cable-tool drills were steam powered in the late 19th and early 20th centuries.

The rotary drill was more common in mineral exploration. Its sharp rotating drill bits were first powered by steam engines and later by gas and diesel. It was more reliable but heavier than the cable-tool drills. Therefore, it was more expensive to transport. Although the diamond drills, which were a more modern version of the rotary drill, could be expensive because of the diamonds, they were generally more economical than either the cable-tool or conventional rotary drills because they were far lighter in weight and therefore less expensive to transport. Diamond drills required fewer men to operate. Nevertheless, for many years diamond drills were not acceptable for oil exploration on government land. The Lynch Brothers would help change that.

Not surprisingly, government regulations were behind the times when Dick and Pat formed the company in Alaska. The federal leasing regulations stipulated that bore holes for oil exploration had to be at least six inches in diameter. Diamond drilling in that era produced core samples of three inches in diameter or less. These samples proved to be just as reliable as the larger holes drilled by conventional outfits like cable-tool and rotary drills, but they did not meet government standards.

In 1922 the Lynch Brothers asked Dan Sutherland, the non-voting delegate to the U.S. House of Representatives for the Alaska

Territory, to personally deliver a letter to the Secretary of the Interior. "Fighting Dan" Sutherland was a miner himself. He had prospected for gold in Nome during the 1890s, but later moved to Juneau where he was co-owner of a mining company. Sutherland was eager to intervene on behalf of the Lynch Brothers.

In January 1922, during the administration of President Warren G. Harding, Sutherland handed the Lynch letter to the Interior Department, requesting a reconsideration of drill requirements on government land in Alaska. The Secretary of the Interior was the notorious Albert Fall, who would become the first cabinet member in history sentenced to prison. Fall accepted bribes from oil companies in exchange for government contracts in what became known as the Teapot Dome Scandal. Fall was out of Washington D.C. in early 1922, perhaps working on his "secret" deals with the oil tycoons. Therefore the response to the Lynch Brothers' request came from Acting Secretary Edward C. Finney. Finney himself would be implicated, vigorously interrogated, but never convicted in the Teapot Dome Scandal.

Department of Interior
Washington D.C.

Mr. Dan Sutherland
Alaska Delegate
House of Representatives
Washington, D.C.

My Dear Mr. Sutherland:

Referring to the letter from Lynch Brothers dated Jany. 9th 1922, regarding the use of diamond core drilling in Alaska on Government lands:

The regulations of governing prospect work on Government lands provide that within one year (3 yrs. In Alaska) from a certain date the permittee must drill one or more wells not less than six inches in diameter to a depth of at least 500 feet each, unless valuable deposits of oil and gas are encountered sooner.

It does not seem advisable to change the regulations reducing the diameter of the hole in prospect wells, but I appreciate that there are in many cases when diamond drill work would be perfectly satisfactory in order to test out land. It is my belief that in certain cases the Secretary of the Interior will be willing to waive the requirement as to the diameter of the hole provided of course that he is satisfied the work will be carried on in a workmanlike manner and for the purpose of actually testing out the area. Obviously each case must be handled separately and it would be my suggestion for anyone wishing to sink diamond core drill holes to meet the requirements of the permit, that they petition the Secretary of the Interior to be granted permission to do so.

Very truly yours,
E.C. Finney
Acting Secretary

While the Lynch Brothers awaited U.S. government permission on a case by case basis they continued in their own "workmanlike" manner, setting up a temporary office in Vancouver, British Columbia where the provincial government encouraged the use of the lighter diamond drill outfits for oil exploration on remote government lands.

Robert Davis Longyear, in his article for *American Association of Petroleum Geologists,* explained a 1921 Lynch Brothers' job in a remote section of northeast British Columbia.

"Last year Lynch Brothers shipped a diamond drill outfit into the Peace River District for the British Columbia Provincial Government. This outfit was capable of drilling 3-inch holes to a depth of 1200 feet and 2-inch holes to a depth of 2000 feet. No figures on the actual cost are available, but the writer is informed that the outfit weighed thirty tons. This included sectional boiler, camp, supplies for all winter, drill rods, tools, 1000 feet of 3-inch flush joint casing, and 2000 feet of 2-inch flush casing. "

"The outfit was shipped 250 miles by boat from Peace River, and then 26 miles on horse-back over tundra so soaked with water that in places only one hundred pounds could be carried by horse. Drilling was commenced in 47 days after leaving Peace River. From 700 to 1100 feet has been drilled each month, the highest footage being made in December with the thermometer standing at 45 degrees below zero. It would have been impossible to have taken a standard rig into the site without building a road over 26 miles of water-soaked tundra. The cost would have been prohibitive."

"In the fall of 1920 to a more easily accessible locality in the same district, a standard rig was moved in on sleighs, and up to August, 1921, had drilled a total of only 800 feet. The diamond drill started nine months later and at the same date had drilled over 2500 feet."

Longyear went on to explain why diamond drills were actually more economical than the standard cable tool drills or rotary drills. According to Longyear a cable tool outfit able to drill 3500 feet weighed 250 tons. A rotary outfit of the same capability weighed 350 tons. But a comparable diamond drill outfit weighed just 60 tons. The savings in transportation costs, especially to remote areas like the Peace River District, could be substantial.

Many years later, Dick Lynch was the subject of an article in *The Escanaba (Michigan) Daily Press.* The article was mostly about the Lynch Brothers' work on the Grand Coulee Dam, but it also mentioned their Upper Peninsula roots and the work they had done two decades earlier on the Peace River.

As *The Daily Press* explained it, "The heavy, cumbersome drilling machinery, food supplies and other materials had to be hauled into the wilderness by horse pack and sleds and during the long, severe winter months the crew worked at times in temperatures that dropped to the almost unbearable degrees of 60 to 70 below. Mrs. Lynch (Sabina), who has often accompanied her husband on these trips, has, on occasions, been the only white woman ever to set foot in these wild regions."

Arthur L. McCready, writing for the *Oil Trade Journal* in August 1922, reported on another Lynch Brothers' job in the same area.

"In northern British Columbia, west of Hudson's Hope, the Consolidated Oil & Development Syndicate of Minneapolis and Duluth has made further examination of the Moberly Lake district and has contracted Lynch Bros. of Vancouver, BC for two core-drill tests. The rate is reported to be $10 a foot, but the difficulties of bringing in material are tremendous. Lynch Bros have an outfit now in the field used last season for a series of tests for the British Columbia Provincial Government near Hudson's Hope; if this is available the Consolidated #1 will start drilling late in June or in early July, but otherwise drilling will not likely commence till the end of August."

In 1922, while continuing with exploratory oil drilling in northern BC, the company was simultaneously core drilling for the Lake Cushman Dam near Tacoma. They had outbid Grant & Smith Co. by $5000 to win the Cushman contract.

In 1925, Pat Lynch travelled to Panama to supervise a crew while Bill lined up new contracts and Dick, Dan and Fred supervised them. There is evidence to suggest that Pat brought his nephew Fred Lynch with him to drill in Panama. In fact, Pat Lynch had almost certainly worked in Panama before. Sullivan Brothers did some of the drilling for the construction of the Panama Canal at the time that both Pat and his big brother Dan worked for them.

The Lynch Brothers were seemingly everywhere during the 1920s and 30s and their willingness to bid low earned the company an extraordinary number of contracts. They did their small part in alleviating the unemployment lines during the Great Depression. Many men worked for the Lynch Brothers during both the Roaring Twenties and the Depression. Some, like Earle "Dusty" Rhoades, stayed with the company for more than twenty years. Rhoades career with the Lynch Brothers spanned the entire Skagit River Project in the early 1920s to the end of the Grand Coulee contract in the 1940s.

But taking on so many different jobs was not without its legal challenges. The decision to explore for mineral deposits could be risky and many poor decisions were made by investors. The ill-fated Southern Oregon Exploration Company sued the Lynch

Brothers in 1925 for alleged "failure to fulfill an oil drilling contract." The details of the "failure" are not clear, but the court ruled in favor of the Lynch Brothers.

That same year the Lynch Brothers won a contract for core drilling at what would become Dam #1 of the Bull Run Reservoir, which continues to provide drinking water for the city of Portland, Oregon. The dam, completed in 1929, would impound 8.8 billion gallons of water.

The Lynch Brothers were so busy during the Roaring Twenties that they occasionally sounded desperate for more drillers. An ad in the March 31, 1926 Seattle-Times sought, "Three or four diamond-drill runners at once." It asked applicants to report to the Lynch Brothers office at 503 Pioneer Building. The office later moved to 34th and Stone Way near Seattle's Gasworks Park.

From 1926 through 1927, the Lynch Brothers were employed by the Brook and Federal Light & Traction Co. to do the core drilling for the Cowlitz River Canyon Dam near Chehalis, Washington. And in 1929 they drilled for the Northwestern Electric Company's proposed Boulder Dam site on the Lewis River near Ariel, Washington. *The Seattle Times* reported on their progress in the November 24, 1929 issue.

"Lynch Brothers, who are doing the drilling on the site, have six outfits, three working on each side of the river, making tests of foundation conditions." It was a big project. The company eventually drilled 26,000 feet of core at $5 per foot.

In 1928 and 1929, the Lynch Brothers drilled for Cushman Dam #2 on the Skokomish River in Mason County, Washington. And in 1930 they drilled for the Merwin Dam site in Cowlitz County, Washington. Raymond Lynch and Dusty Rhoades supervised that operation.

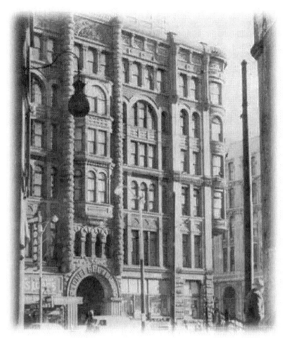

*The Lynch Brothers Diamond Drilling Company was headquartered in Seattle's
historic Pioneer Building during the busy 1920s.
The company later purchased a building near Gasworks Park.
Photo courtesy for National Parks Service.*

Another Lynch job in the late 1920s was at a copper deposit near Baker City, Oregon. The company also did drilling for the spectacular Owyhee Dam, an irrigation dam on the Owyhee River in southeastern Oregon. Dan sent his youngest son Kendall, by now a veteran of the First World War, to supervise the Baker City job. From there Kendall Lynch moved on to The Dalles, Oregon to join a Lynch drill crew at the site of the Bonneville Dam which had been initiated two years earlier. The Lynch Brothers were not the only drill crew at Bonneville, which was built by Six Companies under the direction of the Army Corps of Engineers. The Lynch crew drilled at what was called the Ruckles Slide area of the Bonneville project. Simultaneously, Kendall's brother Fred, by then a radio star in Seattle, supervised drilling at a gold mine in Klamath County, Oregon.

Around 1930 the brothers produced a four page promotional flyer on the company. It featured two pages of photographs showing drilling operations on the famous Skagit River Project. The appropriate heading: **"Lynch Bros.' Drills Go Everywhere."** On the backside were close-up photographs of the company-designed diamond drill, which they manufactured and sold. It weighed 2000 pounds and had a "Pump capacity of 25 gallons per minute at 150 pounds pressure."

Drill In Detail ...

ABOVE is shown a side view of the machine, including gas motor.

A separate transmission on the pump gives variable speeds. Pump capacity is 25 gallons per minute at 150 pounds pressure.

Both pump and drilling equipment are driven by a silent link belt.

BELOW A head-on view, showing the drum which moves the machine under its own power, and pulls tools from the holes. At the right side is shown the feed arrangement, which permits drilling holes at any angle.

Shipping Weight Approximately 2000 Pounds

"Now, Your Drilling Problems Are Solved!"

Also included in the brochure was a letter, under the masthead *Lynch Brothers Diamond Drilling Contractors, Pioneer Building, Seattle, Washington.* It was probably written by Bill Lynch, the president of the company.

W. S. LYNCH   P. J. LYNCH   R. T. LYNCH

LYNCH BROTHERS
DIAMOND DRILL CONTRACTORS
PIONEER BUILDING   SEATTLE, WASHINGTON

You will be interested in this greatly advanced diamond drill machine, which has proven highly successful for hydro-electric projects in the West, and in prospecting for minerals in this and foreign countries.

After several years of diamond drill work for hydro-electric projects, we have designed, built and are now manufacturing a complete unit specially adapted for this work. The power, pumping and churn drilling for going through overburden to depth up to 150 feet, with drilling capacity for 1500 feet, is all combined into one unit, which can be easily moved from hole to hole under its own power, regardless of the contour of the country. It is highly practical for prospecting for minerals in inaccessible places, as it can be taken down and transported by pack horses to inaccessible places.

You can appreciate at once the considerable saving in time and expense, and the unusual accuracy obtained from such a machine.

So successful has it been that we have done all recent power site work for the cities of Seattle, Tacoma, Aberdeen, Portland, Eugene, the Northwestern Electric Company of Portland, the California-Oregon Power Company of Southern Oregon, Stone & Webster, and others. We have been called in on difficult government jobs.

We also make a specialty of water testing in rock, by special packer and meter test for pressure and quantity.

We have developed crews that are highly efficient in this specialized class of work — in building suitable rafts, bridges, scows and drilling where others fear the work is impossible. We are prepared to include full service of this type in contract prices, or to quote prices on machines alone, if you wish to do your own work.

Inquiries will be cheerfully answered, and advice given freely.

Very truly yours,

LYNCH BROTHERS

By

{ *P. S.*
Illustrations on
Inside Page }

In January 1932, the Lynch Brothers won a contract from Bureau of Mines for 8,000 feet of core drilling in the Matanuska coal fields of Alaska. The $84,000 contract was one of their largest to date. The coal field was located some twenty miles from the nearest railroad line between Seward and Anchorage. The *Seattle Times* reported that the Lynch Brothers' "equipment will be transported by pack horses."

The Lynch Brothers bid for their next contract was smaller than the Matanuska job at just $68, 415.   But it beat out larger bids from several other companies including Sullivan Machinery. It seemed routine at first glance: exploratory drilling for a dam on the Columbia River in northeast Washington.   Dick Lynch figured it would take about five months. But the job, for the Columbia Basin Commission, turned out to be much more than anyone anticipated. Once the initial contract was fulfilled additional work poured in. Instead of five months, the job would last eight years and become the biggest operation the Lynch Brothers would ever land, on what would be the largest concrete structure ever built: The Grand Coulee Dam.

Ten: The Grand Coulee

The Grand Coulee Dam at completion in 1942.
Courtesy of the Library of Congress.

Pushed by business leaders from towns like Ephrata and Wenatchee, Washington and promoted by politicians from the Pacific Northwest for dozens of years, the idea of building a monster dam on the wild Columbia River finally reached fruition under President Franklin D. Roosevelt. With the goal of irrigating hundreds of thousands of acres of arid farmland in eastern Washington's "Inland Empire," while supplying unlimited electrical energy to the Pacific Northwest, the mammoth Grand Coulee Dam became the biggest construction project of Roosevelt's New Deal and one of the biggest construction projects in world history. Thousands would eventually be employed, and first among them all were the rough and tumble diamond drillers of the Lynch Brothers.

According to Paul C. Pitzer, author of *Grand Coulee, Harnessing a Dream*, the Lynch Brothers received the very first contract to commence work on the dam. They were hired by Jim O'Sullivan on August 1, 1933. O'Sullivan was a major promoter of the dam and secretary of the Columbia Basin Commission. Like the Lynch Brothers, O'Sullivan was an Irishman from Michigan.

Kendall Lynch, son of Dan, had recently married beautiful Irish lass Grace Sullivan. Two of Grace's brothers also worked for the Lynch Brothers, and one brother was also named Jim Sullivan. Jim O'Sullivan might have appreciated that. In the 1930s the second and third generation Irish Americans still looked out for one another.

Workers for both the Lynch Brothers and Rumsey & Company, which dug the test pits in which the Lynch Brothers commenced drilling operations, had to be approved by the Columbia Basin Commission, and according to L. Vaughn Downs, in his book *The Mightiest of Them All: Memories of the Grand Coulee Dam*, these workers were initially paid by the state treasurer for Washington. This was a good-faith effort by the state government, which correctly anticipated that the federal government would eventually approve the bulk of the funding to build the dam. In fact, many future drilling operations that the Lynch Brothers completed at the dam site were paid for by the Bureau of Reclamation or by big contractors hired by the federal government.

The vast majority of the workers at Grand Coulee were white men; but minorities and even some women were hired. One of the few women who worked at the dam site, according to Downs, was the secretary/clerk for the Lynch Brothers Diamond Drilling Company. This was Mary Jane Rhoades, who is listed by Downs as one of the women who worked at Grand Coulee. Mary Jane was the wife of Lynch Brothers' trusted foreman, Earle Dusty Rhoades.

The Spokane Chronicle and its competitors, The Spokesman-Review, and The Spokane Press, regularly reported on the construction of the Grand Coulee Dam, including numerous references to the Lynch Brothers. The September 15, 1933, issue of the Chronicle reported from Coulee under the headline:

CORE DRILLERS AT DAM

"Lynch Brothers of Seattle, core-drilling contractors of the Grand Coulee dam, moved their outfit to the site yesterday. They brought most of their crew with them, as they only employ expert diamond drill operators. Headquarters will be at the dam site."

The Spokane Press, also reported on September 15th, that "Lynch Brothers, recently awarded the contract for core drilling...moved in large shipments of machinery and other equipment today at the Grand Coulee dam site...the contracts call for work to be started before September 20th."

And so it was. Under the headline **Move First Dirt for Coulee Dam,** dated September 18, 1933, the Chronicle reported that:

"The first dirt actually moved on the Grand Coulee Dam project was today as Lynch Brothers, Seattle diamond drilling contractors, began preparations for the core drilling job which will determine the character of the bedrock underlying the site of the dam."

"The "Lynch boys," as they are known wherever diamond drilling is done, from Cuba to Finland and from Brazil to Alaska, are never slow about starting a job once they land it. When a Chronicle reporter visited the dam site Friday, the first of the fleet of trucks carrying drill equipment for the job arrived from Seattle. Two hours later the first truck had been unloaded and was on its way back home, and two more had arrived with additional machinery, all of which was unloaded with minimum delay."

"Red flags spotted about the river banks and back up the steep abutting banks marked the locations of the fifty-odd holes. Some of them will go straight down, some will angle out at the banks to intersect under the river, and some will go down in midstream from drill rigs mounted on barges. Six crews will be working at one time, fifty men altogether. Fifty thousand dollars' worth of black diamonds will be used in the bits, each bit carrying 16 stones of 1 ½ carats each, at the price of $150 per carat. Six weeks will see the drilling completed, it is estimated."

That was wishful thinking. The company would be drilling at Grand Coulee for the next decade. Nevertheless, *The Spokane Review* reported the frenetic pace of the Lynch Brothers' work under a series of headlines on Sept. 18, 1933:

MACHINERY WHIRS AT GRAND COULEE – Site of Giant Dam Comes to Life in Month - WORLD HAS PART- Diamonds from Africa and Brazil Cutting Granite Base.

"Grand Coulee dam site has changed within the last month from a sleepy spot where the Grant County ferry crosses the Columbia, to an area where machines whir day and night. From the top of the Columbia River gorge as one starts the descent to the dam site, a little town of tents and unpainted buildings is seen."

"The west side is dotted with drill rig structures. Lynch Brothers, core drillers, have 30 on the job and four rigs operating. Three more are on the ground ready to be placed in operation; and additional men will be put to work to operate them."

Possible employment opportunities were a big focus for most newspapers as America was in the Great Depression and jobs were hard to come by. The reporter, who went by the name R.A.S., went on to explain that he had visited the site with U.S. Senator Clarence Cleveland Dill, who was married at the time to the famous suffragist Rosalie "General" Jones. Joining Dill was Frank Banks, the federal engineer in charge of the Grand Coulee construction and for whom a massive reservoir would be named.

According to the report, "This was the senator's first visit to the dam site since drilling operations began. The party's first stop was to the shack where the diamond drill bits are set. E.D. Rhodes (sic), foreman, explained how it is done." *(This is the same Earle*

"Dusty" Rhoades who proved his mettle on the hazardous Skagit River Project a decade before. Rhoades would supervise Lynch Brothers operation at Grand Coulee continuously into the 1940s.)

"(Rhoades) displayed a handful of yellow diamonds from the Kimberley fields of South Africa and also black diamonds from Brazil. The diamonds, which are tougher and less subject to fracture than the white diamonds that ornament women's fingers, are the cutters that bite through solid granite. These diamonds, about three-sixteenth inch in diameter, are set in holes drilled in a steel bit which looks something like an ordinary piece of heavy pipe."

"The party went to a river bank where a drill was in operation. An engine was chugging away, turning, at 400 revolutions a minute, a heavy pipe of tough steel. A few feet of this pipe projected from the ground. The drill bit was cutting through solid granite at the rate of an inch per minute 142 feet away at a 45-degree angle. The bit was then 65 feet below ground and out under the river."

"The machine was operated by three men, one of whom had charge of the rig. Beside the drill rig was a box of cores, labeled to show what hole they came from and at what depth. An unbroken core of fine-grained white granite five feet long had been brought up a little while before the party arrived."

The following day the Spokane Chronicle included a picture of Dick Lynch supervising the unloading of a diamond drill unit.

Two days later *The Spokesman-Review*, reporting from Almira, Washington, a few miles east of the dam site, announced that the Lynch Brothers had already reached bedrock. "Preliminary work on the Grand Coulee dam is well under way. Lynch Brothers, contractors, report that bedrock has been reached and diamond drills are in operation."

The Spokesman-Review of September 24, 1933 elaborated under the headline **SOLID GRANITE BASE FOR DAM – Grand Coulee Test Drill Bores through 25 Feet of Material.**

"Solid granite foundations are being found at Grand Coulee dam site by Lynch Brothers, core drilling contractors. Six core drills were in operation yesterday. J.E. McGovern, member of the Columbia Basin Commission, visited the dam site Friday and saw cores from one of the drills. This drill has brought up 24 feet and seven inches of cores from one hole, and all are pure granite."

Spokane Chronicle, Sept. 19, 1933. Wallis and Marilyn Kimble Northwest History Database. WSU Libraries.

Two days later *The Spokane Chronicle* reported that "Dick Lynch of Lynch Bros. of Seattle, successful bidder for core drilling at the Grand Coulee dam site, reports that six core drills are now in operation and that solid granite foundations are being found."

The journalist R.A.S. sent in a much more detailed report for *The Spokesman-Review* on October 1, 1933. The bold headline read: **DIAMOND DRILLS CHARM VISITORS AT GRAND COULEE DAM PROJECT.**

A series of sub-headings followed: **Bring Up Cores of Rock to Test Solidity of Foundations at Dam Site – EAT THROUGH GRANITE – Compass Needle, Set in Gelatin, Tells Direction of Bore Deep Underground.**

The story that followed by R.A.S. is an excellent layman's explanation of the diamond drilling process. But who was R.A.S.? No one seems to know. The current archivist for *The Spokesman-Review*, could not find the answer. It seems that he only wrote two articles for the paper; both about the diamond drilling at Grand Coulee. Could R.A.S. have been a pseudonym for a member of the Lynch Brothers crew? Was it Raymond (Lynch) and Sellers: the two young men who would eventually become the owners of the company? One thing is for sure, the company could not have asked for better public relations than they got from the Spokane newspapers, particularly *The Spokesman-Review*.

Here is the extensive description of diamond drilling at Grand Coulee by the mysterious R.A.S.

"Visitors to the Grand Coulee dam site on the Columbia display curiosity about the core drilling machines that are burrowing into the prospective dam foundations. They want to know how they work and what they are for."

"Core drilling operations were explained to the writer by Frank T. Banks, federal engineer in charge of dam construction, and by drill operators. The purpose of the drilling is to test the dam foundations, and most people know that, but few know that the drills really bring up a solid core of rock. They work on rock much the same as you might take the core out of an apple with a cylindrical corer."

"These cores are one and a half inches thick. Drilling operations usually break these cores into short lengths, but occasionally an unbroken five-foot core is brought up. Five feet is the maximum length of core that can be taken in one piece by the rigs operating at the dam site."

"The popular conception of a drill is a pointed bit of some kind that grinds metal or rock to powder as it bores through. Rock core drills are quite the surprise to the uninitiated. The drill bits have a flat working face. Into this face are set diamonds which are about three-sixteenths inch in diameter. The diamonds are set around the outside diameter of the hollow, pipe-like bit, and around the inside diameter. They project slightly from the bottom of the bit face, and slightly from the outside circumference of the bit, and slightly from the inside circumference."

"They are set by drilling holes in the steel of the bit, and placing the diamonds in these holes and fixing them in position by punching in some soft metal, such as copper. The diamonds are of various kinds and are used to meet different conditions. Black diamonds from Brazil and yellow diamonds from South Africa are being used at the dam site by Lynch Brothers, core drilling contractors."

"These diamonds are much harder and tougher than granite, and when ground against rock, pulverize it. The diamonds must be reset after drilling about eight feet. The drill bit has an inch and a half hole in the center, and the heavy steel pipe on which the drill bit is screwed also has an inch and a half hole. The bit is revolved at speeds varying 100 to 400 revolutions a minute, depending on the rock being drilled."

"As it revolves, it eats away a circle of rock, converting it to dust, which is conveyed to the surface by a stream of water pumped down to the drill bit through the hollow drill rod. The drill leaves a core of rock, which tells faithfully what the foundation conditions are. The drill rods consist of 10-ft lengths of heavy pipes, which are screwed together to make a rod of any length. The drills at the dam site will go down 200 feet or more."

"Around the drill rod is a casing, through which the dust laden water flows to the surface. A heavier casing, six-inches in diameter, goes down to bedrock and is drilled into the rock deep enough to exclude water from the drill hole, except the water that is pumped down to the drill. This big casing is drilled into the rock by revolving it, the same as the small drill rod is sunk."

"The motion is given to the drill rod through a chuck operated by an automobile engine. In some cases electric motors or compressed air motors are used, but at the dam site gas engines are used exclusively. The engine and drill machinery are mounted on heavy timbers with sled-like runners. The heavy drill rods are drawn out of the hole by use of the engine power. The drills can be set at an angle. Those at the dam site run perpendicularly or at 45-degrees."

"When the drills go deep they sometimes wander off their proper course. The angle at which they are operating can be determined by several kinds of tests. One of these tests is known as the fluoric acid test. A glass tube partly filled with fluoric acid is placed in a drill rod and lowered into the hole. Fluoric acid eats glass slowly. It will leave a record of its level in the tube. From this it can be determined if the drill is running true."

"Another test is to place a compass needle in gelatin and place it in the rod. The needle will swing north in the soft gelatin, and when the gelatin solidifies, a reference point will be left from which the direction the drill is running can be determined. Drill rig operators from long experience know how their drills are running by observation of the action of the drill rig. Vibrations of the rod inform them of conditions below surface. Measurement of pressure on bearings at the drill chuck lets them know whether the drill is being fed against the rock at the right speed."

"Drill cores are laid in open boxes and are so labeled that an experienced person can know what hole they came from and at what depth."

The Wenatchee Daily World filed this report from the dam site three days later:

GRAND COULEE, Oct. 4. – "Let's start off with something good. Monday was pay day in Lynch brother camp. To the boys who "reef and tug" at the steel casings being driven into the ground to protect "cave-ins" for the diamond core drilling, it was a true "ghost walk" and, at least some 38 or 40 of Washington's former unemployed were made happy again.   Lynch Brothers are building a huge log raft on the Grant county side of the river at the proposed bridge site. The raft will support diamond drill equipment for the first test drilling in the river bed."

The Spokesman-Review's chief competitor, *The Spokane Chronicle,* did not seem to have a comparable expert on their Grand Coulee beat in 1933. On Oct. 10th *The Chronicle* mixed up the work of the Lynch Brothers with Rumsey & Co., giving credit to Lynch Bros. for the test pits (done by Rumsey & Co.), and credit for core drilling to Rumsey, when it was actually done by the Lynch Brothers. Nevertheless, the drilling stats were impressive.

"After going down through surface material for 30 to 40 feet, the drills ran into solid granite, 35 feet deep on a straight drill and 50 feet in length on a 45-degree angle drill. The deepest hole drilled so far is 382 feet. This is being drilled out under the river bed at a 45-degree angle and will probably go 800 to 900 feet in length."

Ten days later the *Chronicle* reported that the company was drilling in the middle of the Columbia River.

"In the middle of the river, workmen for the Lynch Brothers have floated a huge raft, about 50 by 50 feet, with a derrick at one end, from which they will swing a core driller to sink test holes down below the river's bed." The core samples brought up by the Lynch Brothers were examined and admired by engineers, including Frank Banks.

Sample of Granite Underlying Dam Site

Fred. K. Jones.   Frank A. Banks.

This photo was taken Wednesday at Grand Coulee dam site, when a group of Spokane business men visited it under the auspices of the Chamber of Commerce. Mr. Jones, president of the chamber, and Mr. Banks, federal engineer in charge of Grand Coulee dam construction, are holding a five-foot piece of granite ore brought up by one of the diamond drills testing the dam foundations.

This piece came from several hundred feet beneath the surface. It is pure, fine grained and unusually hard granite.

Mr. Banks has stated that the dam site foundation material is the best he has seen anywhere.

As drilling and excavation began in earnest many independent entrepreneurs moved in to provide goods and services for the workers. As was the custom of the times, many of these small businesses did not have licenses or contracts to set up shop. The Columbia Basin Commission sent in an intrusive bureaucrat named Joe B. Mehan to evict them. But Mehan ran into trouble when he encountered Al Meyers, proprietor of the Dam Site Cafe which served many of the Lynch Brothers workers. Meyers refused to shut down and chased Mehan off with a wrench, claiming that Jim O'Sullivan himself had approved the café.

Contacted at his office in Yakima, O'Sullivan intervened and the Dam Site Café remained. The November 24, 1933, issue of *The Spokane Review* reported that, "Yesterday saw the removal of the last of the early landmarks at the dam site, with the exception of Meyers café, first on the ground. All others, unless under contract for specified services to Lynch Brothers or Rumsey & Co., had vacated."

Meanwhile the dangerous work went on. "Lynch Brothers are drilling on a raft in the river, near the west bank, for the bridge pier there, five drill rigs being operated elsewhere." *(Spokane Chronicle,* Nov. 20, 1933). On December 14th *The Chronicle* featured a picture of three Lynch Brothers' workers preparing diamond bits for a drill operation. The men are not identified, but the man in the background could be Dick Lynch.

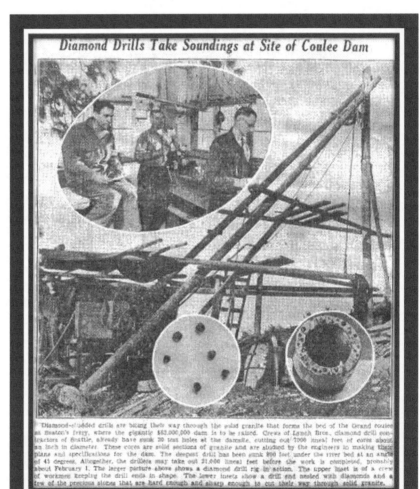

Diamond Drills Take Soundings at Site of Coulee Dam

Two days later *The Spokane Chronicle* featured a photograph of a Lynch Brothers drilling raft.

Diamond Drill Tests Coulee Bedrock

On this float in the Columbia river at the Coulee dam site Lynch Brothers, contractors of Seattle, are operating one of their six diamond drills, which are testing the ground and bedrock for the great dam. This drill is close to the left bank of the river, just below the ferry. They are employing 35 men, working five-hour shifts and four shifts a day.

The Spokane Chronicle, December 16, 1933, From the Wallis and Marilyn Kimble Northwest History Database, WSU Libraries.

Here Is the Headquarters for the Diamond Drillers at the Grand Coulee

"Camp Lynch:" The Lynch Brothers Camp at Grand Coulee. (Spokane Chronicle, December 2, 1933. From the Wallis and Marilyn Kimble Northwest History Database, WSU Libraries.

Workers for the Lynch Brothers, and most of the brothers themselves, liked to share a drink or two when a hard day's work was done. And on "Holy Days of Obligation" these sturdy Irish Catholics might have felt even more obligated to drink.

On page 90 of *Grand Coulee*, Pitzer writes that, "On Christmas Eve 1933, drillers working for the Lynch Brothers got drunk and damaged the camp, completely wrecking one small building. Such incidents occasionally livened things, but otherwise the work proceeded uneventfully."

One man who was not drunk that night was Dick Lynch, co-founder of the company. He was back in Seattle recovering from a long illness. *The Spokane Chronicle* announced Dick's return to Grand Coulee in the January 4, 1934 edition.

DRILL AT COULEE DAM TILL APRIL

COULEE CITY, Jan. 4.—(Special.) —Dick Lynch, of the firm of Lynch Bros., diamond drillers has returned here from his home at Seattle, where he has been since Thanksgiving. He expected to return to the works at the damsite sooner, but a protracted siege of influenza detained him.

Mr. Lynch stated that the diamond drilling contract would not be completed until about April 15. The date previously set for its completion was January 10. Because of high water, he said, no drilling has been done in the river.

More Drilling Necessary.

Acceptance of plans by the reclamation department for the ultimate construction of the high dam make a great deal more drilling necessary, both in the river and for abutments.

Mr. Lynch, who, since starting drilling operations at the damsite, has made his headquarters at the Thompson hotel here, is very enthusiastic over the progress of work at the damsite. He lamented the absence, however, of a good heavy duty road to transport the heavy machinery and material to the damsite.

Spokane Chronicle, January 4, 1934. From the Wallis and Marilyn Kimble Northwest History Database, WSU Libraries.

When Dick Lynch states in the above article that the contract had been set for completion on January 10th, but would need to be extended into April, he is talking about the initial drilling contract that the company signed with the Columbia Basin Commission. There would be many more contracts. In fact, the Lynch Brothers Diamond Drilling Company drilled at the Grand Coulee for nearly ten years.

During the first contract the Lynch Brothers had fifty men working on the Grand Coulee drill sites. Keeping the health and safety of their men a priority, the company signed a contract with Western Hospital Association to provide health care for the workers. A doctor remained in the area and a first aid center was set up until a permanent hospital was constructed in the New Deal town of Mason City where the Lynch Brothers would eventually build a company headquarters and most of the later work crews would live.

The work picked up steam in February, 1934, with the *Chronicle* reporting that "Granite 'as solid as the Rock of Gibraltar' will serve as anchorage for the huge dam in the Columbia River at Grand Coulee."

"Diamond drill borings have been pushed 700 feet through solid granite in six test holes," wrote *The Chronicle*, "proving beyond doubt that the foundation is nearly perfect, from an engineer's point of view."

Although the article reports that a total of 43 test holes and 13, 485 feet had already been drilled, the magnitude of the dam would require much more. The enterprising Lynch Brothers, never a company to lose a bid, would improvise depending on the nature of the job. Besides the standard diamond drill, which they were now producing, the brought in churn drills and the giant calyx drills. In late February, to take core samples in the middle of the river for the axis of the dam, the Lynch Brothers utilized a big churn drill. It could bore larger holes in the thick overburden of the river bed in order to reach bedrock where they could commence the deeper diamond drilling.

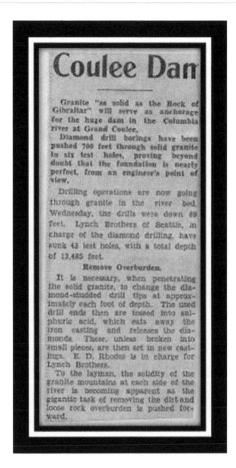

Coulee Dam

Granite "as solid as the Rock of Gibraltar" will serve as anchorage for the huge dam in the Columbia river at Grand Coulee.

Diamond drill borings have been pushed 700 feet through solid granite in six test holes, proving beyond doubt that the foundation is nearly perfect, from an engineer's point of view.

Drilling operations are now going through granite in the river bed. Wednesday, the drills were down 80 feet. Lynch Brothers of Seattle, in charge of the diamond drilling, have sunk 43 test holes, with a total depth of 13,485 feet.

Remove Overburden.

It is necessary, when penetrating the solid granite, to change the diamond-studded drill tips at approximately each foot of depth. The used drill ends then are tossed into sulphuric acid, which eats away the iron casting and releases the diamonds. These, unless broken into small pieces, are then set in new castings. E. D. Rhodes is in charge for Lynch Brothers.

To the layman, the solidity of the granite mountains at each side of the river is becoming apparent as the gigantic task of removing the dirt and loose rock overburden is pushed forward.

Spokane Chronicle, Feb. 2, 1934. From the Wallis and Marilyn Kimble Northwest History Database, WSU Libraries.

On March 27, 1934, a massive mud and rock slide disrupted efforts by the David Ryan Company and Crick & Kuney Company to construct a highway and rail line for the purpose of transporting heavy equipment to the dam construction site. The Lynch Brothers, who were still engaged in the initial core drilling contract for the dam site, were hired, according to reports by *The Spokesman-Review,* to determine the elevation of bedrock beneath the slide.

In late June, *The Spokane Chronicle* gave a detailed summary of the first year of dam construction, which included the following:

"Lynch Brothers of Seattle, core drilling contractors, have sunk 90 holes to a total depth of 19,948 feet. Nearly 10,000 feet of the drilling was in surface material, from which no cores were removed. After reaching solid rock, contractors removed 8,975 feet of core. By "reading" the core, engineers determine the exact nature of the underlying rock. Much of the drilling was in solid granite. The deepest hole went to a depth of 800 feet."

The Seattle Times similarly reported the core drilling results on June 24, 1934 under the headline: **8000 FEET OF GRANITE CORE AT COULEE SITE**

"More than 8000 feet of solid granite core, crated in scores of crate boxes here, tells the story of the foundation on which work will soon start for the construction of the giant Grand Coulee Dam. Core-drilling operations by Lynch Brothers of Seattle, who started work some time ago, are practically ended, and the results are most satisfactory to Frank Banks, Reclamation Bureau engineer, in charge of the work. The core is generally one and three-quarters inch in diameter."

After sharing the same details as *The Spokane Chronicle* regarding depth and number of holes plus total feet of core samples, *The Times* continued by quoting Jim O'Sullivan on the quality of the core samples.

"Many outstanding engineers have examined the core, including the Board of Army Engineers, and all pronounced the core of outstanding quality," said James O'Sullivan, secretary of the Columbia Basin Commission. 'It's really a most interesting and educational sight to see thousands and thousands of feet core, much of it taken from hundreds of feet below the surface."

Most of the big test pits from which the Lynch Brothers set up their drilling outfits were dug by another Seattle business, J.W. Rumsey & Company. Rumsey & Co. was the second business to land a Grand Coulee contract after the Lynch Brothers. Most of their test pits were finished by the end of 1934.

The Columbia Basin Commission, which was headed by Jim O'Sullivan, represented the interests of the State of Washington and worked in conjunction with the Bureau of Reclamation, under the auspices of the Interior Department, to raise funds and allocate contracts for the Grand Coulee Dam. As the first anniversary of construction approached, and with it a planned visit to the site by President Franklin Delano Roosevelt, O'Sullivan proposed to give another $10,000 for additional core drilling and, since the Lynch Brothers were already under contract and had their drilling outfits already on site, he decided that they should get the additional work. Initially, Frank Banks, the chief engineer for the Bureau of Reclamation agreed with O'Sullivan that the Lynch Brothers should do the drilling for the dam's first powerhouse, as well as the proposed highway and railway locations.

But Banks also wanted the Lynch Brothers to do an additional 37 test holes on top of their original contract. Since the $10,000 available from the CBC would not cover it all, Banks had the Lynch Brothers continue with the test holes for the dam itself. By the end of the first year of work the Lynch Brothers had completed over $70,000 worth of core drilling for the Columbia Basin Commission. That is roughly $1.3 million in today's dollars.

On August 15, 1934, the Lynch Brothers signed a contract with the Silas H. Mason Group, a third of the newly incorporated MWAK Company, which through combining assets and ingenuity won the overall bid from the Bureau of Reclamation to build the Grand Coulee Dam. The MWAK companies were the Mason Group of New York; Walsh Construction Company of Davenport, Iowa; and Atkinson-Kier Company of San Francisco.

The three groups had successfully outbid a group called Six Companies, which was nearing completion of the Boulder (later renamed Hoover) Dam in Arizona. Six Companies was headed by the formidable shipbuilder Henry John Kaiser. His company had not only built Hoover Dam, but Bonneville too; and he was not the type to give up easily. Kaiser saw his opportunity through the promotion of a "high dam," the controversial opinion, shared by many, that the Grand Coulee Dam should be much larger than originally planned.

MWAK's winning bid for the original lower dam was just under $30 million. The final cost of the extended high dam would be ten times that amount, or in today's dollars, about three and a half billion dollars.

When the decision was made in 1935 to go with the high dam, MWAK joined forces with Kaiser and his Six Companies to form the Consolidated Builders Incorporated (CBI) which produced the bid necessary to finish the Grand Coulee Dam. But in the summer of 1934 the eventual size of the dam was still a much debated topic. Either way, the Lynch Brothers were certain of work.

That August the *Spokane Press* announced that the Mason Group wanted the Lynch Brothers to do the core drilling for the two cofferdams that would narrow the mighty Columbia while the two ends of the dam were being built; and they wanted to start immediately. The Lynch Brothers got to work on the cofferdam sites two days later.

The Spokesman Review revealed the following day that in addition to the new contract with the Mason group, the "Lynch Brothers are still dong some work for the commission, at $2.95 to $3.50 a linear foot of core. The company will ask the commission at its next meeting to increase the price on extra work, because of added difficulty. Drilling is now being done high above and far away from the river bank, necessitating pumping of water a long distance."

On August 30th *The Spokane Chronicle* reported that the Lynch Brothers, "With the aid of the historic Sam Seaton cable ferry," had set up mid-river drilling operations the previous day to continue their work for the Mason Group. Dusty Rhoades directed the hazardous operation.

The following evening, while the crew worked into the night, a beam from a tripod that provided cable-support for a drill, fell and struck Frank G. Morehead. Morehead was an experienced diamond driller. The 59 year-old had a 36 year-old son who also worked for the Lynch Brothers. Banged up and suffering with a few cracked ribs, Morehead was lucky to be alive. He left the job, but his son Albert kept working for the Lynch Brothers at Grand Coulee into the 1940s.

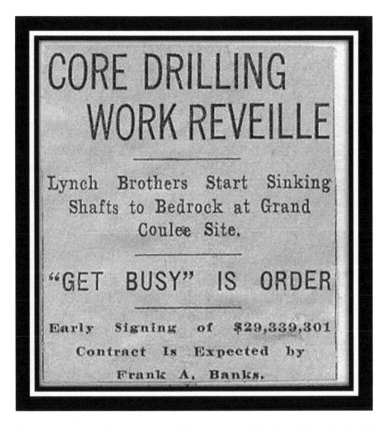

The Spokesman-Review, Aug. 29, 1934. From the Wallis and Marilyn Kimble Northwest History Database, WSU Libraries.

According to Paul Pitzer in his book <u>Grand Coulee, Harnessing a Dream</u>, "Considering the size of the undertaking, the number of people involved, and the speed of the work, Grand Coulee Dam proved to be a comparatively safe work place." In fact, thousands were injured during the construction of the dam, some seriously. In any given month over 200 workers would get hurt. But figures for fatalities were comparatively small, less than ten per year, or 82 total during construction of the dam. Most were crushed by heavy machinery, drowned in the river, or fell from high places. It is not known if any member of a Lynch Brothers crew was among those killed.

Bad luck continued for the Lynch team drilling to determine the necessary depth for the cofferdam pilings. On September 3rd the Sam Seaton's Grant County cable ferry, employed by the Lynch Brothers to move men and equipment on the river, was nearly destroyed. According to *The Spokane Chronicle* "The old Sam Seaton cable ferry was severely damaged when it loosened from its cable and started a precarious journey downstream Saturday afternoon."

"The ferry was being used by Lynch Brothers, diamond drillers, for river drilling, when suddenly it broke loose. The "apron" beam was snapped in two and the wheels used to wind up the cable were likewise demolished. The vessel wound it its wild excursion opposite the post office building, a quarter-mile downstream. Claire Seaton, young son of Sam Seaton, veteran operator, tried vainly to push the big craft upstream with his small outboard motor as it was careening down the river."

Before the accident the Grant County cable ferry was already doomed. When the beautiful Grand Coulee Dam Bridge was completed the following year, the cable ferry was obsolete. But the end of his livelihood was just the beginning of the problems facing Sam Seaton. His barren farm stood at what was to be the north end of the dam. The federal government intended to purchase all of the surrounding land including ten towns that would be buried by Roosevelt Lake and other reservoirs. Seaton joined forces with a few displaced neighbors to demand more money from the federal government. According to Paul Pitzer, "Altogether their disputed property totaled 1,101.63 acres that the government appraised at $15,443." Seaton and his fellow displaced neighbors demanded $5 million!

"The trial ran until August 2, 1935," wrote Pitzer, "when the jury awarded the landowners $17,338.92. *The Spokesman-Review* estimated that their lawyers charged them over $10,000." The furious landowners took the issue all the way to the United States

Supreme Court, which refused to hear the case. After losing his land and his business, Seaton was still able to purchase a piece of property in Elmer City where he became a disgruntled landlord. He died in 1971.

Most residents of Washington's arid Inland Empire, both white and Native American, fared no better than Seaton. The federal government intended to purchase 90% of the surrounding land for the massive reservoir lakes that would be formed by the Grand Coulee Dam. According to Pitzer, "Water eventually covered (the towns of) Peach, followed by Keller, Lincoln, Gerome, Gifford, Inchelium, Daisy, Kettle Falls, Marcus and Boyds. Kettle Falls moved to Meyers Falls, a smaller incorporated community. With the larger numbers, the displaced Kettle Falls residents then voted to annex Meyers Falls to Kettle Falls and changed the name of the new entity to Kettle Falls. Meyers Falls' people never forgave them for that."

In mid-July of 1934, James O'Sullivan announced to the press that President Franklin D. Roosevelt, First Lady Eleanor Roosevelt, and Interior Secretary Harold Ickes would visit the Grand Coulee construction site in early August. He further stated that about 100 "guests" would greet the president at a special platform built for the event near the dam site. O'Sullivan knew that the popular president would attract thousands of spectators, despite the rural nature of the area.

Roosevelt arrived in Oregon on August 3rd and made a stop at the Bonneville Dam, 450 miles downriver from the Grand Coulee, but 300 miles by car. Bonneville was being built by Kaiser's Six Companies under the direction of the Army Corps of Engineers. A smaller Lynch Brothers crew was just one of several drilling outfits at Bonneville.

That night FDR rested in Ephrata, Washington before continuing on to Grand Coulee where, just as O'Sullivan expected, a large crowd of over 20,000 had flocked to see the president. But where were the 100 or so dignitaries to join Roosevelt on the big stage specially built for the occasion? There was Washington's governor, and major Grand Coulee promoter, Clarence Martin;

Washington's two U.S. senators, Homer Bone and Clarence Dill; an assortment of small-time politicians; and officials from the Bureau of Reclamation and Columbia Basin Commission, including O'Sullivan. But O'Sullivan still feared that the big stage would look empty for such an important visit and so he went looking for men with suits.

Dick Lynch had a suit back in his room in the Thompson Hotel. And he could certainly set up his nephew Raymond. Bill Lynch was there too, since the company was in negotiations for further drilling contracts with the Mason Group. Bill's wife Jean and Dick's wife Sabina, were also available. And so it was that members of the Lynch Brothers Diamond Drilling Company sat on the big stage with President Franklin D. Roosevelt.

It was appropriate that the Lynch Brothers were represented on the presidential platform. After all, they were the original contractors on the job. Furthermore, the Columbia Basin Commission planned to present Roosevelt and other distinguished guests with paperweights made from core samples bought up by the Lynch Brothers.

FDR made his usual charming speech, drawing in the whole crowd as if the building of the Grand Coulee had been a shared idea and venture by all in attendance. "We are in the process of making the American people dam-minded,' roared Roosevelt. He justified the great expenditures on the project; promoted the idea of a "high dam," which would indeed be the final plan; and finished to prolonged cheers with these words:

"I am going to try to come back here when the dam is finished and I know that this country is going to be filled with homes not only of a great many people of this State, but by a great many families from other States of the Union—men and women and children who will be making an honest livelihood and doing their best successfully to live up to the American standard of living and the American standard of citizenship. So I leave here today with the feeling that this work is well undertaken; that we are going ahead with a useful project; and that we are going to see it through for the benefit of our country."

FDR did return in 1937, well before completion of the dam.

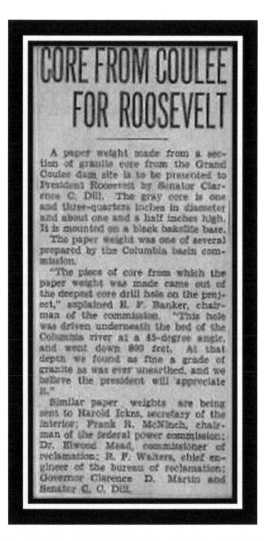

CORE FROM COULEE FOR ROOSEVELT

A paper weight made from a section of granite core from the Grand Coulee dam site is to be presented to President Roosevelt by Senator Clarence C. Dill. The gray core is one and three-quarters inches in diameter and about one and a half inches high. It is mounted on a black bakelite base.

The paper weight was one of several prepared by the Columbia basin commission.

"The piece of core from which the paper weight was made came out of the deepest core drill hole on the project," explained H. F. Banker, chairman of the commission. "This hole was driven underneath the bed of the Columbia river at a 45-degree angle, and went down 880 feet. At that depth we found as fine a grade of granite as was ever unearthed, and we believe the president will appreciate it."

Similar paper weights are being sent to Harold Ickes, secretary of the interior; Frank R. McNinch, chairman of the federal power commission; Dr. Elwood Mead, commissioner of reclamation; R. F. Walters, chief engineer of the bureau of reclamation; Governor Clarence D. Martin and Senator C. C. Dill.

Spokane Chronicle, June 16, 1934. Wallis and Marilyn Kimble Northwest History Database. WSU Libraries.

Later that hot August day in 1934 FDR and Eleanor took a driving tour of the construction site. They came upon a drill pit set near the road and stopped to chat with the men. Roosevelt purportedly asked one of the supervisors, probably Dick or

Raymond Lynch, but now in dusty work clothes and down in a pit, "Haven't I seen you someplace before?" The answer was, "Yes, Mr. President, I was on the platform with you today."

Raymond Lynch, Bill Lynch and Dick Lynch (tipping hat) at the Lynch Brothers Grand Coulee headquarters, in August, 1934. The women are Jean Muldowney Lynch (Bill's 2nd wife) and Sabina Lynch (Dick's wife). This photograph was likely taken as the group prepared to join the stage with President Franklin D. Roosevelt.

FDR Tours the dam site, August, 1934.
Courtesy Spokesman-Review, WSU Archives (Image sh92-562)

On September 10, 1934, *The Spokane Chronicle* reported that "Core drilling by Lynch Brothers reveals the river floor in the area to be approximately level, which made engineers at the Silas Mason Company smile as it aids them in the construction of the (coffer) dams. Away from this location the river bottom is featured by several deep crevices which would have made sheet-pile driving considerably harder."

Three days later the main office in Seattle was burglarized. The *Seattle Times* reported that the "burglars who took two bottles from the shop of Lynch Bros., diamond drillers, last night will be pleasantly surprised when they take out the corks. According to a report made by William G. Lynch, one bottle contained $75 worth of commercial diamonds and the other $75 worth of placer gold."

A total worth of $150 wouldn't be a "pleasant surprise" to a modern outlaw; but it was a nice haul in 1934. The equivalent today would be $2,648.

The Lynch Brothers commenced core drilling for the MWAK railroad bridge on September 18th. Up to that date they had already completed $68,415 worth of drilling contracts for the dam site. As the New Year began nearly 3,000 men were gainfully employed at the dam site. That number would continue to grow as thousands of men from every corner of America flocked to the Inland Empire in search of jobs that were so scarce during the Great Depression.

On January 3, 1935, The Spokane Chronicle announced that the Lynch Brothers had signed a new contract with MWAK to do extensive churn drilling in the slide area. They were to drill large holes and then fill them with perforated pipes, surrounded by gravel. Floats would then be inserted to determine if pumps sunk on the other side of the slide were actually lowering the water level that was causing the slide.

Another local newspaper, *The Quincy Herald*, from nearby Quincy, Washington, explained the job a little differently than the *Chronicle*, but also revealed that the Lynch Brothers had been ordered to drill deeper holes in the bedrock along the west shore of the river so that engineers could determine where water was flowing into that section of bedrock.

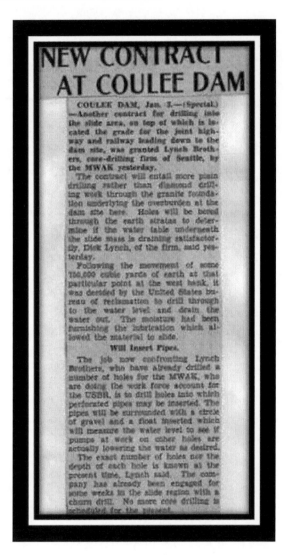

The Spokane Chronicle, January 3, 1935. From the Wallis and Marilyn Kimble Northwest History Database, WSU Libraries.

> ## DRILLING AT GRAND COULEE
>
> GRAND COULEE DAM.—The 36-inch Calyx drill holes bored into the granite bedrock on the west shore will be drilled deeper, it is reported. There are at present 11 of these large drill holes, 30 feet deep, in the granite floor at that point, but further information about the rock upon which the dam is to rest is demanded by the reclamation engineers, it is said, so Lynch Brothers have been ordered to deepen the holes. Engineers can climb into these holes and study the granite formation in place. A fault in the floor through which water is flowing is probably the reason for deepening the holes. Contractors say the drill-rig is capable of sinking holes 50 feet deeper—or more if desired.
>
> In addition to deepening the 36-inch west side holes and probably drilling a set of similar holes in the east side floor, Lynch Brothers will drill a series of 3-inch holes into the roofs of the 1900 feet of drainage tunnels in the granite underlying the slide area for the purpose of draining the clay beds overlying the granite and completing the drainage of the slide area in hopes of stopping further sliding.

The Quincy Herald, January 3, 1935, Wallis and Marilyn Kimble Northwest History Database, WSU Libraries.

The following summer, with the cofferdams in place, excavation of the earth where the west end of the dam would be located proceeded at a furious pace. Solid granite bedrock was reached on July 13th at 880 feet, which was, according to *The Spokane Chronicle*, "Approximately the level predetermined by the Lynch Brothers' core-drill rig."

In the autumn, crews were set to work "waterproofing" the rock where the dam would be anchored on the west shore. *The Spokesman-Review*, explained in a report filed November 19, 1935 that "Large crews are drilling and blasting a tunnel into the west abutment. By last Thursday they had permeated 98 feet, and the tunnel will run in about 475 feet when completed. From this tunnel holes will be drilled and from these holes, grout, which is cement and water, will be forced into the seams and crevices of the rock. Air pressure of from 50 to 500 pounds per square inch will be used."

"The grout will seal the rock against the tremendous pressure of water back of the dam. The first grouting done at the dam was on the west side, where a 50 foot hole drilled by Lynch Brothers took 265 sacks of cement."

The "tremendous pressure of the water back of the dam" was hardly an overstatement. The Franklin Roosevelt Lake, which is held back by today's Grand Coulee Dam, is 151 miles long and covers 125 square miles. It is 300 feet deep at the dam. But the massive concrete base of the dam extends to the bedrock another 200 feet below the bottom of the lake. Nevertheless, a rupture in the Grand Coulee Dam would be catastrophic. That is why the abutments on the shorelines needed to be equally thick and impervious to water pressure.

While tunnels were being drilled into the abutment, the Lynch Brothers were using giant calyx drills to provide more information for the actual foundation of the west side of the dam. The calyx drill is a large rotary drill capable of drilling holes as much as two meters thick and 300 feet deep. But it is also slow, laborious and expensive.

The Wenatchee Daily World of December 24, 1935, (and reprinted by the *Ephrata Journal* on January 3, 1936) reported that the Lynch Brothers, "the oldest contractors at the dam site," were to deepen eleven 30-foot holes so that engineers could descend and study a water flow in part of the west bedrock. Dusty Rhoades would supervise. The paper also revealed that the Lynch Brothers would be drilling the three foot wide calyx holes for the east end of the dam foundation while simultaneously drilling the relatively small three-inch holes from a tunnel placed under the notorious slide area to assist in water drainage.

"These holes," reported the Wenatchee newspaper, "spaced every 50 feet, will be bored through the rock from the tunnels until they reach the clay overhead. When completed, this set-up, it is hoped, will give additional drainage to the slide area."

But what really proved to be the solution was an idea by Raymond Lynch. The saturated land made it nearly impossible to drill. Ray suggested bringing in giant refrigeration units and placing them underground to freeze the ground water, which might make it possible to drill. It worked. Drainage tunnels finally brought the slide under control. Work could proceed at the Grand Coulee.

As they strove to solve problems at the Grand Coulee the *Seattle Times* reported on September 13, 1935, that the company had been awarded a contract by Seattle's Board of Public Works to do "test drilling on the site of City Light's proposed Ruby Dam on the upper Skagit. Four holes, each of them 150 feet deep, will be drilled to determine the character of the rock foundation."

Seattle City Light's Diablo and Gorge Dams, which the brothers had drilled for in the early 1920s, had been completed, but the third dam, which became the Ross Dam, and where they also had done some drilling more than 15 years earlier, had not yet been built. The new drilling was a minor operation compared to what they continued with at the Grand Coulee.

Also in 1935 the Lynch Brothers were hired to drill for sulphur on top of Washington's majestic Mt. Adams. Wade Dean (1885-1960), a land speculator and mining advocate from White Salmon, Washington knew that the 12,276 ft. tall Mt. Adams had a large deposit of sulphur beneath the surface of its summit, and he was determined to exploit it. He formed the Glacier Mining Company, which became the Pacific Sulphur Company of White Salmon. Dean built a mule trail all the way to the summit of Mt.

Adams where he erected a small mining shack to store supplies. He then hired the Lynch Brothers to drill exploratory holes. It was a challenge to move the drilling equipment up the mule trail to the top of a Cascade mountain, but in 1935 the Lynch Brothers dug eight test pits and drilled sixteen exploratory holes on the summit. Their samples revealed a high percentage of sulphur in the ground, but the numbers didn't work out for Wade Dean. It would be too expensive to extract and transport the mineral.

Dean abandoned the project and the Lynch Brothers abandoned their equipment. According to Tim Lynch, the son of Ray, it was too expensive and difficult to transport the equipment back down the mountain. They simply wrote it off as a business expense.

It is unclear if any of the Lynch Brothers equipment remains on Mt. Adams today, buried beneath snow and ice. But the dilapidated remains of the mining shack that Dean built for the operation is still visible on summer days. Mt. Adams is the only mountain in the entire Cascade Range to have been mined on its summit and the Lynch Brothers was the only company ever to receive permission to drill atop a Cascade peak.

The old mining shack on top of Mt. Adams (photo by Jonathon Ley).

In the summer of 1936 a celebration was held to commemorate the third anniversary of the start of construction for what would be the greatest concrete structure ever built. Only one individual was mentioned in *The Spokane Chronicle's* announcement of the event: President Franklin Delano Roosevelt. And only one company was mentioned: The Lynch Brothers Diamond Drilling Company. Yet, virtually every history of the construction of the great dam available today; from Pitzer's excellent book to the American Experience documentary on the project, either scarcely mention or fail to mention at all, the Lynch Brothers' contribution.

One year later, on October 6, 1937, the *Wenatchee Daily World* reported on the 4th anniversary of the project. The first company mentioned in the article was the Lynch Brothers Diamond Drilling Company of Seattle. They were called the "first pioneers" of the project, along with the company that dug the test pits for them, Rumsey & Co., also from Seattle.

Contracts for the Lynch Brothers unique and apparently affordable services at Grand Coulee continued to pour in with each passing year of the giant project. *The Spokane Chronicle* ran a bold headline on June 25, 1938 that went across the entire page. It read: **Lynch Brothers Start Huge Drilling Operations Under Dam at Grand Coulee**

"Drilling for the world's largest 'dentistry job' was resumed here Friday by Lynch Brothers of Seattle. The company has a contract to drill about 200,000 lineal feet- 38 miles of holes-in the bedrock under the Grand Coulee dam. After the dam's height has been increased considerably, grout will be forced down the holes, which will be about 200 feet deep, to seal small fissures in the granite foundation. About 38 miles of shallow holes have been drilled and grouted under the dam to care for fissures near the surface."

The choice of the phrase "world's largest dentistry job" wasn't used in jest by the *Chronicle*. Diamond drillers used the term "dental work" when referring to the filling of cracks or boreholes with grout.

COULEE PROJECT HAS ANNIVERSARY

Workmen continued their drive today for completion of the Grand Coulee-Columbia river diversion dam as residents in the vicinity of the project celebrated the third anniversary of the beginning of construction of the giant power-reclamation project.

Three years ago today Lynch Brothers of Seattle unloaded their diamond drilling equipment to determine the exact foundation for the huge mass of concrete. It was upon the findings of the drilling that hung President Roosevelt's willingness to allocate $63,000,000 for dam construction.

Since then more than 1,000,000 yards of concrete have been poured in the foundation. In the vicinity of the workings 12,000 persons live. Financial benefits of the project have spread into all parts of the United States.

The Spokane Chronicle, September 14, 1936. Wallis and Marilyn Kimble Northwest History Database, WSU Libraries.

"A big calyx drill is being used to take sample cores from the concrete at the eastern end of the spillway section. The cores will be 18 inches in diameter. The cores will be tested under pressure to determine the strength of that portion of the dam."

The Lynch Brothers would keep a working crew at the Grand Coulee Dam until its completion. Bill Lynch had died during the construction of the dam and Pat Lynch was in poor health. Dan was getting old and wanted to spend more time with his children, grandchildren and his ailing wife, Mate. Only Dick stayed active, but even he spent most of his time managing the company from Seattle or his Hood Canal home in Silverdale. His nephew, and adopted son, Raymond Lynch, was taking more control of the company affairs and Dan's sons, Fred and Kendall Lynch, were still supervising jobs. But the man in charge of the Grand Coulee crew to the end continued to be the dependable Earle "Dusty" Rhoades.

Lynch Brothers made the news in connection to the Grand Coulee Dam for something other than drilling in the summer of 1940. A brush fire broke out on the day after Independence Day, leading one to speculate that leftover fireworks could have been involved. The fire reached the edge of Mason City where it destroyed a few supply buildings and the office of the Lynch Brothers Diamond Drilling Company. And in the process it destroyed company records that would have provided a much clearer picture for future historians regarding the importance of the work accomplished at the Grand Coulee Dam by this largely forgotten company.

On January 17, 1942 *The Spokane Chronicle* announced the end of the Lynch Brothers work at the Grand Coulee under the headline: **LYNCH BROTHERS DRILL LAST HOLE**

COULEE DAM, Jan. 17. (Special Report) - "Grand Coulee Dam's pioneer contractors, Lynch Brothers of Seattle, who started core drilling on September 18, 1933, two days after the first operation – sinking test pits – was started, will leave the project in about a week, its hard work finished. The company has had a crew here continually for eight years."

"The company is completing the drilling of 167,800 linear feet for CBI (Consolidated Builders Incorporated). Previously it drilled 21,200 feet for the state Columbia Basin Commission and about 20,000 for the Mason-Walsh-Atkinson-Kier Company. The 209,000 feet total about 39 ½ miles.

"The first drilling was in the river and along the shore at the dam site. Some holes punctured the granite 800 feet. The work established general contours and the continuity of the granite. More recently the company has been drilling grout holes in bedrock under the dam. A mixture of cement and water was forced into the holes to close cracks in the granite. Holes were drilled also to drain seepage water."

"When President Roosevelt visited the project for the first time on August 4, 1934, a Lynch Brothers drill rig was set up on the road to show him that some activity was taking place."

In the winter of 1942 that activity would move elsewhere.

Eleven: Kendall Lynch, The Soldier-Poet

Kendall Oscar Lynch, better known as Ken, was the younger brother of Fred and Harriet, and the namesake of his famous uncle, Oscar Kendall. Ken spent more of his early years with his parents at mining camps than either of his siblings. He grew up around adults; many of them hard-drinking, rugged men. And it seems he took after them. A diamond driller for most of his life, he also served his country during World War I. Ken was a tough man who wrote sentimental poetry, as revealed by the following poem that he composed for his mother, Mate Lynch. He may have been the only person who saw his mother in glowing terms. But he did carry her last name as his first and spent much more time with her during childhood than had with either of his siblings, Fred and Harriet.

My Mother

Mother, who with tender care
Didst teach to me my first wee prayer,
Who was the first to comfort me
When I fell and skinned my chubby knee;
Who calmed my troubled days and nights
And gave me all my young delights;
Comfort me too, when I shall go
Into the world of sorrow and woe.
Send me on life's rugged way
With the will to work and always pray,
Make me choose what's right and wise,
Make me see through Christian eyes.
Catholic may I always be
In everything I do and see.
Ungrateful though I sometimes am
Help me, Mother, all you can.
Then when I shall meet my King
In Heaven above, the first song I'll sing
Will be 'plauded By God and every other,
"I am safely here because of my Mother."

The poem is a bit sappy and was probably written when Ken was a boy or a very young man. But it is remarkable in its affection for a woman that few other people, except her faithful husband Dan, and a few adult friends, seemed to feel much affection for.

Equally affectionate toward his wife Grace, Ken composed numerous Valentine poems for her. Perhaps the most interesting, and humorous, follows.

A Valentine for you dear wife,
Your sparring partner all through life.
Let's lay aside our boxing gloves
And be like two young turtle doves.
We're getting too darn old to fight.
Besides, you know I'm always right.

And while Ken loved his mother and wife, he also loved his dog.

Skippy

He is only a mongrel
Yet he means more to me
Then your blue ribbon mutts
With a long pedigree.
His father a terrier
His mother unknown
But he's my dog
And mine alone.

Others can pet him
He'll wag his tail
They can feed him beefsteak
Chicken or quail.
So long as I am there to tell him O.K.
But if I am not around
He will just run away.

And when I come home
From work or afar
I know he'll be waiting
Where I park my car.
He will jump on my leg
And dirty my clothes
And fondle my hand
With his cold little nose.

He is only a dog
And like all dogs you see
He never misses

A post or a tree.
There is only one person
On earth he can see
And somehow I am glad
That person is me.

He is only a dog
But this much I know.
If dogs have a heaven
That's where he will go.
For no human being
Ever born of man
Could love and be faithful
Like my Skippy can.

Ken spent many cold nights at mining camps and with drill crews in the far north. Some of the jobs were in British Columbia, the Yukon Territory and Alaska. Like his brother Fred, and many other miners, he became a fan of the long narrative poems written by Robert Service. Fred coveted a book by Service that he received from his uncle, Albert Kendall, on Christmas, 1925. And Ken memorized Service ballads like "The Shooting of Dan McGrew" and "The Cremation of Sam McGee."

Perhaps Ken was spending New Year's Eve at a lonely drill site in the far north, without the comfort of his wife Grace, when he tried to imitate Service with a rather somber and depressing ballad. How much of it was personal cannot be known. But when Ken had too much to drink, and too much time to think, he could have dark moods.

The following poem is about a lonely man who has lost his faith and is descending into hell or simply despair. Its attack on the church is startling for an Irish Catholic from the Lynch clan. Suffice to say it could never have been written by Ken's jovial and very religious brother Fred.

ME

Happy New Year.

The old year is past; the New Year is here,
And all the best wishes received.
But what can it hold for me but despair
My life's hopes are just empty dreams.

I have built my air castles with faith from on high.
I've prayed and I've played the game square.
But the cold church stands by with a sneer in its eye,
And I'm slowly descending the stairs.

What use to appeal to a church that can't feel?
It is heartless and colder than snow.
There is no helping hand; there is no place to stand,
So I'm slipping and sliding below.

I once was a fool, but I'm not the first,
I was young and wanted a wife.
I thought she'd shoot square, and I married her there,
In that church, where I ruined my life.

And now I just wander and drift with the tide,
With never a place of my own.
Run with the ones who would love me and hide,
In the camps, in the place I call home.

The world's dark and cold and I'm growing old
Life is half over for me.
All I ask from above is someone to love,
And a young one to hold on my knee.

Every man in this world has a mission to fill,
My life has just been a joke.
But I'm paying the bill for that one youthful thrill,
And I guess I will pay till I'm broke.

I laugh and I play in my own carefree way
And nobody ever could tell,
That my heart is like lead, and my hopes are all dead.
And I'm suffering the tortures of hell.

And so I receive the cards of good cheer,
From my friends who never will know,
That with church standing by with hypocritical sighs,
My soul is descending below.

Kendall Lynch tries to relax in his cabin after a hard day's work on a drill crew. He has a picture of his parents, Dan and Mate, on the table next to him and a picture of his wife Grace on the shelf above him. Everything about the photograph projects loneliness.

Ken came from a Catholic family that believed in good and evil; heaven and hell. Perhaps he thought his weaknesses condemned him to hell. Another part of the poem is confusing, but might have an answer. He refers to a marriage that ruined his life. But he could not be referring to his marriage with Grace Sullivan, a woman he loved deeply and who gave him two sons. So who was he talking about?

The late Betty Biner Fulton, Ken's niece, had a picture of her beloved uncle as a young man with an unknown woman. On the back of the picture she wrote "Uncle Ken's first wife." Betty's sister Fritzi recalled that her mother Harriet (Kendell's sister) had confided that her brother "was married briefly when he was young but the marriage was annulled. Things like that were scandals in those days and not to be talked about." But no one else in the family, including Ken's son Jack, who was 15 years younger than his cousin Betty, had any knowledge that Ken Lynch had been married before he met Grace Sullivan.

Ken's letters to his siblings while he was engaged in World War I are not as sappy or depressing as his attempts at poetry.

Ken enlisted on August 3, 1917 and was assigned service number 1822812. He worked in the naval shipyards, served on a sub-chaser and a destroyer and finished his service aboard the famous transport ship *USS Hancock,* which had seen action during the Spanish- American War. He was discharged on November 12, 1919.

In 1916 the U.S. Navy purchased the grounds and buildings of the Panama-California Exposition which ran from 1915 to 1916 in San Diego's Balboa Park. The picturesque location was turned into San Diego's first Naval Training Center. Kendall Lynch was one of thousands who reported to San Diego for training.

The following are letters written during the final months and immediate aftermath of World War I. These letters are presented as they were written. In the first letter Ken inquires about his new niece, Betty Biner, the daughter of his sister Harriet. Betty was born on February 20, 1918; six months after Ken enlisted.

Harriet and her husband Billy lived in the copper boomtown of Phoenix, BC where Billy was the brewmaster of his father's Phoenix Brewery.

All four letters were sent to Harriet and Billy, whom Ken calls bro, in Phoenix. Ken also calls Billy the "fat Dutchman." Biner was not fat, but he was short and stout. Nor was he Dutch. In fact, he was a boxing champion and the son of Swiss immigrants; however, his father did speak German, a language similar to Dutch, and sided with the Germans during WW I.

The Naval Training Center at Balboa Park in San Diego in 1917. On the back of the photograph Kendall wrote, "The command's stand at ease. Behind is the Y.M.C.A. just for our own use. Notice the people crowding around the edge of the parade ground. It is like that every day until dark then all women are put out of the park.

Sept. 24, 1918

Dear Sis,

I guess you think I have quit writing entirely. Well I have just about. Gee I do not have any chance at all anymore. We are going all the time. Just stop and take on coal and shove off again. I suppose we will have to stop some time for repairs. Each trip we expect to stop for repairs but we always have to make one more.

Well Sis I received your letter also the money and thanks ever so much. I have not written to hardly anybody for a long time and don't know when I will get caught up with my writing again.

Well Sis how is my niece getting along. I am waiting for more pictures. Gee I sure like to receive pictures. How is the fat Dutchman? Tell him if he ever wants to reduce weight to join the navy as a fireman. I fire three ___ on a scotch boiler. The slice bar weighs about 75 lbs. and the hoe about 40. We slice one up, push one back and coal one over, then start over again. Its lots of fun.

Well Sis I don't know what to write about. We have to be careful what we write now as there is so much hell a popping about telling our movements through the mail.

Well I guess I had better close as the mess cooks are getting down the tables for chow.

Good bye With Love, K.

Parade grounds at the Naval Training Camp in San Diego's Balboa Park, 1917. On the back of this photograph Kendall wrote: "Our Battalion drilling. The building with the X on it is our sleeping quarters. There are ten buildings like it for sleeping quarters only."

Harriet Lynch Biner, the only sister of Fred & Kendall Lynch, with her baby, Betty, in the British Columbia mining town of Phoenix. The Phoenix Brewery, owned by her father-in-law, is in the background. The entire town of Phoenix, once the highest town in Canada, is now gone; bulldozed for an open pit mine in the 1950s.

In this next letter, Ken again refers to Germans as "Dutch" and says he is anxious to get back on a D.D. (destroyer). He mentions that he wrote to Mary Biner, Billy's younger sister, who was already married at the time. He calls his niece "Little Billy;" suggests she is too good-looking to be the child of her "Maw & Paw" and acknowledges his brother-in-law as a cartoonist.

Nov. 17, 1918

Dear Sis and Bro,

I am going to write again because I know darn well that you are not getting half of my letters or you would answer them. We are at sea now but we hit port tomorrow night and hears hoping there will be a lot of mail waiting me.

Well we put it over on the Dutch men didn't we. Not meaning myself very strange in that we bit the U.S. in general. We were figuring on furloughs when we get in port this time but I suppose this peace will change that now as we have a lot of work ahead of us that will take some time. I don't know if there will be any chance to buy out later on or not but I will sure try. I (am) anxious to get back on the old D.D. again. I have been on this job long enough and anyhow I believe they will be able to get along now without my aid.

I believe I will mail this letter in Norfolk Va. If I do I will just about freeze to death. I have been around tropical climates now for five months except one day we spent in Phillia.

I wrote Mary B. a long crazy letter butting into all her private affairs. I don't know what made me write so much foolishness except that I got one of my streaks that I wanted to write and if I want to write I must have something to write about. I don't blame her if she is sore at me for butting into her own affairs.

Well Sis how is the kid. Has she learned to wash bottles yet. Gee I never will forget the time I washed kegs and blistered my hands all up. Gee little Billy is sure a cute kid. Funny she don't take after her Maw or Paw. She looks something like Billy only she will be good looking. I guess that don't make you sore. Send more pictures when you have them also some of her Maw.

I am sending a real pretty picture. I would like to have you get it framed and hang it in the house across the way. It would look quite appropriate. The fellows with me are really good fellows although I'll admit their looks are again them. You will notice that my Adam's apple is still with me and just as active as ever. In fact I believe it is growing. I'm afraid I will have to have my collars made to order when I get in civilian life again. The fellow on my left is Irish, you can probably guess it by his face. His name is McCabe. Don't you think he is intelligent looking. The one on my right is from Boston. His name is Nickels and everyone takes us for brothers. We both feel flattered. Being from Boston he always kicks about the chow unless there is baked beans however he has little occasion to kick. Notice his neck. It reminds me of an ostrich that had swallowed a baseball. Billy is a cartoonist isn't he? Well if he needs inspiration he should be able to get it from that picture.

Well Sis I am not getting any thinner neither am getting fatter but I have not been sick a day in sixteen months and guess I have no reason to (be) sick. I am not working hard now. I have not been in the fire room for three months. I am working for the machinist running a big forty fat gas boat when in port and running a small hoist while at sea. I have been pretty lucky.

Well I have got to close for today. I might as well anyhow as I have not written any news. So good bye.

With love,

Bro Kendall

Kendall Lynch, center, flanked by Navy buddies he identifies as Nickels and McCabe.

USS Hancock
Jan. 20, 1919

Dear Sis and Bro,

We are staying a couple days in Charlestown on our way to the Isles. So I want to let you know I received the box on the same day we left Norfolk. And thanks ever so much for everything. It sure was swell. I know it was the best box that has come aboard. We sure had some good feeds. I also got Mothers and Fred's the same day so you can imagine how we stuffed ourselves for a few days. Gee Sis you made a hit with the fellows with your divinity fudge. It was sure swell.

Say I wrote Mary Biner sometime ago especially to thank her for the candy and I don't believe I thanked her after all. It was sure swell candy. The hanker chief and sox are fine – I won't have to use (?) anymore.

Well Sis there are a whole bunch of men leaving for home today with honorable discharges. I made awful hard try to get out but no chance yet for a while. However, I think I will be out within three months more. Gee there are sure some sore fellows today also some happy ones.

Well we a leaving on a six weeks cruise this time. We have on a bunch of Marines. It don't look as though were ever going across again. Well how is the kid getting along. I have got to close now and have a lot of letters to write to day. With love to all and thanks. Ken
P.S. Did you make those sox yourself? They fit fine.

Kendall Lynch, left, with three Navy buddies in an unknown location.

A deadly flu pandemic paralyzed the entire world in 1918 and 1919, killing approximately 50 million people. It was called the Spanish flu and many thought its origins were in the European trenches of WW I. Soldiers were quarantined (or held in detention as Ken calls it in the following letter) until it could be ascertained if they carried the virus, which seemed to strike young adults more than any other segment of the population.

After months crisscrossing the Atlantic and stopping at ports along the East Coast, Kendall finally returned to San Diego, where he and his fellow soldiers spent three weeks in isolation. Ken claims not to be interested in any of the girls who flirt with the soldiers and he wonders how the "beerless beer" is coming along. Billy Biner, anticipating Prohibition in America, was experimenting with "near-beer" recipes at the time.

USN Station San Diego, California
(undated but probably written in 1919)

Dear Sis and Bro,

Just a few lines to let you know I am in San Diego now. I did not know I was going until about 45 min. before I left. I am writing this sitting on the floor of my tent with a book on my lap. So you will have to excuse the writing.

Well they have us all in detention camp. I guess we will have to go into isolation every time we go to a new camp or ship. You see it is to protect the other men. We are kept here for 21 days to make sure we are not carrying any disease. So we will not get any liberty or be allowed to mix with any other men until our 21 ds are up. We are divided up into sections of 30 or 36 men and put in separate yards with a guard at the gate. We sleep and eat out under the sky. We have no tables or anything to write on.

Gee it sure is hot here in the day time but it's swell at night. We are camped in the old fair grounds and it is sure pretty. All little lakes and big palm trees. You can buy oranges for 50¢ a box here and they are good ones too.

I think I will like it fine when I get out of detention camp. We are treated a lot better by the officers here. Gee it sure is a nice trip by boat. We traveled first class on one of the best boats. Gee we sure get treated fine by cyvillions especially the girls. We get treated lots better than the army men. We can pick up any girl we want. But I don't want any. I have not spoken a dozen words to any girl since I left home.

Well Sis write and tell me all the news and how the beerless beer is working.

With Love, Bro Kendall

Kendall finally meets his niece Betty after his discharge.

When he returned from his service in what was called the Great War, Ken went right to work for the Lynch Brothers. He had been on many jobs before he was old enough to work. Now he would spend most of his adult life on the drilling crews. He often served as a supervisor, but his unique talent was bringing worn diamond bits back to life.

Kendall Lynch at drill camp circa 1930.

When Ken wasn't resetting diamond bits that had been worn down, he was on the move. He drilled for ore deposits and dam locations in Alaska, Washington and British Columbia; Patterson, Idaho and Oregon's Owyhee Canyon. He drilled for copper and gold deposits, under contract with the Bureau of Mines, in the mountains near Baker City, Oregon. In short, he went wherever his dad or uncles sent him.

Ken supervised exploratory drilling for what would become, many years later, the Boundary Dam along the Washington-British Columbia border in NE Washington. It was there, in the nearby town of Metaline Falls, where he met the love of his life; the diminutive, pretty Grace Sullivan.

Grace Sullivan Lynch

Ken's somewhat erratic behavior was tempered beautifully by his charming wife. Grace was everything that her name suggested.

She became a regular at the drilling sites and Ken found work with the company for two of her brothers: Jim and George Sullivan. She also gave birth to two sons: Daniel, born near a drilling camp in Oregon in 1930, and Jack born two years later in Washington.

Everyone fell in love with Grace Lynch, according to her niece Fritzi Biner Bernazani.

"She was an adorable redhead and had one streak of white hair in her left temple. I got to live with them (Kendall and Grace) for a while when Mom and Dad lived in Port Orchard. Aunt Grace was a treasure and so much fun. We all loved her dearly."

Grace Sullivan Lynch, right, with a friend at a drill camp near the Washington/British Columbia border.

*Danny Lynch, son of Kendall & Grace Lynch, at a drill camp in Oregon's
Owyhee Canyon, circa 1932.*

*Drilling for the Owyhee Dam was treacherous.
It was the highest dam in the world at the time of completion.
Photo courtesy of the Library of Congress.*

The Owyhee Dam after completion.
Photo courtesy of the Bureau of Reclamation.

A diamond drill near Baker City in Grant County, Oregon, where Kendall and
his Lynch Brothers crew worked a contract for the Bureau of Mines.
Photo courtesy of the Library of Congress.

For reasons not entirely known, but likely due to a combination of his drinking problems and his slow disenfranchisement with the Lynch Brothers as his cousin Ray took over, Kendall stopped drilling and pursued other options to make a living.   During World War II he planted a "Victory Garden" in his parent's yard near Green Lake.   Potatoes were his crop of choice.   But he also helped the war efforts by taking a job in the pipe shop of a Seattle shipyard cranking out vessels for the military.   The experience led him once again to poetry.

We Have a War To Win

There are clever shipyard poems
On the day shift and the swing,
The rivalry existing there
Is quite a funny thing,
The day shift thinks that every job
Is ruined during the night
And they're the only ones on earth
That really do things right.

The swing shift blames the day shift
For everything that's wrong,
They claim they hide material
And keep the prints too long,
And so the battle wages--
Beefing, knocking, day and night--
Neither side can realize
That neither side is right.

If the Germans bomb Seattle,
And the Japs are at our door
Through lack of good destroyers
To keep them from our shores,
I wonder if they'll then realize
How petty was the fight,
When by working all together
They could all be in the right.

There isn't any use to beef
And knock your fellow men,
You'll never win a war that way,
But here's a way you can,
If you must fight, don't use your mouth,
Just grab a gun and go,
Help plant the stars and stripes on
Rome, Berlin and Tokyo.

Let's work together, every man--
Build ships and planes and tanks,
Lay petty squabbling aside
And help those fighting yanks.
We haven't time for private quarrels,
We found that out before,
We have a man-size job to do--
We've got to win a war.

'Til water lilies bloom 'round
Old Mussolini's grave
And the slant-eyed son of heaven
Is a cringing Chinese slave,
'Til the Fuehrer, Adolph Hitler,
And his murdering Nazi crew
Are hanging from a scaffold
With their necks near stretched in two.

Let's get along together
And work in harmony,
Like the parts of our destroyers
That sail across the seas,
'Til Satan, opening up the door
Of his hottest fiery well,
Says, "Welcome home, mine Fuehrer,
Welcome back to hell."

Ken also tried his hand at poetry in different dialects. Certainly
he was familiar with the Irish accent, but in the shipyards he
became accustomed to Scandinavian accents and the accents of
southern blacks. According to the Northwest Digital Archives

website, Scandinavians "were struck by the Pacific Northwest's physical similarity to their Scandinavian homelands. The abundance of mountains, forests, and waterways provided economic opportunities in familiar vocations, namely logging, boatbuilding, and fishing." Whole communities of Finns, Swedes, Danes and Norwegians were established up and down the Northwest coast. Astoria even had a Finnish language newspaper.

Seattle Times journalist Don Magnuson wrote a derogatory piece about shipyard workers claiming they were inefficient and wasted time. Kendall Lynch took exception to the article. He was in the shipyards every day and saw things quite differently. His poem attacking Magnuson was penned in a Scandinavian dialect and meant to be sung to the tune of *Yankee Doodle Dandy.*

Ve left our vives to run the farm,
Ve'd like to pack a gun,
But some of us are too damn old,
And some are too damn young.

Ve came from Minnesota and
From Maine and Tennessee,
To build some ships to beat the blitz,
And keep our country free.

Ve are shipyard vorkers,
Ve work for Uncle Sam.
For Seattle Times and Magnuson,
Ve just don't give a damn.

Now some of us are farmers and
Dare some are business man,
Ve don't know much of building ships,
Ve do de best ve can.

Don Magnuson a yournalist,
He taute he vas so vise,
He should be in da army now,
Instead of viting lies.

Ve are shipyard vorkers,
Vork seven days a veek,
Dat Mister Magnuson he say,
Ve yust stand around and sleep.

Ve launch ten big destroyers,
And it's very hard to see,
How ve can stand around all day,
And get that Navy "E".

Ve building ships and buying bonds,
Believe me vere not fooling,
Ve ask you Mister Magnuson,
Yust vot have you been doing?

Ve are shipyard vorkers,
Ve know ve are O.K.
Ve'll build da ships and vork like hell,
No matter vat you say.

The Navy E was an efficiency pin that shipyard workers were awarded for excellent production. And no doubt Ken had a legitimate beef with Magnuson, who went on to become a U.S. congressman with financial support from big business tycoons who liked the cut of his jib. One of those supporters was Henry Kaiser, known as "The Father of Ship Building." Kaisers' Six Companies had built the Golden Gate Bridge, the Hoover Dam and had assisted in the Grand Coulee and Bonneville.

The biggest Kaiser shipyard was just north of Portland, Oregon in a town established by the government. It was called Vanport and during World War II it became the second largest city in the state. Thousands of African Americans flocked to Vanport to work in Kaiser's shipyards. Vanport became one of the most integrated cities in America. 40% of the families were black and many were still hard at work after the war when, in 1948, a monstrous flood took Vanport off the map. Even the dams that Kaiser helped build could not prevent Mother Nature from destroying his shipyards. Many descendants of the Vanport shipyards live in

Portland today. And while so many black Americans worked at Vanport, thousands also worked in the Seattle shipyards where Ken Lynch took note of their dialect.

Ken claimed to have written this humorous poem about love and marriage using a southern black family as the main characters.

LOVE

Melindy fell deep in love,
With a colored boy she knew,
But it was quite the proper thing,
For she was colored too.
She hastened home and told her Pop
That shortly she would wed
One likely Mr. Rufus Brown,
When Pop looked up and said,
"No, honeychile, you can't do that
Yo haf to find another,
Don' tell you Mom but Rifis Brown
Am sholly yo haf brother."
Melindy shed a few salty tears
Then went her lonely way
And soon she met another boy
And hastened home to say:
"Now Pop I'se goin' to marry
Dat Smith boy down the street
He ain't got no bad habits
And he dresses up so neat,
He never swears 'cept when he's drunk
At bootleggin' he's fine
He says date Packard Limousine
Am jest the same as mine."
Pop slowly shook his head
And looked across at Mother
And said, "No chile, you can't do that
Dat Smith boy is you half-brother."
Melindy wailed, Melindy moaned
In hopeless grief she cried
Until her Maw across the room

Called her to her side.
"What you and Pop conspiring' far?"
She said, "From dawn till night,
And why you cry yo eyes out,
Till you're a dreadful sight?"
Melindy then forgot her oath
And blurted out to Mother
"Pop says I can't marry Rufus Brown
'Cause he is my half-brother,
And then I turn to Samuel Smith
Although' it seemed like treason
But Pop says I can't marry him,
For just the self-same reason."
Then Maw said, "Honeychile don' cry,
Put on you weddin' cap,
And marry either one you like,
Yo ain't no kin to Pap."

But was Kendall Lynch the original author of this poem? Similar
versions can be found online, including an abbreviated version
called "A Redneck's Love Story." But no author is ever credited
and the versions were typically printed well past the time that
Ken typed his version of the poem. One thing seems likely: the
poem originated near the end of World War II.

Ken took another attempt at humor when his father, Dan Lynch
got in trouble with his mother Mate.

Father's in the Doghouse

Father's in the doghouse! That's what Mother said.
When I've disobeyed her I'm sent up to bed.
When I'm being punished I'm kept in from play,
But she deals with Father in a different way.

Don't know what has happened. Something's gone astray.
When he tries to kiss her she pushes him away.
If he starts to chuckle Mother wears a pout
Says there's really nothing she can laugh about.

Father's being punished. Wish I knew just why.
When he asks a question Mother won't reply.
"Picture show this evening?" Mother mutters: "No! I can buy my
tickets when I want to go."

"Mothers right!" he told me, "I've been naughty, too!
And I'm being punished just the same as you.
I am in the doghouse!" That can't be I know,
We don't keep a kennel where a dog can go.

Father's in the doghouse! Mother's face is grave.
Says she's going to teach him how he should behave
But I hate to see him moping around about
Guess I'll go and ask her please, to let him out.

Working in the shipyards of Seattle seemed to mark the end of
Kendall's association with the Lynch Brothers Diamond Drilling
Company, which must have been a disappointment to his aging
father, who was busy trying to stay out of Mate's doghouse! Ken
had spent most of his life in mining camps or dam locations and
was employed by the company for nearly 30 years. But according
to Ken's son Jack, his father had a falling out with Raymond
Lynch. Ray and Juanita Lynch were once close friends with Ken
and Grace. The two couples spent a lot of time together. But that
seems to have changed as Ray was being groomed by Dick Lynch
to take over the company. Ken was the odd man out and
apparently not interested in working under his younger cousin.

In fact, after years of diamond drilling or pipe fitting in a shipyard,
by the late 1940s Ken was ready to move away from the hard
manual labor that had defined his life. He was a man of diverse
interests and talents, and proved quite creative in his attempts to
make a living. Somewhere along the way he learned how to
massage and started K.O. Lynch Massotherapy with an office at
147 East 57th Street in Seattle. He offered evening appointments
for medical massage at "Office or Your Home."

He opened a lunch fountain near Everett and purchased the Lake
Cassidy Resort, a small fishing camp near Lake Stevens,
Washington. The camp had three cabins and a boathouse with

nineteen boats, which Kendall rented out for recreational fishing. The shallow lake was stocked with bass, crappie, perch, cutthroat and rainbow trout. It had a view of scenic Mt. Pilchuck.

This was the ideal location for Ken, who loved the outdoors. He would entertain his brother Fred; brother-in-law Billy Biner; nephew Bob Biner and Betty's husband Pat Fulton. All of the men liked to fish, smoke, tell jokes and, equally important to Ken, imbibe in a strong drink.

Fred Lynch, Pat Fulton, Bob Biner and Billy Biner (kneeling) get ready for a day of fishing and drinking with Kendall Lynch.

Things seemed to be going well, but trouble lurked within. As some of his poems suggested, Ken had a haunted soul. Well-liked by both intimate and casual acquaintances, he was handsome, charming, quick-witted and could be the life of the party, until he had too much alcohol. When he drank he could say inappropriate things that put him on the wrong side of friends and family members alike. And sometimes his drinking got him into trouble with the law.

In the summer of 1947 Ken was charged with negligent driving when he collided with another vehicle on the old Seattle-Everett Highway, also known as the Pacific Highway. According to police reports, he pulled out in front of another vehicle while attempting a U-turn from behind a parked car. The occupants of the other car, which included a young couple returning to Everett after securing a marriage license in Seattle, sustained minor injuries. Ken fractured his shoulder and broke several ribs. After a brief stay in Everett's Providence Hospital, he spent weeks recuperating at home.

During this time Ken either started or joined a small company called Northwest Business Investments and had an office on Roosevelt Way in Seattle. He advertised as a real estate broker in Seattle under the same name he used in his "massotherapy" - K.O. Lynch.

One of the first properties he attempted to sell, in January, 1948 was the lunch fountain near Everett.   The heading of his advertisement in the *Seattle Times* was **Sacrifice – Sickness,** which probably referred to his incapacitation following the car accident. Since Ken was at fault in the accident he likely paid a hefty fine and owed money to those he injured. The location of the fountain shop was listed as an Everett suburb on Hwy 99. Ken may have been pulling out from that shop when he had his accident a few months earlier.

"Sacrifice - Sickness – Fountain Lunch. Everett suburb, Hwy 99. $7,300 one month ago. Will take $6000 for quick sale. All new equipment."

Whatever he made off the sale it was not enough. Exactly two months later he listed his beloved fishing camp for sale. It was advertised as a "long-established" seven-acre fishing resort with buildings, boats and a seven-room house. The asking price was $15,000. He sold it, as his son Jack recalls, "to a man named Parr." Shortly thereafter the entire camp - cabins, boats and boathouse included - burned to the ground. Today the shallow lake has one small boat ramp and campground, located on the same spot where Kendall Lynch once dreamed of retiring to an easy life of fishing.

In 1949 Kendall and Grace took what money they made from his job as a real estate broker and moved to 4121 Creston Ave. in Vancouver, Washington. Ken's sister Harriet was living across the Columbia River in Portland, where her husband Billy owned and operated Leipzig's Tavern. Initially Ken helped Billy at Leipzig's while he looked for other opportunities.

Ken thought that offering French Dip sandwiches at the tavern would be profitable and Billy gave it a go, until it proved otherwise. But Ken could experiment to his heart's content when he became the proprietor of his own bar: the Barrel Inn Tavern on Portland's Macadam Avenue. The Barrel Inn was located right across the street from the Oregon Furniture Manufacturing Company, making it a convenient watering hole for men when they got off work. Leipzig and Barrel Inn were on opposite sides of the Willamette River, and just over two miles apart via the Sellwood Bridge.

On November 8, 1950, *The Oregonian* newspaper, under the headline **Pinball Machines Cited In Arrests** reported a strange coincidence without connecting the dots.

"Charges of conducting gambling, by use of pinball machines, were lodged Tuesday against two employees of taverns, according to a police vice squad report. Taken into custody were Leslie G. Holt, 41, Leipzig Tavern, 8081 SE 13th Avenue, and Mary J. Darden, 28, Barrel Inn, 5131 SW Macadam Avenue. A pinball machine was taken from each establishment."

Justice was swift. The following day Municipal Court Judge J.J. Quillan found both Holt and Darden guilty of conducting gambling operations by offering payoffs on pinball machines. Holt was fined $100 and Darden $50. What *The Oregonian*, and apparently the vice squad, never seemed to realize was that the owners of the two taverns were brothers-in-law. Another employee of Leipzig at the time was C.P. "Pat" Fulton, the husband of Kendall's beloved niece Betty Biner.

Pat Fulton and Billy Biner at Leipzig's Tavern in Portland.

A few years later a man named Paul Whittman purchased the Barrel Inn, and with it the custom of gambling. In January 1958 Whittman and three others were arrested for operating a gambling operation at the tavern. Kendall Lynch was not involved. He had other things on his mind. He was dying.

The author of this history recalls visiting the home of Kendall Lynch during his illness. Harriet Biner and Fred Lynch were there to say goodbye to their little brother. The author, just four at the time, and his siblings, were oblivious to the nature of the visit. They stayed outside, throwing rocks into a small pond. But a glimpse of what appeared to be a very old man on his death bed is the only memory that the author has of Uncle Ken.

The end came on December 12, 1958. Contrary to the eyes of a small child, Ken was not an old man. He was just 61 years old. His older sister Harriet would live another 20 years; his older brother Fred another 24 and his wife Grace would be a widow for 44 years. Kendall Oscar Lynch, the hard-drinking soldier-poet-diamond driller, is buried in Portland's Willamette National Cemetery.

Ken's son Daniel Lynch, named for his grandfather, died six years later at the age of 34. He suffered from diabetes. Grace Sullivan Lynch died in 2002 at the age of 98. Only Jack survives, though a recent stroke has slowed him down a bit. Jack has fond memories of his childhood, when his dad worked as a diamond driller in what seemed like exotic places for a young boy. He recalls one specific drill site on a river. Though too young to recall the exact location, he was not too young to forget that he slept with his dad in a tent attached to a raft in the middle of a river. A taste of Huck Finn's life is something no child could ever forget. Jack's dad had many such experiences as a boy. And Kendall Lynch, like his father Dan and brother Fred, always remained a boy at heart.

Kendall Lynch with his niece Betty, who clearly adored him. Circa 1930.

Danny and Jack, the sons of Kendall Lynch, flank their grandfather Dan Lynch in this photograph taken at the Lynch home near Green Lake in Seattle, Washington, circa 1945.

Twelve: Ray Lynch & the Final Years

A month before the Lynch Brothers wrapped up at Grand Coulee, old Dan Lynch, the first diamond-driller in the family, was visiting his daughter Harriet and her family in Ellensburg, Washington. His son-in-law, Billy Biner, was the brewmaster at the Ellensburg Brewery. The date was December 7, 1941 and word had just reached the mainland about the Japanese attack on Pearl Harbor. Talk around the dinner table that night included the possibility that Dan's two grandsons, Bill and Bob Biner, would have to fight the Japanese. Dan Lynch told the boys not to worry.

"We'll just drop a few bombs," proclaimed the old Irishman, "and the whole island will burn up."

It was actually a fairly prophetic statement, if nearly four years premature. Bill and Bob Biner did go to war, but not against the Japanese. They fought in the European Theatre of action, as a bombardier and belly gunner respectively. They flew in a combined 101 missions and both boys wrote dozens of letters home to Grandpa Lynch and other family members with details about training camps and actual combat flights. Both boys made it home safely at the end of the war and their letters are the subject of the book *Brewmaster's Bombardier & Belly Gunner.*

The Skagit River dams and the Grand Coulee were the two most famous projects that the Lynch Brothers Diamond Drilling Company engaged in, but this company, despite its humble setting and staff, was never a one-trick pony.

The brothers were not of a mind to focus on one job at a time. They had crews all over the West working on multiple projects. Each project was usually supervised by one of the brothers; by a trusted employee like Dusty Rhoades or Charles Sellers; or by a son or nephew; like Fred Lynch, Kendall Lynch or Raymond Lynch. In 1938 the Lynch Brothers initiated the drilling for what would become the Shasta Dam. They were hired by Frank Crowe through the Bureau of Reclamation. And in 1939 they signed a contract with the Alaska-Pacific Consolidated Mining Company for coal exploration on the Anthracite Ridge.

William "Bill" George Lynch (1880-1936), first president of the Lynch Brothers Diamond Drilling Company.

During the Great Depression the Lynch Brothers tried to venture beyond drilling by opening a miniature golf course in Seattle. Perhaps they concluded that amateur golfers, who couldn't afford the real links, might settle for a fix on a mini course instead. It didn't work. Also during those bleak days brother Bill was known to wander the streets of Seattle offering to buy lunch for destitute men. Bill was gaunt and looked like he could use a meal himself and some of the down-and-out he tried to help brushed him off as a joker. On January 21, 1936, the Good Samaritan was rushed to Seattle's Providence Hospital. He was suffering from a "heart ailment." Five days later the president of Lynch Brothers and the 2nd youngest son of Cornelius and Bridget Lynch died. He was just 55 years old. He left no children. His first wife, Laura Shannon, like Bill the child of Irish immigrants, had died three years earlier. Buried at the foot of her grave in Seattle's Calvary Cemetery is little Patricia Biner, infant child of Harriet Lynch Biner and granddaughter of Dan Lynch.

Bill Lynch, with second wife Jean Muldowney, shortly before his death.

While the attempt to start a miniature golf course didn't pan out, Dick and Pat had more success marketing the diamond drill bits patented by their nephew, Raymond Lynch. They formed the Diamond Bit Corporation of Seattle in 1938. Raymond and co-inventor Clarence Carpenter, applied for a patent the same year. The application, followed by one of the drawings, took up several pages. Excerpts of the application follow.

DIAMOND DRILL BIT ...Clarence E. Carpenter and Raymond C. Lynch

"Seattle, Wash., assignors to Diamond Bit Corporation, Seattle, Wash., a corporation of Washington Application October 20, 1938, Serial No. 235,978
Claim. (01. 255-1) This invention relates to improvements in diamond tools and is specifically directed to the provision of a diamond drill bit particularly adapted for drilling holes which do not require the taking of core.
It is one of the objects of the present invention to provide a diamond drill bit which is so constructed that it will completely bore or drill a hole in hard rock and not merely form an annular cut with a central core which must be cut away.
More specifically the present invention provides a diamond drill bit in which the working face of the bit is concaved, the diamonds set in this concave face pointing toward the axis of rotation of the bit. All of the diamonds are offset from the center line of the bit so as to sweep" or have movement about the axis of rotation of the bit as the bit is rotated, to provide the desired cutting operation. By providing this concaved face it will be apparent that the edges of the bit are in advance and while there are no diamonds at the exact bit center, nevertheless they are in such close proximity to the axis of rotation that we are assured that all of the rock formation."

The application went on for several pages, detailing the new diamond bit in excruciating detail, as evidenced here by the conclusion.

"Bit, said waterway extending to the outside of the bit and along the outside face of the bit, and diamonds set in said concaved working face and extending toward the axis of rotation 01' the hit, all of said diamonds being offset radially from the axis of rotation of the bit, some of said diamonds being disposed intermediate the inner end of the waterway and the axis of rotation of the bit."

- RAYMOND C. LYNCH, CLARENCE E. CARPENTER.

The language of the patent application is a "bit" hard to follow but is an interesting example of the detailed process. Raymond Lynch and Clarence Carpenter worked together on other diamond drill bit patents and in 1946 registered patents for a hydraulic power transmission mechanism and a drill rod that improved the joining of sections of rods used in diamond drilling.

A drawing that Lynch and Carpenter submitted with the drill bit patent application is reproduced on the following page.

One of the first contracts for the new drill bits was with the Alaska-Pacific Consolidated Mining Company which had already hired the company to drill for gold deposits. The Lynch Brothers also did the core drilling for the New Kettle Falls Bridge on the Columbia River in 1939 and 1940. And while these projects were underway they still had a big crew at Grand Coulee. Their success was even noticed "back home" in Michigan's Upper Peninsula.

According to a feature story on Dick Lynch in the September 15, 1940 issue of *The Escanaba (Michigan) Daily Press*, the Lynch Brothers drilled "Over 250,000 feet in the Coulee dam project." A slight exaggeration as it was actually closer to 210,000 feet.

The article quoted Dick Lynch as saying that the Coulee project was, "Much larger than even the Panama Canal and enough concrete is (was) used with construction to build a highway from the Pacific Coast to New York and back with plenty left over."

The Daily Press went on to explain the process of diamond drilling.

"Foundation drilling enables the geologists to take tests of the various rock and mineral formations at different depths and obviates the necessity of blasting which upsets the foundations. Cores varying in size from an inch to thirty six inches are taken. When the tests holes are completed the test holes are tightly sealed with concrete."

"Diamond drilling, of course, has played a most important role in the development of the Upper Peninsula and it was in the Copper Country where some of the first diamond drills were used in this country."

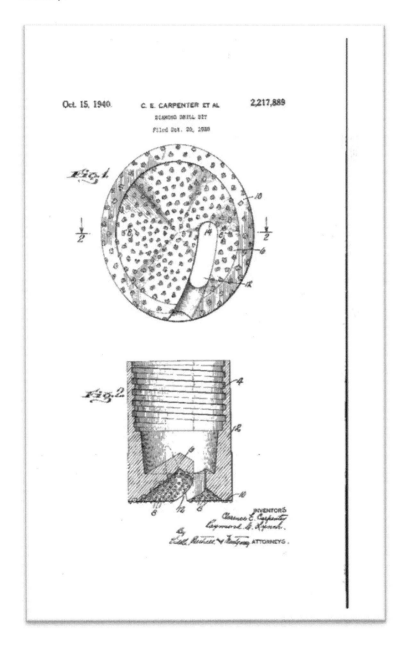

The paper referred to the Lynch Brothers as, "One of the largest diamond drill companies in this country, (having done) exploratory work from South America to the Arctic Circle, in the wilds of northern Canada and Alaska and in all parts of our vast northwest. Much of the work being done now by the Lynch brother's drilling units is foundation testing and their projects have included all of the larger dams in the northwest."

"Even today many people do not realize that diamond drills are so called because diamonds are used in them as the cutting bit to penetrate the rock...Mr. Lynch said that until about twelve years ago white diamonds costing $180 or more per carat were used exclusively. However, experiments showed that black diamonds or borts were almost as useful and could be had at a fraction of the cost of white diamonds."

"Lynch's company has done practically every type of drilling, seeking gold, coal, tin, copper and even oil, since they completed their first project in Alaska's Yukon country many years ago. One single project for the Kennecott copper mines in Alaska was in operation for over sixteen years and was only recently completed."

Dick and Sabina owned a summer home near Silverdale, Washington on the Puget Sound's Hood Canal. Aptly named "End-O-Kare," it became a welcome retreat for the entire Lynch clan. Bridgy Lynch was accustomed to the small life of Republic and Seattle must have been a difficult transition for her. She loved her outings to Hood Canal where she could tend to flowers and commune with nature in her own natural world of silence. One of the pleasures for the extended family visiting End-O-Kare was the good cheer and gentle love of Aunt Bridgy, to say nothing of the maternal generosity and compassion from Aunt Sabina.

Bridgy Lynch was just 60 years old, and seemingly in good health, when, on August 20, 1939, she had a heart attack and died while attending a picnic at Sandy Beach on Seattle's Lake Washington. Her brothers, Dan, Dick and Pat, buried her near their brother Bill in Calvary Cemetery. Besides the three brothers in Seattle, only

Con, living in Los Angeles, and Mary, in Wisconsin, survived as America entered World War II.

Dick Lynch with his sisters Mary and Bridgy at his "End O' Kare" property near Silverdale on the Hood Canal in Washington.

Sabina and Mary Lynch McCarthy at "End O' Kare."

In 1942 the Lynch Brothers drilled the Turk Deposit in Stevens County, Washington which produced one and a half million tons of magnesite. The following year they signed a contract with Bureau of Mines to drill a lignite (brown coal) deposit near Toledo, Lewis County, Washington. The actual drilling for the lignite took place between March and November of 1945 and involved both churn-drilling for the overburden and two and an eighth-inch diamond core-drilling for the strata exploration. The combined drilling amounted to 4,278 total feet. The Bureau of Mines, in a report written by Albert Toenge, Louis Turnbull and Willard Cole for the Department of Interior, had high praise for the Lynch Brothers.

"The drillers were experienced and cooperated faithfully in securing good samples."

The report went on to say that borium bits were used to drill though clay while the bort diamond bits were successful in coring lignite. The report also revealed how much the Bureau's engineers relied on the experience of the Lynch Brothers.

"The interpretation of drilling results required the samplers to record depth of holes when changes in the strata occurred. These changes were indicated by the drillers' experience in the operation of the drill in different formations and by observing return water and character of the cuttings. This record was designated as the 'driller's log.' "

The Lynch Brothers did the initial core drilling for what was originally the Foster Creek Dam near Wenatchee, Washington in the spring of 1944. Although the company completed its job in a timely fashion, it would be another 35 years before the dam itself was complete under the new name of Chief Joseph Dam.

On September 10, 1945, the youngest sibling, Patrick Lynch, who had started the diamond drilling company with his brother Dick in 1914, died in his home at 325 Olympic Place in Seattle after a long battle with stomach cancer. He was just 60 years old. Pat left behind his wife Florence Lowney Lynch and an adopted son, Larry. In *The Seattle-Times* obituary the work on Shasta,

Bonneville, Grand Coulee and Skagit was mentioned. It also said that Patrick Lynch was a member of the Arctic Club, Washington Athletic Club, Knights of Columbus and the Juneau Lodge 420 of B.P.O.E. (Benevolent and Protective Order of Elks).

The home of Pat & Florence Lynch in Seattle, Washington.

Jack Lynch, son of Kendall, remembered his Uncle Pat as a friendly, handsome man who took him to baseball games when he was a boy. He also remembers that, like his own father, Pat Lynch, the godfather of Fritzi Bernazani, was a heavy drinker.

Between June 17 and Oct 22, 1945, with Dick still at the reigns, the Lynch Brothers conducted core drilling for the Alaska Railroad Eska Coal Mine under contract with the Bureau of Mines. In March, 1946, they were awarded the contract for foundation exploration at the proposed Paradise Dam on the Clark River in Sanders County, Montana. Also in 1946 the Lynch Brothers were one of three companies invited to bid on core drilling for seven prospective dam sites in Oregon's Willamette Basin, including one near Hoskins on the Luckiamute River and one near Wren on the Mary's River. Neither dam was built.

The company also drilled for dam foundations on Oregon's wild Rogue River. Several dams were built but most have since been removed, restoring the Rogue to its near pristine state as one of America's most beautiful wild rivers.

Irish green was the color for the Lynch Brothers in 1947. That year they won a contract to do core drilling for the Green Peter Dam near Sweet Home, Oregon. However, they lost a bid to Vivian Brothers of Kellogg, Idaho to do the foundation exploration for what would become the Howard A. Hanson Dam on the Eagle Gorge of Washington's Green River. It was a rare defeat for the Lynch Brothers as they were underbid by just $770.

In December 1947 and January 1948, the Lynch Brothers drilled at a limestone deposit on Marble Mountain, a few miles south of Grants Pass, Oregon. They were hired by Electro Metallurgical Company, which became part of Union Carbide. Although a fine deposit of limestone was confirmed by the Lynch Brothers, it was not enough to commence extraction. The earlier removal of a rural railroad line to the nearest town of Wilderville made transportation of the limestone prohibitively expensive.

Death came to Richard T. "Dick" Lynch on June 25, 1951, at the age of 72. Dick had no offspring of his own, but left behind three adopted children who mourned him; Raymond Lynch and Tillie's daughters by Moses Aubrey; Marjorie and Catherine. Dick was remembered as easy-going, nice to everyone, and the "main man" of the Lynch Brothers. His beloved wife lived without him for ten years. Dick and Sabina Lynch rest, side by side, in Seattle's Calvary Cemetery, not far from the grave of Sabina's dearest friend, Tillie.

Shortly after the death of Dick Lynch, his namesake, Dick Lynch II, son of Raymond, would go off to fight in the Korean War as part of the U.S. Navy. He survived the experience and returned to Washington to become a member of the Lynch Brothers.

After the deaths of Bill, Pat and Dick Lynch, ownership of the diamond drilling company was transferred to Raymond Lynch and Charles Sellers, a longtime employee of the company. Under the guidance of Ray Lynch the company remained active, particularly in drilling for the foundation of dams, but also for minor jobs that no one could have expected. From the late 1940s through the early 1960s the Lynch Brothers were willing to supply the drilling toward any dream; even if it meant drilling for buried treasure.

A few years after Lewis and Clark reached the Oregon coast, New York industrialist John Jacob Astor sent two parties, one by land and one by sea, to establish a trading post at what became Astoria; the oldest settlement in Oregon. Those who crossed the continent arrived as living skeletons, but largely survived. Those who sailed around South America aboard the *Tonguin* faced a much more deadly future.

The captain of the *Tonguin*, Jonathan Thorn, was a regular Captain Bligh who demanded complete obedience from his passengers and crew. After dropping some off at the mouth of the Columbia he continued north to trade with coastal Indians. He was not a good negotiator. After he unceremoniously tossed a chief overboard into Vancouver Island's Nootka Bay, angry warriors boarded the ship and massacred Thorn and most of his crew. The following day the natives returned to size up their booty, unaware that the ship's clerk was hiding below deck ready to explode a barrel of gunpowder. This early version of a suicide bomber exacted a terrible revenge as the entire ship and all of its conquerors were blown to bits.

Among those lucky enough to have been left behind at Fort Astoria was a young Canadian fur trapper named Thomas McKay. McKay's father, Alexander, had perished with Thorn when the Indians attacked the ship in Nootka Bay. The younger McKay married a Chinook Indian woman named Timmee Tikul Concomly Tchinook. It was probably from his wife and her people that McKay heard about the legend of the Spanish treasure.

According to the oral history of both the Chinook and Tillamook tribes, a Spanish galleon had landed on the Oregon Coast near Neahkahnie Mountain in the late 1600s or early 1700s. As the story went the Spanish sailors scampered up the side of the mountain and buried a large chest. Then they sacrificed a black slave and buried him on top of the treasure to protect it from would be treasure hunters.

McKay was one of the first to seek the treasure and some think he found it. According to Finn J.D. John on his wonderfully quirky website *offbeatoregon.com*, McKay searched long and hard for the treasure. And then he "suddenly walked away from the mountain, quit his job and disappeared."

But historian J.A. Hussey in his book *Champoeg: Place of Transition* reveals that Thomas became the stepson of Dr. John McLoughlin, the "Father of Oregon" after his widowed mother of Canadian-Indian descent married McLoughlin. McKay was a well-known man in the Willamette Valley, where he purchased a piece of property and, according to John, "seemed oddly flushed with cash, not to the point of being flashy about it, but never worried about money either, and was quite generous with it among friends."

The possibility that McKay found the treasure and made off with it rarely deterred other treasure hunters from combing the earth beneath Neahkahnie Mountain. One of the first was a pioneer named Hiram Smith (1812-1876) who purchased land on the mountain, raised a family there and spent every spare moment digging for the elusive treasure.

Others would follow. Mysterious stone carvings were found and many thought they were clues to the location of the treasure. A tavern owner near the mountain found what appeared to be the handles to a very old chest on his property. A mystic followed her visions to where the treasure should be and came to the tavern owner's property - but no treasure was found.

After Hiram Smith passed away one of his sons, Patrick Henry Smith (1851-1928), continued the quest and before his death brought on an enterprising partner named Charlie Pike (1872-1955). Pike refused to give up and continued the futile search long after the death of Pat Smith. Pike hired a crew to dig as deep as they could and when they hit bedrock he hired the Lynch Brothers Diamond Drilling Company to search for caverns. And so it was in the year 1947 that the very company that had helped determine the site of the Grand Coulee Dam drilled for the legendary, and very likely fictitious, Spanish treasure of Neahkahnie Mountain.

The Lynch Brothers were able to confirm that a stream had been intentionally diverted on the mountain many years earlier; but they found no sign of a buried treasure. It has since been determined that an earthquake on the scale of 9.0 magnitude rocked the Oregon Coast in 1700, which could have diverted the creek and even disrupted the location of the treasure, if it had ever been there in the first place.

In the 1950s the Lynch Brothers resumed more conventional searches as they received contracts to help determine the best locations for The Dalles Dam in Oregon; Albeni Falls Dam in Idaho; Glen Canyon Dam in Arizona and the Casad Dam in Washington.

The Glen Canyon Dam on the Colorado River created the great reservoir known as Lake Powell. But Glen Canyon was a tricky dam to build. After suitable bedrock was located it was discovered that one bearing cliff was too narrow to withstand the pressure of the proposed reservoir. The creative mind of Ray Lynch came up with a novel solution. Ray bolted the cliff to a much thicker cliff that stood but a few meters away. After the cliffs were bolted together a framework was built between the two and reinforced concrete filled the space. The dam was then constructed and holds back Lake Powell to this day.

Ray Lynch suffered from Undulant Fever, or Brucellosis, which he contracted as a young man after he consumed contaminated milk. The disease nagged him for the rest of his life and he was often bedridden when he would prefer to be on the job. But what bothered him most was that the disease eliminated him from consideration for the armed forces during World War II. Ironically, Ray would find the opportunity to serve his country after the war. In fact, he helped save the U.S. military from an embarrassing oversight.

Following World War II, the United States entered a "Cold War" with the Soviet Union as both countries engaged in a dangerous build-up of nuclear weapons. Hyper-paranoia seized America as citizens built underground bomb shelters; school children ducked and covered in worthless drills; and Senator Joe McCarthy went on a modern-day witch-hunt for communist sympathizers.

If citizens were going underground for safety it seemed logical that military installations do the same. The McCord Air Force Base near Tacoma, Washington decided to construct underground facilities. But after constructing thick concrete subterranean walls for barracks, offices, mess halls, etc., a glaring oversight was discovered. Contractors neglected to install tunnels between the rooms for water pipes and electrical conduit tubing.

The Lynch Brothers were called in to save the day. They bored holes through concrete and bedrock to connect each room with necessary services. But they didn't talk about their patriotic rescue of the McCord Air Force Base. In those days virtually everything was "top secret."

In 1952 the Lynch Brothers submitted a boring bid for the Rainier Ave overpass to the Lake Washington Floating Bridge. But Raymond's company was outbid by the ironically named Raymond Concrete Pile Company. However, the Lynch Brothers did win a contract to do exploratory drilling for a copper deposit near the north fork of Washington's Skokomish River for the Copper Mountain Mining Corporation of Princeton, BC. The job commenced in the summer of 1955.

Four years later they completed drilling for the Wenatchee Hydro Project (Rocky Reach Dam) in Washington and won a contract for the core drilling for Dam 2 of the Bull Run Watershed in Oregon. That dam, completed in 1962, currently provides drinking water for the Portland metropolitan area, and has a capacity of seven trillion gallons.

Also in 1956 the Lynch Brothers shared a contract with R.S. McClintock Co. of Spokane for the core drilling of the Boundary Dam on the Pend Orielle River in Washington. It was the same site where Kendall Lynch met his bride Grace Sullivan nearly 30 years earlier.

In the early 1960s the Lynch Brothers landed contracts for Hells Canyon Dam; Oxbow Dam; Brownlee Dam and Foster Dams (all in Oregon). Nevertheless, according to Mike Lynch, Raymond's son, with typical Lynch humor, recalled that the hydroelectric jobs begin to "dry up" in the 1960s. At that time Raymond Lynch transferred management of the company to Jim Muldowney, the brother-in-law of the late Bill Lynch, first president of the company.

"When Jim took over," Mike recollected, "they were doing very minor concrete drilling jobs." But the company also did exploratory drilling for the proposed Satsop Nuclear Power Plant. Construction of that controversial facility, which was never finished, occurred long after the company was sold.

Raymond Lynch decided to sell the company in 1964. At first, according to Raymond's son Tim, he tried to sell it directly to the Roman Catholic Archdiocese of Austin, Texas. Raymond's wife Juanita was opposed to the deal. But the archdiocese was only interested in large projects and the mainstay of the Lynch Brothers had always been their willingness to take on small jobs. In June, 1964, the R.S. McClintock Diamond Drill Company of Spokane, Washington, headed by W.J. Whinnen, purchased and absorbed the remaining contracts of the Lynch Brothers Diamond Drilling Company. But the bishops in Texas that Juanita Lynch mistrusted would still realize a profit from the sale. A major interest in R.S. McClintock was Equity & Capital Corporation of

New York City, which leased much of the McClintock equipment from the Roman Catholic Archdiocese of Austin, Texas.

Fritzi Biner Bernazani has found memories of her mom's cousin Raymond; who seemed more like an uncle to her.

"Cousin Ray was one of the nicest men you could ever meet, I loved him. He used to pick me up at the bus station in Seattle and take me out to Aunt Sabina's and Uncle Dick's with my cousin Katherine, his daughter, who was a year younger. He always took us out to eat and once took us to "The Twin Teepees" which I thought was terribly exotic! At any rate he always made my trips memorable and his wife Nita was also a sweetheart. We visited them late in life, not long before Ray died and Nita was recovering from a broken arm. She joked that she "fell off a bar stool"."

Postcard showing Seattle's historic, and now gone, Twin Teepees, where Ray Lynch would entertain his children and young cousins.

The end was tough for Raymond Lynch. He had dedicated his entire life to the Lynch Brothers. He was behind many of the bids, and the diamond bits, that made the Lynch Brothers so successful. His son, Mike Lynch, recalled that his dad "had an uncanny ability to calculate bids and get jobs done within budget. Dad was a practical and methodical person. He had an education that ended at the 8th grade but he had business savvy and a college educated engineer's mind. I would see him in evenings, sitting down at the table with large pieces of paper and a ruler and designing actual drill equipment that Lynch Bros and other companies would later adopt. Just good business sense I think made the difference."

But the final difference was death.

Earle "Dusty" Rhoades died on July 28, 1971 at the age of 78.
Raymond Lynch died of cancer on September 11, 1980, having
outlived his sisters by 70 years. His cousin Fred Lynch, the last of
the early diamond drillers, died in 1982. No remnant of the Lynch
Brothers Diamond Drilling Company, save the memories of a few
aging employees from the later years, exists today.

Raymond Lynch, with his beautiful wife,
Juanita Edith Leafdahl, who is also shown below.

Raymond Cornelius Lynch, son of Timothy Lynch and Tillie Trenerry and adopted son of Dick Lynch and Sabina Norman. Ray was the owner of the Lynch Brothers Diamond Drilling Company in its final years. Here he is in front of the company office in Seattle, at the time of its sale to R.S. McClintock Company of Spokane.

Raymond Cornelius Lynch (1905-1980) and Juanita Leafdahl (1908-1985) had five children: Richard (1930-1971); Kathryn (1932-2004); Mary, who died as an infant in 1939; Raymond Timothy and Michael Bruce Lynch. Tim and Mike Lynch shared valuable insights into the Lynch Brothers Co. and their remarkable father for this history. Both men, like so many descendants of the Lynches, are educators, and Mike Lynch has a bit of an international following on YouTube as "Ukulele Mike."

Thirteen: An Irish Clan Drifts Apart

A 1907 postcard sent to Fred Lynch from his cousin Loretta in Gladstone, Michigan shows a brand new horse-drawn carriage, which Loretta calls "our bus," completely enclosed with windows. It would suggest that Dennis McCarthy, the husband of Mary Lynch, was doing just fine as a railroad dispatcher. Nevertheless, Dennis and Mary, along with five of their children, joined the Lynch family in Seattle around 1920. Two sons worked for the Lynch Brothers. But it seems the climate of the Pacific Northwest caused some conflict. In 1930 Mary and Dennis, with their two youngest sons, were in Fond du Lac, Wisconsin. But this too was temporary. Mary and Dennis returned to Seattle where Dennis, minus one leg from diabetes, managed an auto accessory store. He died on January 20, 1934 at the age of 66, and is buried in Seattle's Calvary Cemetery.

In the 1940s the widow Mary moved to Greenleaf, Wisconsin to be near some of her children. She died at the age of 84 on May 17, 1953 in Green Bay, where her son Claude was a dentist and her son William an attorney. Another son, Richard, was a Catholic priest and may have presided over his mother's funeral.

The descendants of Mary Lynch have scattered with the wind and are no longer in contact with their Lynch family. All of Mary's children are long gone. And of those children, the author of this book could only locate descendants of one. Mary's daughter Loretta spent most of her life in Stambaugh, Iron River, Michigan. She was a school teacher and taught the immigrant children of miners that hailed from many different countries and spoke many languages. Loretta's husband, William J. Kofmehl, served as the town doctor for 50 years. Komfehl Street in Iron River is named for the popular couple. Loretta had one child, Joan Komfehl Sacia, who ended up in Portland, Oregon, where she earned a master's degree in social work. After William Komfehl died, Loretta McCarthy Komfehl spent her final years near her daughter in Portland. She died in 1981. Her daughter Joan Sacia, died in 2000, but Joan's children, Bill Sacia, Jennie Robbins and Marie Hill, still live in the Pacific Northwest.

Loretta McCarthy, first cousin to Fred, Harriet, Ken and Ray Lynch, with her husband, Dr. William Komfehl and daughter Joan.

Loretta's sister Mary married Joseph Weins and had three children; Theodore, Loretta and Mary. After her husband died Mary Weins moved with her children to Green Bay to be near her mother and brothers. She died in 1980 at the age of 89.

Mary Lynch McCarthy, the sister of the Lynch brothers, with her husband Dennis McCarthy. Note that Dennis is missing a leg, which had been amputated due to complications from diabetes. Sitting next to Dennis is Loretta McCarthy Komfehl and her daughter Joan. In the back are the sons of Mary & Dennis; Raymond, Dennis, Richard, Claude, John and William. The photograph on the previous page shows Mary & Dennis McCarthy many years earlier with all of their children, including daughter Mary Weins, the only one missing from the reunion photograph.

Con Lynch was 83 when he died in Los Angeles on January 14, 1956, having outlived his wife Jane McKenna by eight years, as well as all of his siblings. Con had moved to San Gabriel in the Los Angeles area in 1924. After retiring from the mines he worked for a dairy and later as an electrical engineer. Con and wife Jane, aka "Jenny", shared an acre of land in South San Gabriel with son Howard and daughter Mary "Doll" Philothea. Con's granddaughter Susan Twomey recalls three homes and no fences on the property. "I remember feeling like I actually lived in three houses then," Susan relates, "We all came and went so freely between them, at the cost of preferred privacy sometimes." The

McKenna brothers (siblings of Con's wife) built a house for Con's son Neil Lynch a few miles away, next door to the brother of Carol Saunders, Neil's wife. Neil and Carol Lynch had two daughters: Sharon Marie (1940-1999), and Sheila Eileen.

The three surviving children of Con Lynch; Howard, Philothea (Doll) and Cornelius (Neil), all died within three years of each other in the 1970s. Howard had married Marjorie Bob. They had no children but their niece, Susan Twomey, recalls that "Howard always wanted to work in the mines...to be a mining engineer like his father. He did work some in the mines starting at the age of 10, but his father wanted him to have a better life. Howard worked all of his life for the telephone company, AT&T/Pacific Bell at the time."

Doll Lynch

The beautiful Doll Lynch, who married John Twomey in 1930, was a public school teacher. "She loved to teach," said Susan, herself a music teacher in Eureka, California. Doll had a special interest in American History. "Every summer we travelled somewhere to explore this country and its history. She also seemed to know the name of every plant and flower she saw. She was very proud of the fact that she went to UCLA and got her teaching credential there in 1925."

Doll and John Twomey had three daughters: Jane Ann, born in 1936; Sally Jean (1939-2003) and Susan.

Neil Lynch was a popular teacher of agriculture at Pierce College in Los Angeles. His daughter Sheila Lynch Brooks shared that he was "Much loved and respected in his career, his devotion to his students was an inspiration. I was honored when he donned the cap and gown to help lead the procession when I graduated from Pierce in 1965. He loved going to school every day of his life, and it was in watching him that I decided to teach also."

Sheila, who is married to Dennis Brooks, became an educator and spent 27 years as a 4th grade teacher in Connecticut. But like so many in the Lynch clan her life was also filled with unexpected tragedy. Her father Neil Lynch, was tragically killed by a drunk driver on February 26, 1975, shortly after his retirement from Pierce College. And Sheila's highly decorated son, Lt. Colonel Timothy Brooks, died of cancer at the age of 37 and is buried in Arlington National Cemetery. But the Con Lynch family continues to expand through Sheila's offspring. Timothy and his wife Kim Johnston had four children; Meghan, Brian, John, and Stephen. Sheila's oldest daughter Maureen and husband Robert Ross are the parents of Alicia and Brett. Son Neil and wife Michelle Barr are the parents of Jack, Morgan, Abigail, and Samuel, and her daughter Ellen and husband Keith Suarino have two sons, Peter and Kyle.

As the years passed by Mate Kendall Lynch, who suffered from diabetes, weakened in health. Dan tried to keep her blood sugar in check by faithfully administering insulin injections every day. Mate's helplessness was enough to keep Dan close to home in the Green Lake neighborhood of Seattle.

According to his granddaughter, Fritzi, Dan did most of the cleaning and cooking and tried to make life easier for Mate, which included affixing small wheels on her favorite chair so that she could roll around their home without having to get up. Nevertheless, she would accompany Dan to visit her children and grandchildren in places like Ellensburg, Washington and John Day, Oregon in her final years.

Daniel Samuel Lynch, who introduced his younger brothers to the diamond drilling business, then worked for them as a supervisor of drilling operations, lived to be 84 years old. The first of the Lynch family born in America, Dan died on November 27, 1951 in Seattle. By then two of his daughter Harriet's children had given him six great-grandchildren. His seventh great-grandchild, the fourth child of Betty Biner Fulton, was born on December 3, 1951; less than a week after his death. She was named Mariette, in honor of Dan's surviving wife Mate.

Dan Lynch loved his wife Mate until death did they part.

The "invalid" Mate had somehow outlived the doting Dan; but not for long. In her final days she reported visits from her departed husband. She "saw" him standing in her doorway checking in on her. Mate died on January 13, 1952, less than two months after Dan; a final testament to the fact that she could not live without him. They are buried side by side and lie near Dick and Sabina in Seattle's Calvary Cemetery.

In fact, Seattle's Calvary Cemetery is the final resting place of thirteen members of the Lynch clan, including Dan, Mate, Dick, Sabina, Tillie, Bill, Bridgy, Fred and Mollie Lynch, and Betty Biner Fulton, the first grandchild of Dan and Mate.

Tim Lynch, son of Raymond and grandson of Timothy, recalled his uncles, Dan and Dick Lynch, as "jovial, tall leprechauns." By contrast he remembered his Aunt Mate Lynch as a cranky old woman. But Jack Lynch, a grandson of Mate, recalled that Dick, who was married to the saintly Sabina Norman, was "very fond of both Dan and Mate." And daughter-in-law Grace Lynch used the exact same words to describe her own parents regard for both Dan and Mate. Mate was a hard-boiled egg who was a bit soft inside. You just had to spend some time with her to figure out what made her smile.

Bob Biner, another grandchild of Dan and Mate, remembered living with his grandparents prior to his service as a belly gunner in World War II.

"While attending Seattle University in the winter semester of 1941, I lived with my grandparents, Daniel Samuel Lynch and Mariette Kendall Lynch. I had a room in the basement of their Green Lake District home at 2333 North 57th Street in Seattle, Washington. Their house was a one story house with two bedrooms, bath, living room, dining room, kitchen and a large enclosed front porch and a full basement. My sister, Fritz remembers sleeping on the front porch and taking hot bricks to bed to keep warm in the winter."

"My most vivid memories of Mariette Kendall Lynch were of the years she was crippled and sat in a chair on wheels in the dining

room. She was diabetic and her legs were not strong. She listened to the radio and read while sitting in her chair and did not leave the house very often. I don't recall her doing any housework. Her husband Daniel Lynch did the housework and cooking. He was a good cook. He made a very special coffeecake while smoking his pipe. The family said the coffeecake was so good because Grandpa's pipe ashes would fall on the top of the cake. He had a vegetable garden and I remember the rhubarb in his garden. He always grew sweet peas and nasturtiums. He did all the gardening. Everyone had a Victory Garden during World War II. Uncle Ken Lynch, their son, plowed his front yard and grew potatoes".

"Grandpa had a car, but he would ride the street car into town. The grocery store was within walking distant of their home. Grandpa would help Grandma take her urine test and he would give her insulin shots each day. He was very attentive toward her."

"My mother, Harriet Veronica Lynch Biner, and my sister, Fredericka Ann Biner (Fritzi) also lived with Grandpa and Grandma when my dad, Bill Biner, was moving from Ellensburg to Port Orchard between brewery jobs."

"After the War, while attending the University of Washington, I spent most Sunday afternoons at my grandparent's home. Grandpa Lynch always made a good Sunday dinner. On holidays Aunt Mollie Wittanen Lynch, wife of Fred Lynch, and Aunt Grace Sullivan Lynch, wife of Ken Lynch, would prepare dinners at grandpa and grandma's house. Grace and Ken's sons, Danny and Jack Lynch, would also attend these dinners."

Bob's final recollection was that, *"The Lynch family members were always very supportive of each other."*

The numerous living descendants of Daniel Samuel Lynch and his siblings have many different occupations, but none of them are miners.

Some of the descendants of those Irish miners, who mined the earth from Waterford to the Upper Peninsula; from Butte to Alaska, continue to practice the Catholic faith, but most are only vaguely aware of the Irish blood, sweat and tears that made their lives possible.

Irish immigrants like the Lynch clan were forced to leave their ancestral homes and literally carve out of the earth a new life in America. But they remained proud of their heritage and despite being constantly on the move, strived to keep it alive. Today most Americans of Irish descent celebrate Irish heritage only on St. Patrick's Day.

Like the Irish of the 19th century, those of us who are descendants of Irish immigrants have departed on an exodus as well. But it is an exodus from our past. As we move on with our own life adventures, our family histories are left with the old, or lost with the dead. The goal of this brief history is to help save some roots in one Irish clan from withering away completely, even if it is just a reprieve for a generation or two.

With just oral tradition Native Americans carried the stories of their ancestors for scores of generations. We might yet learn something from the indigenous people of this spacious land that lured our own ancestors from their ancient place of birth. We have far more tools at our disposal to carry on family history and therefore little excuse to dismiss our ancestors as irrelevant to our lives today. For all of us surely must feel, if deep inside, that they were not only relevant, but essential to our own existence.

As the author James Baldwin observed...
"The great force of history comes from the fact that we carry it within us, are unconsciously controlled by it...and it is literally present in all we do."

ADDENDUM

Many more great-grandchildren of Dan and Mate would come into the world following the birth of their first, Barbara Ann Biner, in 1946. Their son Fred had no children and just one of Kendall's two sons, Jack, who married Mary Jo Bruner, had two children of his own; Therese, born in 1961 and Dan, born in 1963. Therese is the mother of Olivia Lynch, and Dan, who is married to Melanie Richardson, is the father of Anna, Jack and Sean Lynch.

Harriet, the only daughter of Dan and Mate, was the mother of six children, four of whom survived infancy and produced 25 grandchildren for the beloved "Nanny" Biner, who died in 1978.

Granddaughter Betty Biner Fulton had ten children (all of them born in Portland, Oregon) and they in turn have produced 18 children of their own and, as of this writing, seven grandchildren: the great-great-great grandchildren of Dan and Mate Lynch.

Betty's offspring with Charlton Paschal Fulton are as follows:

William Henry Fulton, born 1947, married to Diane Sanders and the father of Charlton Fulton II.

Charlene Patricia Fulton, born 1948, married to Charles Collora and the mother of Andrew (married to Melissa Mascara), Alicia, Nicole, Mariette and Jeanne. Alicia and husband Brian Meza are the parents of Noah and Balin; daughter Nicole and husband John Wood are the parents of Nina and Caroline Betty (born on the birthday of Betty Biner Fulton).

Charles John Fulton, born in 1949.

Mariette Fulton, named after Mate Lynch, was born in 1951. Married to Chuck Olson, she is the mother of Erik (married to Talia Schwartz) and Hattie Olson. Hattie is named in honor of Harriet Lynch Biner, the daughter of Dan Lynch.

Leslie Ann Fulton, born in 1953, married to Bill Boniface and the mother of Dan Liz and Erin Boniface. Dan and wife Erica Walker are the parents of Beckham Boniface, and Liz and husband Shawn Bookey have two children, Gwynne and Oliver.

Joseph Edward Fulton, born in 1954, the author of this book, married to Debra Hascall and the father of three children, Chloe (married to Blake Martin), Leland (partner Megan Janssen) and Rhea (partner Jonathan Haase).

Daniel Stephen Fulton (named in honor of Dan Lynch), born in 1956, married to Beth Marcotte and the father of Nathan (married to Valerie Vorderlandwehr), Alexander and Parker Fulton.

Robert Joseph Fulton, born in 1958, married to Lauren Mack and the father of Olivia Fulton.

Frederick Peter Fulton (named in honor of Fred Lynch), born in 1960, and married to Rose Trentacoste.

Thomas Anthony Fulton, born in 1963, married to Jenn Drueke.

William Daniel Biner, grandson of Dan Lynch, married Maxine Gray and had four daughters:

Barbara Ann Biner, born 1946, married David Jimenez and is the mother of Dominic, (married to Karen Lawson and the father of Lola), and Christina Jimenez.

Susan Louise Biner, born 1949, married Terrance Burke and is the mother of William Burke.

Karen Lynn Biner, born 1950.

Joan Michelle Biner, born 1957, is the mother of three children, Kyle, Jamie and Stacy, with Neil Beckman. Joan is also the mother of Stephen and Robert Tucker from a previous marriage. Robert is married to Stephanie Marie Deleo.

Robert Joseph Biner, grandson of Dan Lynch, married Louise Andos and has three children:

Timothy Robert Biner, born 1964.

Mary Louise Biner, born 1966.

William Joseph Biner, born 1970, married to Rachel Perez and the father of Isabella and Olivia.

Fredericka (Fritzi) Biner, granddaughter of Dan Lynch, and named in honor of Fred Lynch, is married to Paul Bernazani and has a large family. Her children are:

John William Bernazani (1954-1989)

Joseph Anthony Bernazani, born 1956, married to Margaret Bedford and the father of Anthony, Melissa and the late Sara Bernazani.

Mary Clare Bernazani, born 1957, married to John Webster and the mother of Matthew Moore, married to Nicole McCarthy, and Eric Bernazani. Eric is married to Marina Sizow and has two children: Natalia Fredericka and Dmitri Benjamin.

James Patrick Bernazani, born 1958, married to Julia Ann Jordan. David Paul Bernazani, born 1959.

Elizabeth Ann Bernazani, born 1960, married to Wayne Harper and the mother of Kevin and Brian Harper.

Rita Louise Bernazani, born 1961, married to Benton Field, and the mother of Alicia (married to Bryceon Shulman), Rachel, Erica and Daniel Field.

Daniel Charles Bernazani, born 1962, married to Krissy Hearn. He is the father of Angela and Nicolas Bernazani.

Chronology of Lynch Brothers Mining & Drilling History

1865 -1900 – Irish immigrant Cornelius Lynch, Sr. works in the copper and iron boomtowns of Michigan's Upper Peninsula. First born son Michael killed in accident. Other sons follow father into mining industry.

1897 – Dan Lynch (first son born in America) becomes diamond drill supervisor for Sullivan Brothers Machinery Co. in Dickinson County, Michigan (iron).

1901 – Dan Lynch becomes diamond drill supervisor for Sullivan Brothers Machinery Co in Hancock, Michigan (copper).

1900-1910 –Tim, Con and Dick Lynch work in the mining boomtown of Butte, Montana. Tim killed in accident. John "Jack" Lynch moves to Great Falls, Montana, works in Barker Mine.

1902-1904 – Dan serves as a mining engineer at the Isabella Gold Mine in Cripple Creek, Colorado and the Silent Friend Mine in Leadville.

1907 – Dan supervises drilling operation for United Verde Works in Jerome, Arizona.

1907-1911 – Dan supervises drilling operations at Britannia Beach, BC. Son Fred works with him.

1907 – Pat Lynch supervises drill crew for Sullivan brothers in Iron River, Michigan.

1908-1924 – Con Lynch works at mines in Tombstone, Arizona; Northern Mexico; Idaho; Butte, Montana and with his brothers in Republic, Washington. Con is the last Lynch to leave Butte, Montana.

1910-1911 – Pat Lynch supervises drill crew for Sullivan brothers in Chile.

Circa 1911 – Dan Lynch supervises drilling in West Africa.

Circa 1912 – Pat and possibly other Lynch Brothers work on Panama Canal.

(An article in the 1930s suggests that the Lynch Brothers also worked in Brazil, Cuba and Finland).

1912-1915- Dan Lynch supervises drilling jobs in Phoenix, BC (copper) and at Curlew and Republic, WA (gold).

Circa 1912 – Pat and Dick Lynch move to Juneau, Alaska. Nephew Fred works with them on some jobs.

1913 – John Michael "Jack" Lynch dies in Great Falls, Montana.

1914 – Dick and Pat Lynch form the Lynch Brothers Diamond Drilling Company in Juneau, Alaska. Will Lynch, back in Minnesota, provides financial support and becomes president of the company.

1914-1917 – Lynch Bros. drill for the Perseverance Gold Mine near Juneau, completing over 75,000 feet of drill holes and establishing their reputation in the diamond drilling business.

1916- Lynch Bros. drill 1,680 ft. horizontal hole for Alaska Gold belt Co. It was a record for Alaska and the 2nd deepest horizontal hole ever drilled at the time. The record was held by E.J. Longyear Co at, ironically, the Quincy Mine in Hancock, Michigan.

1917 – Lynch Bros. drill for Gould & Curry Company and for Alaska Treadwell Gold Mining Company.

1917 through the 1930s- The Lynch Bros. continue long-term contracts in Alaska including; Kennecott copper mine, at the time the largest copper mine in the world; Jualin gold mine; the Ellamar copper mines near Valdez; the Latouche copper mine and the El Capitan marble quarries. Fred Lynch, son of Dan, is in charge of the crew at El Capitan.

1918- Lynch Brothers Diamond Drilling Company headquarters moved from Juneau to Seattle.

1919-1922 – The Lynch Bros. complete their first major dam project, to determine the sites of the Diablo and Gorge Dams for Seattle City Lights on the treacherous upper Skagit River in the North Cascades. They drilled to find at least 250 uninterrupted feet of bedrock before any dam could be built. This was the contract that led to jobs on most of the dams built in the Pacific Northwest over the next forty years.

1920 – Drilling for copper for Spider & Northern Light Group near Prince Rupert, BC. Cornelius Lynch, Sr. dies in Republic, Michigan.

1921 – The brothers send a drilling crew for oil exploration near Medford, Oregon.

1921- 22 -Oil exploration for British Columbia Provincial Government near Peace River in northern B.C.

1921 – Oil exploration for Seattle Inland Company near Prosser, Washington.

1921 – Drilled for gold at the Premier Mines near Stewart, BC for Alquacuin Syndicate of Belgium.

1922 – Lynch Bros. drill for the Lake Cushman dam site near Tacoma.

1923- Drill for oil exploration for the Consolidated Oil & Development Syndicate of Minneapolis and Duluth near Moberly Lake in northern British Columbia.

1925 – Pat Lynch supervises more work in Panama.

1925- Lynch Bros. win contract for core drilling for what would become Dam 1 of the Bull Run Reservoir, which provides drinking water for the city of Portland, Oregon. The dam, completed in 1929, would impound 8.8 billion gallons of water.

1925 –Lawsuit against Lynch Brothers by Southern Oregon Exploration Company for alleged failure to fulfill an oil drilling contract ends in favor of the Lynch Brothers.

1926 – Lynch Bros. drill for the site of Glines Canyon Dam on the Elwha River near Port Angeles, WA.

1926-1927 - Brook and Federal Light & Traction Co. hire the Lynch Brothers to drill in the Young and Dunn Canyons near Chehalis, Washington to determine location of the proposed Cowlitz River Dam.

1929 -1930 – Northwest Electric Company hires the Lynch Brothers to drill for a proposed dam site on the Ariel River near Woodland, Washington and for the proposed Boulder Dam on the Lewis River.

1928-29 – Lynch Bros. drill for Cushman Dam #2 on the Skokomish River in Mason County, Washington.

April-Aug. 1929 – Fred Lynch supervises a driling job in Klamath County, Oregon.

Late 1920s through early 1930s – The Lynch Bros. supervise drilling operations for copper near Baker City, Oregon and for the Owyhee Dam on the Snake River.

1930 – Lynch Bros. drill for the site for the Merwin Dam in Cowlitz County, Washington.

1930s –Lynch Bros. supervise drill operations near Calgary, Alberta; Trail, B.C.; and on the Peace River, some 800 miles north of Edmonton, Alberta. Raymond Lynch, son of Tim and adopted son of Dick, patents special diamond drill bits for the company.

1932 – Lynch Bros. win contract from U.S. Government for 8,000 feet of core drilling in the Matanuska coal fields of Alaska.

1933 – 1942 - The Lynch Brothers Diamond Drilling Company awarded the coveted first contract for the mammoth Grand Coulee Dam in eastern Washington. They determine the site for the largest concrete structure ever built. Work for the Columbia Basin Commission, U.S. Bureau of Reclamation and private contractors. Meet FDR, who visits one of the drilling operations.

1934 – The Lynch Bros. core drill for the Bonneville Dam (Ruckles Slide area) on the Columbia River.

1934 – Exploratory drilling for gold at the Goo Goo claim in Ketchikan Mining District of Alaska which led to the formation of Evis Mining Corp.

1935 – Lynch Bros. drill for sulphur deposit on the summit of Washington's Mt. Adams for the Pacific Sulphur Company.

1935 – Contract from Seattle City Light for core drilling for Ruby Dam (later renamed Ross Dam).

1936 – Will Lynch, president of the Lynch Brothers, dies.

1936 - The Lynch Bros. drill for the Shasta Dam in California and for coal exploration on the Anthracite Ridge in Alaska.

1938 – Dick and Pat Lynch form the Diamond Bit Corporation of Seattle.

1939 – Lynch Bros. Diamond Bit Corp sign contract with Alaska-Pacific Consolidated Mining Company for drill bits.

1939-40 - Lynch Bros. Core drill for New Kettle Falls Bridge, Columbia River.

1940s – Lynch Bros. drill for proposed dam site on Oregon's Rogue River.

1942 – Lynch Bros. drill the Turk Deposit which produces one and a half million tons of magnesite in Stevens County, WA.

1943 – Lynch Bros. sign contract with Bureau of Mines to drill the Lignite (brown coal) deposit near Toledo, WA.

1944 – Lynch Bros. do core drilling for Foster Creek Dam in Washington (renamed Chief Joseph Dam).

1945 - Lynch Bros. drill for the Eska Coal Mine in Alaska.

1945 – Pat Lynch, youngest brother and co-founder of the company, dies.

1946 – Lynch Bros.is one of three companies invited to bid on core drilling for seven prospective dam sites in Oregon's Willamette Basin, including near Hoskins on Luckiamute River and near Wren on Mary's River.

1946 – Lynch Bros. win bid for foundation exploration for proposed Paradise Dam, Clark Fork River, Montana.

1946-47 - Exploratory drilling on limestone deposit near Grants Pass, Oregon for Electro Metallurgical Co. which became part of Union Carbide.

1947 – Lynch Bros. lose bid to Vivian Brothers of Kellogg, Idaho for Eagle Gorge Dam site. The company was rarely underbid.

1947 – Lynch Bros. win contract to do core drilling for the Green Peter Dam near Sweet Home, Oregon.

1947 – Lynch Bros. drill for Spanish treasure on Oregon's Neakahnie Mountain.

1949 – Win contract for foundation exploration for Columbia River Bridge (also known as Bridgeport Bridge) near Chief Joseph Dam.

1950s- Lynch Brothers Diamond Drilling Company, now under the leadership of Raymond Lynch and Charles Sellers, a longtime employee of the company, receive contracts for the drilling to determine sites of The Dalles Dam in Oregon; Albeni Falls Dam in Idaho; Glen Canyon Dam in Arizona and Casad Dam in Washington. They also drill for McCord Air Force Base underground facilities.

1951 – Both Dick and Dan Lynch pass away in Seattle, Washington.

1952 – Test-boring bid for Rainier Ave overpass to the Lake Washington Floating Bridge. Outbid by Raymond Concrete Pile Company. One of the few times the company was ever outbid.

1955 – Lynch Bros. drill for copper deposit near the north fork of the Skokomish River in Washington for the Copper Mountain Mining Co. of Princeton, B.C.

1956 – Con Lynch, the last of the Lynch Brothers, dies in Los Angeles at the age of 83.

1956 – Lynch Bros. complete drilling for Wenatchee Hydro Project (Rocky Reach Dam) in Washington.

1956- Lynch Bros. win contract for the core drilling for Dam 2 of the Bull Run Watershed in Oregon. The dam, completed in 1962, has a capacity of seven trillion gallons.

1958 – Kendall Lynch dies.

1961- Lynch Bros. share contract with R.S. McClintock Co. for core drilling of Boundary Dam on the Pend Orielle River in Washington.

1960s – The Lynch Bros. contract for drilling at Hells Canyon Dam; Oxbow Dam; Browlee Dam and Foster Dam (all in Oregon).

1964 – Raymond Lynch sells the Lynch Brothers Diamond Drilling Company to the R.S. McClintock Co. of Spokane which absorbs the remaining contracts.

1971 – Earle "Dusty" Rhoades, longtime Lynch Brothers supervisor, dies.

1980 – Raymond Lynch dies in Seattle, Washington.

1982 – Fred Lynch dies in Seattle, Washington.

1984 – Will D. "Bob" Jenkins, who worked for the Lynch Brothers in the 1920s, publishes Last Frontier of the North Cascades, which includes some anecdotal history of the Lynch Brothers work on the Skagit River Project.

1988 – Jim Muldowney dies in Seattle.

2014 – The 100th anniversary of the founding of the company and the 50th anniversary of its ending. Dam Right! The first history of the Lynch Brothers Diamond Drilling Company is published in Oregon.

Workers for the Lynch Brothers:
Family members 1st Generation:

Dan Lynch
Dick Lynch
Pat Lynch
Bill Lynch
Jim Muldowney (brother-in-law of Bill Lynch)
Mose Aubrey (2nd husband of Mrs. Tim Lynch)

Family members 2nd Generation:

Fred Lynch (son of Dan)
Kendall Lynch (son of Dan)
Raymond Lynch (son of Tim, adopted son of Dick)
Raymond McCarthy (son of Mary Lynch McCarthy)
Dennis McCarthy (son of Mary Lynch McCarthy)
James Sullivan (brother-in-law of Kendall Lynch)

Family members 3rd generation:

Bill Biner (son of Harriet Lynch, grandson of Dan)
Bob Biner (son of Harriet Lynch, grandson of Dan)
Richard Lynch (son of Raymond Lynch)
Michael Lynch (son of Raymond Lynch)
Tim Lynch (son of Raymond Lynch)

The following are non-family employees who worked for the Lynch Brothers Diamond Drilling Company. Most worked either at the Skagit River Project or on the Grand Coulee Dam. This is certainly an incomplete list. Dozens more worked for the Lynch Bros. on their many projects.

Chester Barton	Ed O'Connor
Bert Bechand	Clarence Olson
Charles Belangee	Einer T. Olson
Milo Bishop	Bill Patton
Wayne Bozart	Howard Paul
Bill Brazinet	Lawrence Phillips
Austin Burnett	James Quann
EverettBursell	Earle "Dusty" Rhoades
Edward Buzley	Mary Rhoades
Harry Buzley	Norman Rigney
Bill Chapman	John J. Riley
Scott Coleman	Lawrence Roberts
Walter Cook	Henry Rodgers
Nate Davis	C. Morris Sherman
George Ferguson	Raliegh Sherman
Hugh Hayles	Clifford Schrag
Jack Henry	Charles Sellers
Vic Henry	B.J. Squibb
Denny Holcomb	William Steinmetz
Will Jenkins	Olaf Swedman
Steve Kudowitz	Russell Vaughn
Melvin Lynch	Walter Vetter
Jesse Maddux	Alva Walker
Floyd McLaughlin	Tommy Walsh
Jim Miller	Clark Weimer
Albert Morehead	Oscar Weldon
Frank Morehead	Astrid Wenstrom
Charles Neihart	Donald Wilson
Nels Nelson	Rocky Wilson
Robert Neumann	Vic Wilson
Carl Noble	Jack Woodrig
Dave O'Connor	Lloyd Young

Additional Photographs

Mate Kendall, center, with arm on the leg of Dan Lynch, and friends in Republic, Michigan.

*The Catholic faith was important to the Lynch family. Harriet saved
her First Holy Communion certificate from 1904.*

*Dan & Mate Lynch with their
children Ken, Harriet & Fred circa 1917.*

Mate Kendall Lynch with son Fred & daughter Harriet.

Mate Lynch in center, Harriet to far right. Tillie Lynch is 3rd from left. Little Raymond Lynch has his hand on his uncle, Dick Lynch, who stands beside his wife Sabina.

Mate & Dan Lynch with Dick Lynch (far right) at Bear Creek, Alaska.

Florence Lowney Lynch, the wife of Pat Lynch, with her brother-in-law Dan.

Dan, Harriet & Pat Lynch at mining camp.

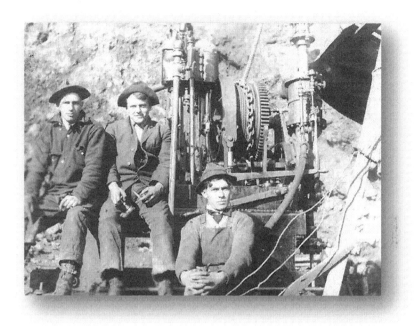

Lynch Brothers drill crew.

Big Fred Lynch, far right, with his drill crew.

Lynch brothers drill platforms at remote locations in the late 1930s.

The ever-jovial Dan Lynch strikes another pose at a mining camp.

When Fred wasn't singing he was leading a drill crew. Fred is at the far right.

Kendall Lynch operates a diamond drill and stands in front of his log cabin at a drill site.

This picture says it all: Dan Lynch adored Mate Kendall.

Con Lynch holds Billy Biner & Betty Biner stands in front. The others, L-R, Harriet Lynch Biner, Doll Lynch Twomey, baby Bob Biner, Jane McKenna Lynch and Howard Lynch.

Ray & Nita Lynch
and Ray Lynch during the drilling for Cushman Dam #2 on the Skokomish River
in Mason County, Washington, 1928.

Richard "Dick" Lynch, (1930-1971), Korean War veteran and son of Ray & Nita,
grandson of Tim & Tillie and the namesake of Dick Lynch.

Back row: Fritzi Biner, Betty Biner Fulton, Billy Biner, Billy Biner Jr., Pat Fulton
Front row: Maxine Gray Biner, Harriet Lynch Biner, Bob Biner.

Brothers Con, Dan & Dick Lynch in one of their final visits together.

Dan Lynch with son Kendall shortly before Dan's death.

Harriet Lynch Biner, the beloved Nanny Biner, with five of her 25 grandchildren, in Portland, Oregon, 1956. Chuck, Mary, Leslie & Charlene Fulton stand around Harriet who holds Joe Fulton, the author of this history.

Appreciation

Most of my information came from the records of my grandmother, Harriet Lynch Biner; my godparents, Fred and Mollie Lynch, and my mother, Elizabeth Biner Fulton. All were very proud of their Irish roots and faithfully saved letters, photographs, newspapers clippings and postcards, which passed on to me after their deaths. By sorting through their collections I was able to piece together the family history. For more information on the Lynch Brothers Diamond Drilling Company I relied heavily on archival information from the digital collections of the Washington State University Library, the Multnomah County Library in Portland and the Seattle Public Library.

The memories of Lynch Brothers' worker Will D. "Bob" Jenkins during the Skagit River Project as published by the Skagit County Historical Society in the book Last Frontier in the North Cascades: Tales of the Wild Upper Skagit offered a rare first-person account of a major Lynch Brothers job.

I would like to thank Fritzi Biner Bernazani and Bob Biner, the grandchildren of Dan Lynch, along with Bob's wife Louise, for their recollections. Mike and Tim Lynch, sons of Raymond Lynch, provided valuable details, including photographs and anecdotal history of Ray Lynch when he was head of the company.

My brother Dan Fulton provided access to U.S. census records, military records and family trees through his membership with Ancestry.com. Megan Janssen and Rick Cooper offered advice on the layout.

Photographs and memories of the Con Lynch family were shared by Susan Twomey and Sheila Brooks, the granddaughters of Cornelius Lynch Jr. Other contributors were Judy Heinrich, the daughter of John Harris Lynch; Bill Sacia, the great-grandson of Mary Lynch McCarthy; Therese Lynch, the granddaughter of Kendall Lynch, and her wonderful father Jack, the son of Kendall Lynch, who graciously sat for an interview, one that neither of us wanted to end.

Finally, my wife Debra Hascall accompanied me on research trips and also served as a proofreader for this book. This is my third book based on interesting figures from my own family. Deb has supported my efforts from the very start and I deeply appreciate her positive assistance.

Bibliography & Sources

"Alaska Historical Collections." Alaska State Library. N.p., n.d.
Web. 10 May 2014.
<http://library.alaska.gov/hist/>.

Battien, Pauline. *The Gold Seekers-- a 200 Year History of Mining
in Washington, Idaho, Montana & Lower British
Columbia*. Colville, Wash.: P. Battien, 1989.

Burke, William A. and the Montana Writers' Project. *Copper
Camp*. New York City, NY: Hastings
House, 1943.

"Chronicling America, Historic American Newspapers." Library of
Congress, Washington D.C.
http://chroniclingamerica.loc.gov/

"Cousin Sam." : THINGS HAPPENING AT GRAND COULEE! [1933].
N.p., n.d. Web. 27 Mar. 2014.
http://cousinsam.blogspot.com/2011/07/things-
happening-at-grand-coulee-1933.html

Downs, L. Vaughn. *The Mightiest of Them All: Memories of the
Grand Coulee Dam.* Fairfield,
Washington. Ye Galleon Press. 1987.

"E/MJ : Engineering and Mining Journal : Free Download &
Streaming : Internet Archive."
Internet Archive. N.p., n.d. Web. 10 May 2014.
<https://archive.org/details/emjengineeringmi102newy>.

"Fowler, IN Train Wreck, Jan 1907." Fowler, IN Train Wreck, Jan.
1907. N.p., n.d. Web. 20 Apr. 2014. <http://www.
gendisasters.com/data1/in/trains/fowlertrainwreckjan19
09.htm>.

Fulton, Joseph Edward. *Brewmaster's Bombardier & Belly
Gunner: The World War II Letters of*

Bill & Bob Biner. Portland, Oregon. Originario Productions, 2013.

Great Falls Daily Tribune, Dec. 22, 1913. Courtesy of Great Falls Public Library, Great Falls, Montana.

Gilfoyle, Timothy J. *A Pickpocket's Tale, The Underworld of Nineteenth Century New York*. New York: W.W. Norton & Co. 2006.

Harris, Lillian and Genevieve. Interview by Margaret Thurston Carlson. Personal interview. 1 June 1971.

Henning, Robert A., Editor. *Alaska's Oil/Gas & Minerals Industry*. Anchorage, Alaska: Alaska Geographic Society, 1982.

Hussey, J.A., *Champoeg: Place of Transition*. Portland, Oregon: Oregon Historical Society, 1967

"In Person! Pictures and Pertinent Paragraphs About the Leading Radio Stars of the Far Western Stations." Sunset Magazine, Aug. 1928: page 67. Print.

Jenkins, Will D. *Last Frontier in the North Cascades: Tales of the Wild Upper Skagit*. Mount Vernon, Wash.: Skagit County Historical Society, 1984.

Lamb, Allison. "The Town the New Deal Built: Mason City, the Grand Coulee Dam, and Visions of New Deal America." Mason City. Great Depression in Washington State Project, n.d. Web. 18 Mar. 2014. <http://depts.washington.edu/depress/mason_city_new _deal.shtml>.

"Locomotive Firemen's Magazine." Google Books. N.p., n.d. Web . 20 Apr. 2014. <http://books.google.com/books?id=03cWAAAAYAAJ&pg =PA396&lpg=PA396&dq=SCHAFF.+big+four+railroad&sou rce=bl&ots=hay-SaTlrb&sig=8aBrHKKxq8aX8QhNv8AHSVowZ88&hl=en&s

a=X&ei=olVUU6_NHImNyATVzoL4Cw&ved=0CCsQ6AEwA
A#v=onepage&q=SCHAFF.%20big%20four%20railroad&f=
false>.

Long, Albert E. *A Glossary of the Diamond-Drilling Industry.*
Washington D.C.. UNT Digital Library.
http://digital.library.unt.edu/ark:/67531/metadc12738/.
Accessed May 28, 2014.

"Lynch Brothers Start Huge Drilling Operation." Spokane
Chronicle. N.p., n.d. Web. 26 Mar. 2014.
<http://news.google.com/newspapers?nid=1338&dat=19
380625&id=MIUzAAAAIBAJ&sjid=K_UDAAAAIBAJ&pg=71
51,5410591>.

Lynch, Fred & Mollie Collection: Photographs, postcards and
newspaper clippings preserved by Fred and Mollie Lynch.

Lynch, Jack. Interview by Joseph Fulton in Kent, Washington,
March, 2013.

Lynch, Raymond C., and Clarence E. Carpenter. "Patent
US2217889 - Diamond drill bit - Google Patents." Google
Books. N.p., n.d. Web. 18 Mar. 2014.
<http://www.google.as/patents/US2217889>.
State University Libraries.

LAMPERT v. REYNOLDS METALS COMPANY. Leagle TM: February
8, 1914

Marquette Mining Journal, July 29, 1871, Courtesy of Central
Upper Peninsula & Northern Michigan University Archives

"Michigan-Iron-Mines." *Michigan-Iron-Mines*. Web. 9 July 2014.
<http://www.miningartifacts.org/Michigan-Iron-
Mines.html>.Mining & Scientific Press. San Francisco.
January 1920.

Merritt, William E.. *A Fool's Gold: a Story of Ancient Spanish
Treasure, Two Pounds of Pot, and*

the Young Lawyer Almost Left Holding the Bag. New York: Bloomsbury Pub. 2006.

Morgan, Murray C., *Skid Road: An Informal Portrait of Seattle*. New York City, Viking Press, 1951.

Morgan, Murray C. *The Dam*, New York City, Viking Press, 1954

Morgan, Murray C., *Puget's Sound: A Narrative of Early Tacoma and the Southern Sound*, Seattle, Washington, University of Washington Press, 1979

Murdoch, Angus. *Boom Copper; the Story of the First U.S. Mining Boom*. New York: Macmillan Co., 1943. Print.

Musser, Kevin. "CopperRange.org presents the Copper Country Historical Page." CopperRange.org presents the Copper Country Historical Page. N.p., n.d. Web. 30 June 2014. <http://www.copperrange.org/index.html>.

Nesbit, Sharon, "Troutdale Historical Society Newsletter," 2009

316 F2d 272 Reynolds Metals Company v. Lampert. Open Jurist. February 08, 2014

Offbeat Oregon History. Finn, J.D.John. Web. 26 May 2014. <http://www.offbeatoregon.com/d-about.html>.

Oregon Digital Newspaper Program (ODNP), University of Oregon Libraries. http://library.uoregon.edu/diglib/odnp/index.html

"Oregonian Historical Archives." Multnomah County Library, Portland, Oregon. https://multcolib.org/resource/oregonian-historical-archives

Pees, Samuel T. "CABLE-TOOL DRILLING." *Oil History*. Petroleum History Institute, 2004. Web. 14 Mar. 2014.

Pitzer, Paul C.. *Building the Skagit: a century of Upper Skagit*

Valley History, 1870-1970. Portland, Or.: Galley Press, 1978.

Pitzer, Paul Curtis, *Grand Coulee, Harnessing the Dream.* Pullman, Washington : Washington State University Press, 1994.

"Postglacial Lahars on the SW Flank of Mt. Adams, Washington." USGS. N.p., n.d. Web. 20 June 2014. <http://pubs.usgs.gov/bul/2161/report.pdf>.

"Roosevelt ,Franklin D. : Remarks at the Site of the Grand Coulee Dam, Washington.." Franklin D. Roosevelt: Remarks at the Site of the Grand Coulee Dam, Washington.. N.p., n.d. Web.   26 Mar. 2014. <http://www.presidency.ucsb.edu/ws/?pid=14732>.

San Francisco Call. (San Francisco [Calif.]), 17 Jan. 1907. Chronicling America: Historic American Newspapers. Lib. of Congress. http://chroniclingamerica.loc.gov/lccn/sn85066387/1907 -01-17/ed-1/seq-1/

Schneider, John. "Seattle Radio History: KJR and KOMO" http://www.theradiohistorian.org/Seattle/kjr%20komo% 20history.htm

"Seattle Times Historical Archives, 1900-1984." Seattle Public Library, Seattle, Washington http://www.spl.org/library-collection/articles-and-research/databases-a-z

Simonds, Wm. Joe. *The Columbia Basin Project. Bureau of Reclamation History Program*, Denver, CO. 1998. www.usbr.gov/projects/ImageServer?ImgName=doc_129 7780309537

"Skagit River and Newhalem Creek Hydroelectric Project." National Register of Historic Places. Dept. of Interior, n.d. Web. 22 Sept. 2013.

http://pdfhost.focus.nps.gov/docs/NRHP/Text/96000416.
pdf

"Spokane Daily Chronicle." Google News.. Web. 13 June2013.
http://news.google.com/newspapers?nid=1338&dat=19
331202&id=6NJXAAAAIBAJ&sjid=7fQDAAAAIBAJ&pg=732
6398378.

"Spokane Daily Chronicle." Google News. Web. 26 Mar1954
http://news.google.com/newspapers?nid=1338&dat=194
20117&id=dmpWAAAAIBAJ&sjid=TfUDAAAAIBAJ&pg=730
0,3647476.

"Spokane Review Digital Collections." WSU Libraries. Washington
State University,
http://content.wsulibs.wsu.edu

"State History. Grand Coulee Dam.." WSU Digital Collections. N.p.,
n.d. Web. 24 Mar. 2014.
<http://kaga.wsulibs.wsu.edu/u?/clipping,15641>.

Toenge, Albert L., Turnbull, Louis A., Cole, Willard A. "Technical
Paper 699, Exploration of a Lignite Deposit Near Toledo,
Lewis County, Wash." U.S. Govt. Printing Office,
Washington D.C. 1947

"United States Federal Census Records, 1870-1940."
Ancestry.com. www.ancestry.com

Wallis and Marilyn Kimble Northwest History Database
(http://content.libraries.wsu.edu/cdm/landingpage/colle
ction/clipping), Washington State University Library

Willison, George F. *Saints and Strangers*. New York City, Reynal &
Hitchcock, 1945.

Diablo Dam, Courtesy of Seattle City Light

Ross Dam (formerly Ruby Dam). Photograph by Debra Hascall.

Other books by
Joseph E. Fulton:

Brewmaster's Bombardier & Belly Gunner:
The World War II Letters of Bill and Bob Biner

ISBN 10 - 0979607213
ISBN 13 -978-0-9796072-1-9

Published by Originario Productions, 2013
Printed by On Demand Books
Cover by Alicia Meza

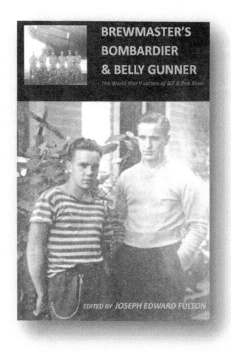

To order any book check online or contact the author directly at:
chiefjoephsxc@gmail.com

From Beardstown to Andersonville:
The Civil War Letters of Newton & Tommy Paschal
ISBN: 978-0-7884-5331-1
Published by Heritage Books, Inc. 1998
Reprinted in 2011
Cover by Rhea Fulton & Sue Crawford

How to Pass the US Citizenship Test
ISBN: 978-0-9796-0720-2
Published by Originario Productions, 2007
Cover by Lynne Moore

INDEX

G

M

Made in the USA
Charleston, SC
15 August 2014